DIALOGICAL DESIGNS

STUDIO AS BOOK
NO. 02

SERIES INTRODUCTION

Studio as Book is a new series of yearly publications that tender the extraordinary creative work undertaken in the Department of Architecture's design studios – in detail. The series includes undergraduate and graduate level work, and is intended to sit alongside the Open Exhibition and catalogue. Each book in the series covers the work of a single design studio over the course of at least two years. Its objectives are:

- To record, archive, and present the pedagogical programme and creative student outputs of a design studio
- To position the work of a design studio within a broader intellectual, scientific or aesthetic field
- To advance the design driven research being undertaken in the Department's design studios
- To provide a reference for future iterations and variations of a design studio

Reducing the creative output of a multi-year design studio to a single volume, using a pre-designed book template is no easy undertaking, and it is necessarily selective. At the same time, it provides a consistent, sure platform for the wide range of approaches to the discipline of teaching architectural design which characterise the department.

Each Studio as Book has been peer-reviewed on the basis of a proposal submitted by the studio's tutors to an editorial committee. In addition to studio briefs and student work, each book includes content that draws out the studio's research and pedagogical agenda. The format that this takes varies from book to book – reflective essays by tutors or past students, interviews, theoretical essays from parallel fields, and so forth. The Studio as Book Series will later be accompanied by a Studio Pamphlet Series for design studios of a shorter duration.

I wish to acknowledge the contribution of the following in bringing this project to fruition: Lindsay Bremner, Director of Research, who was the driving force behind the series, Mark Boyce, author of Sizes May Vary, A workbook for graphic design (Lawrence King, 2008) – and the designer of Studio as Book, and Filip Visnjic, designer of the series' web site, http://www.studioasbook.org.

Harry Charrington
Head of Department of Architecture
University of Westminster

DIALOGICAL DESIGNS
DS03 2012-2015
EDITED BY CONSTANCE LAU

STUDIO AS BOOK
N0. 02

DEPARTMENT OF ARCHITECTURE
UNIVERSITY OF WESTMINSTER

CONTENTS

FOREWORD

DIALOGICAL DESIGNS   6–13
Jonathan Hill

STUDIO INTRODUCTION

THE ARCHITECTURAL NARRATIVE   14–15
Constance Lau

THE ARTS MARATHON PRODUCTION LINE   16–17
Constance Lau

The Pigment Production Line	18–27
The Elizabethan Tailoring Academy	28–45
Bibliography	46–47
Loreta Lukoseviciene	
The Art Factory: A Vertical Production Line	48–53
Restore, Reuse and Regenerate, Up-Cycling and Architecture Conservation	54–75
Bibliography	76–77
Larisa Bulibasa	

**PORTS OF CALL: THE 'DANDELION' FOLLY AND
THE ROYAL BOTANICAL AUCTION HOUSE**   78–79
Constance Lau

The Rhythmical Folly: A Rowing Observatory	80–91
The John Soane Folly at Kew: A Collection of Found, Borrowed and Reconstructed Items	92–115
Bibliography	116–117
Panagiota Kotsovinou	

UNTO THIS LAST: THE CAMDEN WORKSHOP AND SCHOOL OF DESIGN   118–119
Constance Lau

The Arts and Crafts Wood Workshop   120–135
The School of Elemental Drawing   136–155
Bibliography   156–157
Ioana Vierita

Morris' Pleasure Garden: The Viewing Folly   158–167
The Arts and Crafts School of Cabinet Construction   168–189
Bibliography   190–191
Sear Nee Ng

Adaptable Architecture   192–197
Sear Nee Ng

THE INVISIBLE ICON AND THE URBAN OBSERVATORY   198–199
Constance Lau

Garden of Echoes   200–211
Theatre of Transparencies   212–231
Bibliography   232–233
Iga Martynow

Tatlin's Workshop   234–245
The Vygotsky Centre of Evolutionary Anthropology   246–267
Bibliography   268–269
Kyriakos Eleftheriadis

SPATIAL WRITING AND NON-LINEAR ARCHITECTURAL NARRATIVES   270–281
Sotirios Varsamis

MONTAGE AND MULTIPLE INTERPRETATIONS   282–293
Constance Lau

ACKNOWLEDGEMENTS   294–295

FOREWORD

DIALOGICAL DESIGNS

JONATHAN HILL

Some tutors respond to the creative competitiveness of the 'unit system' by adopting a didactic approach; and students join such a unit knowing that they will learn a design method. Other tutors emphasise dialogue, developing a generous community of open-minded individuals. For the dialogical tutor, the aim is to create a coherent position that is also questioning and incomplete, and thus a stimulus to students' creative development, not a limit. Led by Dr Constance Lau and Dr Claire Harper, Design Studio 03 is exemplary of the dialogical model of architectural education. The concern for dialogue is evident both in the studio's educational model and in the designs it encourages.

It is rare in a contemporary architectural school to see such a thoughtful, nuanced appreciation of site qualities—physical, social, perceptual and in terms of patterns of movement and use—as a stimulus to design. Each project is embedded within a site, drawing attention to existing characteristics so that they seem newly discovered, while offering subtle modifications and interventions so that the resulting assemblage is both old and new, familiar and unfamiliar. A technique in which one 'site' is read through another, montage is employed to conceive a drawing as analogous to a site, and vice versa, which demands drawings and models that address multiple temporal, spatial, social and material conditions. The studio's commitment to the creative and critical potential of the drawing includes an impressive array of drawing types but special emphasis is given to ones that explore the relations between design and experience. Creatively expanding conceptions of authorship, the studio recognises the creativity of the user as well as the architect, appreciating site-specific narratives and interpretations as instruments of negotiation and dialogue. In response to Design Studio 03's considerable commitment to creative invention, multiple narratives, and dialogical research encapsulated in this book, I offer a possible pre-history to its ideas and themes. As a reinterpretation of the past in the present, a history is analogous to a design.

Drawing Forth

In the early fifteenth-century, searching through the monastic library at St. Gallen for Latin manuscripts that would support his humanist beliefs, the Florentine scholar Poggio Bracciolini came upon a copy of Vitruvius' treatise *De architectura libri decem*, which was written in the first century BC. The discovery of the only architectural text to survive from classical antiquity was hugely influential. Modelled on Vitruvius' example, Leon Battista Alberti's *De re aedificatoria* (Ten Books on Architecture), c. 1450, was the first thorough investigation of the Renaissance architect as artist and intellectual.[1] Acknowledging that nostalgia can stimulate imaginative and critical responses to the past, Erwin Panofsky characterises the fifteenth-century as a 'nostalgia' for classical antiquity 'that distinguishes the real Renaissance from all those pseudo- or proto-Renaissances that had taken place during the Middle Ages'.[2]

Classical antiquity established the principle that ideas are immaterial and that intellectual labour is superior to manual labour. In *Timaeus*, c. 360 BC, Plato claims that all the things we perceive in the material world are modelled on ideal forms, which are defined by geometrical proportions.[3] Consequently, there are two distinct realms. One consists of ideal originals, which only the intellect can comprehend, the other of imperfect copies subject to decay. Plato distrusted art because it mimicked natural objects, merely adding one layer of misrepresentation onto another. Concerned to affirm their intellectual status, Italian Renaissance artists promoted a concept of beauty based on geometric ideals but undermined Plato's argument that the artwork is always inferior. Introducing a fundamental change in perception, they assumed that the drawing truthfully depicts the three-dimensional world and is a window to that world. The term 'design' derives from *disegno*, which means drawing, and associates the drawing of a line with the drawing forth of an idea. *Disegno* allowed the three visual arts—architecture, painting and sculpture—to be recognised as liberal arts concerned with ideas, a position they had rarely been accorded previously. The command of drawing—not building—unlocked the status of the architect, emphasising the immaterial idea of architecture not the material fabric of building. Alberti notably stated that 'It is quite possible to project whole forms in the mind without recourse to the material'.[4] In the new division of labour, architecture resulted not from the accumulated knowledge of a team of anonymous craftsmen working together on a construction site but the artistic creation of an individual architect in command of orthogonal drawing who designed a building as a totality in a studio. Accordingly, Alberti emphasised that construction was to be undertaken and supervised by craftsmen who were to ensure that a design was completed exactly according to 'the author's original intentions'.[5] The architect associated with *disegno* was established in Italy around 1450, in France a century later and in Britain in the early 1600s.

In the new division of labour, architects acquired complementary means to practice architecture—writing as well as drawing—that were as important as building, creating an interdependent and multi-directional web of influences that together stimulated architects' creative development. To affirm their newly acquired status, architects began increasingly to theorise architecture both for themselves and for their patrons. The history of the architectural book is interdependent with that of the architect, and has been crucial to the architect's status since the Renaissance.

A further stimulus to the imaginative nostalgia for classical antiquity was the bucolic, rural life evoked in Virgil's *Georgics and Eclogues*, which were written in the first-century BC, like Vitruvius' treatise. Emphasising narrative rather than geometry, Francesco Colonna's *Hypnerotomachia Poliphili*, 1499, was the second architectural book by a Renaissance author and the first to be printed with illustrations, establishing the multimedia interdependence of text and image that has been essential to architectural books ever since. The first part of Colonna's title—*Hypnerotomachia*—derives from three Greek words, *hypnos*, *eros* and *mache*, which respectively mean sleep, love and strife, so that they roughly translate as the 'strife of love in a dream'. The second part—*Poliphili*—refers to the principal character, Poliphilo, who has a restless night after being rejected by his love, Polia. *Hypnerotomachia Poliphili* is a fictional narrative illustrated with pictorial drawings, in which love is lost and won in a sylvan landscape among monuments and ruins that are themselves erotic, not just locations for lust and desire. Some of Colonna's designs may have been invented while others were taken from ancient and Renaissance sites in Italy, Greece and Asia Minor. The most impressive structures are composites. The largest consists of varied forms mounted one on top of the other: a plinth, a pyramid, a stone cube, an obelisk and, finally, a winged statue 'revolving easily at every breath of wind, making such a noise, from the friction of the hollow metal device, as was never heard from the Roman treasury'.[6] Stimulating the fascination for architectural and garden narratives, formal and spatial juxtapositions, monuments and ruins, and pictorial representations of architecture, *Hypnerotomachia Poliphili* has been an enduring influence on later speculations on these themes.

Phenomenology of the Eye

Beginning in the mid-seventeenth-century and extending into the subsequent century, the Enlightenment—the natural light of reason—was founded on the assumption that humanity and nature can be understood and progressed by reason. Derived from *empeiria*, the ancient Greek term for experience, the principal British contribution to Enlightenment theory was empiricism, which promoted reason but made it specific rather than generic. Countering the Platonist and Cartesian traditions in which knowledge is acquired by the mind alone, empiricism states that personality and morality develop through a dialogue between the environment, senses and mind.

In drawing attention to the conditions that inform self-understanding to a greater extent than in the Renaissance and baroque, the eighteenth-century fundamentally transformed the visual arts, its objects, authors and viewers. In Britain, the title of architect associated with *disegno* was in its infancy when another appeared alongside it, exemplifying a new type of design and a new way of designing that valued the ideas and emotions evoked through experience. This new design practice focused first on gardens not buildings because they were more clearly subject to time and the changing natural world. Although the pleasures and liberties of the picturesque were limited to the educated and prosperous, notable principles were established. Rather than refer to universal ideas, forms and proportions, design could draw forth ideas that were provisional, changeable and dependent on experience at conception, production and reception.

Rather than follow an inflexible vision, the garden was designed in detailed response to site conditions, and creative adjustments were made during construction. Valuing the individuality of the designer and the occupant, the picturesque acknowledged that beauty is subjective and encouraged varied allegories and diverse interpretations. Rather than being conceived according to the rules of geometry in a distant studio, the garden was designed the way it was experienced, by a figure moving across a landscape and imagining future movements, while special attention was given to drawings that explored the relations between site and experience. Owning several copies of *Hypnerotomachia Poliphili*, the early eighteenth-century architect and landscape designer William Kent represented his garden designs—and often his garden buildings too—in perspectives. In his letter to Pope Leo X, c. 1519, Raphael associated the picture with the painter and the plan with the architect, confirming an opinion earlier expressed by Alberti.[7] However, the value given to experience in the eighteenth-century made this distinction less convincing. Indebted to *ut pictura poesis*—a concept of classical antiquity that means 'as with painting, so also with poetry'—the picturesque landscape was conceived as a spatial poem dependent on all the senses not just vision.

Immersion within a garden stimulates a questioning attitude to vision in which self-reflective viewers perceive themselves viewing, and observe others doing the same, so that their experiences are both personal and social, and equivalent to 'the phenomenology of the eye', as Peter de Bolla concludes.[8] The picturesque draws attention to the problems as well as the pleasures of vision, which is no more than 'intelligent guesswork' 'from limited sensory evidence', writes Richard Gregory.[9] Consequently, informed by memory, 'perceptions are hypotheses. This is suggested by the fact that retinal images are open to an infinity of interpretations'.[10] What we see is affected by what we touch, feel, taste, smell and hear. Even when the garden visitor is static, physical and perceptual movement is implicit because any past or future journey is understood in relation to other potential journeys and is but one part of a complex and changeable whole.

In the Renaissance, the effects of time, nature and weather on buildings were understood to be negative. In contrast, the picturesque adopted the ruin as its emblem—a hybrid of architecture and landscape, nature and culture—that was understood to represent growth as well as decay, the future as well as the past. Rather than a finite object, the ruin acknowledged the effects of time and place, emphasising symbiotic relations with its ever-changing immediate and wider contexts, and celebrating the creative influence of natural as well cultural forces. Rather than only associate the immaterial with timeless geometries, the eighteenth-century increasingly conceived the immaterial as temporal and experiential, not only in the actual absence of matter, but also in the perceived absence of matter seen through mists and storms, establishing a dialogue between the immaterial and material that associated self-understanding with the experience of objects subject to nature and weather.

In the Renaissance, a fragment was understood as a component of a coherent whole, but the eighteenth-century appreciated a fragment for itself, which was seen in juxtaposition to other fragments that need not coalesce into a comprehensible total system. In *Athenaeum Fragments*, 1798, the romantic poet Friedrich Schlegel noted that, whereas 'many works of the ancients have become fragments … many works of the moderns are fragments at the time of their origin'.[11] Fragments were associated with potential rather than loss, and the opportunity for a work of art or architecture to remain unfinished, literally and in the imagination. Though diminishing objects physically, ruination was understood to expand architecture's metaphorical potential: 'for imperfection and obscurity are their properties; and to carry the imagination to something greater than is seen, their effect', concluded Thomas Whately in 1770.[12]

Technology of the Self

Empiricism was a catalyst to new writing conventions as well as new landscape designs. People have written about themselves for millennia but the formation of modern identity is associated with a type of writing that Michel Foucault describes as a 'technology of the self', the process of self-examination by which moral character and behaviour are constructed and maintained in conjunction with other social forces.[13] Objectivity may be an aspiration but no diary is entirely truthful and the diarist cannot fail to edit and reinvent life while reflecting upon it, altering the past as well influencing the future. As Paul de Man remarks: 'We assume that life *produces* the autobiography as an act produces its consequences, but can we not suggest, with equal justice, that the autobiographical project may itself produce and determine the life and that whatever the writer *does* is in fact governed by the technical demands of self-portraiture and thus determined, in all its aspects, by the resources of his medium'?[14]

Focusing on the fate of individuals, the early diaries—autobiographical fictions—developed in parallel with the early novels—fictional autobiographies. In valuing direct experience, precise description and a sceptical approach to 'facts', which needed to be repeatedly questioned, the empirical method created a fruitful climate in which the everyday realism of a new literary genre—the novel—could prosper as 'factual fiction'.[15] In contrast to the epic or romance, which incorporated classical mythologies, the novel concentrated on the lives of everyday people in eighteenth-century society and the individualism it professed. Empirical description and analysis was applied to the novel, which emphasised specific times, peoples and places and sought justification through a combination of reasoned explanation and intuitive experience. Often described as the first English novel, Daniel Defoe's *Robinson Crusoe*, 1719, is a fictional autobiography, as is Defoe's other famous novel *Moll Flanders*, 1722.[16] In each case, the principal character is complex and conflicted, and one voice among others in a changing society. Defoe describes *Roxana* as 'laid in Truth of Fact' and thus 'not a Story, but a History', a claim echoed by other novelists throughout the eighteenth-century.[17] He also characterises *Moll Flanders* as 'a private History' but invites 'the Reader to pass his own Opinion upon the ensuing Sheets, and take it as he pleases'.[18] Even Jonathan Swift's *Gulliver's Travels*, 1726, is teasingly presented as true. The frontispiece to the first edition depicts a portrait of Lemuel Gulliver, a ship's surgeon and captain, who claims to verify his story in a number of ways, including by reference to the stingers of three gigantic Brobdingnagian wasps donated to Gresham College, the first home of the Royal Society, the institution that personifies empiricism.

History's uncertain status at that time supported authors' claims that the first novels were in fact histories. Describing actual events and others of his own invention, Giorgio Vasari's *Le vite de' piu eccellenti pittori, scultori e architettori* (The Lives of the Most Eminent Painters, Sculptors and Architects), 1550, was the first significant history of art and architecture, initiating a new discipline. In the sixteenth-century, history's purpose was to offer useful lessons; accuracy was not necessary. In subsequent centuries, empiricism's emphasis on the distinction between fact and fiction began to transform historical analysis, diminishing the humanist emphasis on literary sources. Rather than Vasari's focus on individual achievements, the historian began to characterise changing cultural, social and economic processes in which the deeds of specific protagonists were contextualised. But this transition was slow and most eighteenth-century histories inherited some of the rhetorical approach of earlier histories.

The relationship between history and design is central to *Hypnerotomachia Poliphili* and Andrea Palladio's *I quattro libri dell'architettura* (The Four Books of Architecture), 1570, which is an analytical manifesto illustrated with orthogonal drawings and thus an alternative to Colonna's literary model. Historical references appear in both books but for different reasons. In one they enrich a specific story, in the other they legitimise generic solutions. Influenced by Colonna and Palladio, in 1714 Kent began a diary, 'Remarks by way of Painting & Archit.', which records his journeys around Italy. Sometimes written in English, at other times in Italian, it recalls buildings, paintings and gardens in words and images, and includes delicate illustrations of perspective techniques in line and wash, recording and stimulating Kent's creative development.[19] Equivalent to a visual and spatial diary, the process of design—from one drawing to the next iteration and from one project to another—is itself an autobiographical 'technology of the self', formulating a design ethos for an individual or a studio. De Man concludes that the autobiography 'veils a defacement of the mind of which it is itself a cause'.[20] Having changed his name from Cant, Kent continued the tradition that Palladio had favoured, who was born Andrea di Pietro della Gondola.

A private design diary is autobiographical. An architectural drawing can also be autobiographical, as well as a means of negotiation between an architect and other individuals, and therefore subject to a more complex authorship. A building or landscape can be an autobiography of its principal author, even if many people are involved in its procurement, design, construction and use. Equally, a building or landscape may be the combined autobiographies of its many protagonists, with some getting more attention than others.

Creative Myth

Architects have used history in different ways, whether to indicate their continuity with the past or departure from it. From the Renaissance to the early twentieth-century the architect was a historian in the sense that an architectural treatise combined design and history, and a building was expected to manifest the character of the time and knowingly refer to earlier historical eras. Modernism ruptured this system in principle if not always in practice. Advocating an architecture specific to the present and breaking from previous educational models, Walter Gropius excluded the history of architecture from the Bauhaus syllabus, while in the 'Manifesto of Futurist Architecture', 1914, Antonio Sant'Elia and Filippo Tomasso Marinetti proclaimed: 'This architecture cannot be subject to any law of historical continuity'.[21] But even modernists who denied the relevance of the past relied on histories to validate modernism and articulate its principles. Books such as Nikolaus Pevsner's *Pioneers of the Modern Movement*, 1936, and Sigfried Giedion's *Space, Time and Architecture*, 1941, identified a modernist prehistory to justify modernism's historical inevitability, rupture from the past and systematic evolution.[22]

To some degree, mid-century modernists merely reaffirmed an appreciation of history that was latent in a work such as Le Corbusier's *Vers une architecture*, 1923, but had been largely ignored.[23] But the Second World War was a more scientific war than the First, and nuclear devastation undermined confidence in technological progress as a means of social transformation, notably for the generation of architects who had seen military service. In the search for stability in the uncertain aftermath of 1945, modernism's previously dismissive reaction to social norms and cultural memories was itself anachronistic. The consequence was not just to acknowledge early modernism's classical heritage but also to place a concern for history at the heart of architecture once again, affirming the liberal humanist tradition that modernism had once seemed to repudiate, and undermining the unnecessary opposition between tradition and innovation that modernism had once seemed to pose.

In Britain a burgeoning romanticism celebrated national identity, affirming the association of a people with a place. The return of history meant the return of the ruin, the enduring emblem of an evolving tradition from the picturesque and romanticism to picturesque and romantic modernism. Equating a history to a ruin, Walter Benjamin remarked: 'Allegories are, in the realm of thoughts, what ruins are in the realm of things'.[24] Our understanding of the past is inevitably partial. Laying bare the processes of construction and decay, a history is both a ruin of the past and a speculative reconstruction in the present. Equally, the novel's origins in the fictional autobiography ensure that a 'life in ruin' is a recurring literary metaphor, representing potential as well as loss, and a challenge to the protagonist, whether he or she is incarcerated on an island or in a prison as in Defoe's two best-known novels, *Robinson Crusoe* and *Moll Flanders*, for example.

Since the early twentieth-century, allegory has often conceived in terms of montage, which acquired prominence because of its dual character as the principal artistic strategy of the avant-garde and the technical procedure of mass-production, including film. Deploying all the techniques of allegory—the depletion of previous meanings and the formulation of new ones by the appropriation and dialectical juxtaposition of fragments set in a new context— montage is relevant to architecture because the experience of a building depends upon a complex reading of many conditions at the same time. Just as the juxtaposition of the parts of the artistic or literary montage can resist easy resolution, the juxtaposition of spaces and uses of the architectural montage can be rich in ambiguity. However, one of the virtues that Benjamin ascribes to montage—the ability to shock people into new understandings—is of little relevance to architecture.[25] Shock wears off very quickly, and most buildings are experienced many times. The purpose of the architectural montage should not be to grab attention, and then sink to acceptability, but to have a more gradual influence, remaining unresolved to be remade anew by each user. Architecture is most often experienced habitually, when it is rarely the focus of attention. But as empiricism made evident, habit is not passive. Instead, it is a questioning intelligence acquired through experience and subject to continuing re-evaluation. Rather than necessarily a deviation from habit, creative use can instead establish, affirm or develop a habit that is itself unexpected and evolving.

Associating designs with stories and histories, Denys Lasdun remarked that each architect must devise his or her 'own creative myth', which should be 'sufficiently objective' and also have 'an element of subjectivity; the myth must be partly an expression of the architect's personality and partly of his time, partly a distillation of permanent truths and partly of the ephemera of the particular moment'.[26] The 'creative myth' can be a private inspiration or a public, collective narrative that is disseminated widely, either to architects, or to users, or to society as a whole. Emphasising that 'I don't mean myth in the sense that it is untrue' Lasdun concluded: 'My own myth … engages with history'.[27]

Lasdun corresponded with Ernesto N. Rogers, who was critical of international modernism and instead promoted appreciation of national and regional architectural cultures. Advocating 'continuity' in 1954, Rogers emphasised that 'No work is truly modern which is not genuinely rooted in tradition, while no ancient work has a modern meaning which is not capable of somehow reflecting our modern temper'.[28] To explain his conception of a building in dialogue with its physical and natural surroundings and contributing to an evolving historical continuity, Rogers quoted from 'Tradition and the Individual Talent', 1917, in which T. S. Eliot emphasises that the present alters our understanding of the past as much as the past influences the present. Admired by Rogers and equally indebted to Eliot's essay, Lasdun noted the value that the poet placed on innovation as well as tradition: 'The existing monuments form an ideal order among themselves, which is modified by the introduction of the new (the really new) work of art among them'.[29] Including Palladio, Nicholas Hawksmoor and Le Corbusier in one evolving 'architectural tradition', Lasdun transformed Eliot's words into his own: 'Context is not only topographical and physical, it is also historical… My concern for context is as an agent of architectural transformation. The place you build actually has formative influences on the nature of the building. And when the building is there it has formative influences and effects on the place it is made'.[30]

Confirming the prevalence of such ideas in postwar architecture, Vincent Scully concluded in 1969 that the architect will 'always be dealing with historical problems—with the past and, a function of the past, with the future. So the architect should be regarded as a kind of physical historian … the architect builds visible history'.[31] As a design is a reinterpretation of the past that is meaningful to the present, each building or landscape is a new history. The architect is a historian twice over: as a writer and as a designer.

Histories and novels each display a concern for the past, present and future. The historian acknowledges that the past is not the same as the present, while the novelist inserts the reader in a place and time that feels very present even if it is not. Whether implicit or explicit, a critique of the present and a prospect of the future are evident in histories and novels. They both need to be convincing but in different ways. Although no history is completely objective, to have any validity it must appear truthful to the past. A novel may be believable but not true. But recognising the overlaps between two literary genres, Malcolm Bradbury notably describes his novel *The History Man*, as 'a total invention with delusory approximations to historical reality, just as is history itself'.[32]

As a design is equivalent to a history, we may expect the designer as well as the historian 'to have a certain quality of *subjectivity*' that is 'suited to the objectivity proper to history', as Paul Ricouer concludes.[33] But the designer does not usually construct a history with the rigour expected of a contemporary historian, and we expect the designer to display other qualities of subjectivity as well, whether personal or cultural.

A design is also equivalent to a novel, convincing the user to suspend disbelief. Part-historian, part-novelist, the architect is *The History Woman*. We expect a history or a novel to be written in words, but they can also be cast in concrete or seeded in soil. An architectural book can be a history and a novel, and so can a building or a landscape. While a prospect of the future is implicit in many histories and novels, it is explicit in a design, which is always imagined before it is built. Creative architects have often looked to the past to imagine the future, studying an earlier architecture not to replicate it but to understand and transform it, revealing its relevance to the present. Twenty-first-century architects need to appreciate the shock of the old as well as the shock of the new.

1. *De re aedificatoria* was first published in 1485, over a decade after Alberti's death.
2. Erwin Panofsky, '*Et in Arcadia Ego*: Poussin and the Elegiac Tradition' in *Meaning in the Visual Arts* (Chicago: University of Chicago Press, 1982), pp. 295–320 (pp. 302–303).
3. Plato, *Timaeus, Critias, Cleitophon, Menexenus, Epistles*, trans. by R. G. Bury (Cambridge MA: Harvard University Press, 1929), p. 121.
4. Leon Battista Alberti, *On the Art of Building in Ten Books*, trans. by Joseph Rykwert, Neil Leach and Robert Tavernor (Cambridge MA and London: MIT, 1988), p. 7.
5. Alberti, p. 309.
6. Francesco Colonna, *Hypnerotomachia Poliphili: The Strife of Love in a Dream*, trans. by Joscelyn Godwin (London: Thames & Hudson, 1999), p. 24.
7. Raphael and Baldassare Castiglione, 'The Letter to Leo X, c.1519' in Vaughan Hart and Peter Hicks, *Palladio's Rome: A Translation of Andrea Palladio's Two Guidebooks to Rome* (New Haven and London: Yale University Press, 2006), pp. 177–192 (p. 188); Alberti, p. 34.
8. Peter de Bolla, *The Education of the Eye: Painting, Landscape and Architecture in Eighteenth-Century Britain* (Stanford: Stanford University Press, 2003), pp. 25, 220.
9. Richard Gregory, *Eye and Brain: The Psychology of Seeing* (Oxford: Oxford University Press, 1998), p. 5.
10. Gregory, p. 10.
11. Friedrich Schlegel, *Dialogue on Poetry and Literary Aphorisms*, ed. and trans. by Ernst Behler and Roman Struc (University Park and London: Pennsylvania State University Press, 1968), p. 134.
12. Thomas Whately, *Observations on Modern Gardening, Illustrated by Descriptions* (London: T. Payne, 1771), p. 131. First published in 1770.
13. Foucault mentions 'four types of technologies' that 'hardly ever function separately': technologies of production, sign systems, power and the self. Michel Foucault, 'On the Genealogy of Ethics: An Overview of Work in Progress' in *The Foucault Reader*, ed. by Paul Rabinow (London: Penguin, 1984), pp. 340–372 (p. 369); Michel Foucault, 'Technologies of the Self' in Luther H. Martin, Hugh Gutman and Patrick H. Hutton, eds, *Technologies of the Self: A Seminar with Michel Foucault* (London: Tavistock, 1988), pp. 16–49 (pp. 18–19).
14. Paul De Man, *The Rhetoric of Romanticism* (New York: Columbia University Press, 1984), p. 69.
15. Lennard J. Davis, *Factual Fictions: The Origins of the English Novel* (Philadelphia: University of Pennsylvania Press, 1996), p. 213. Refer to Ian Watt, *The Rise of the Novel: Studies in Defoe, Richardson and Fielding* (London: The Hogarth Press, 1987), p. 62.
16. Daniel Defoe, *Robinson Crusoe* (Oxford: Oxford University Press, 2007).
17. Daniel Defoe, *Roxana, or the Fortunate Mistress*, ed. by P. N. Furbank (London: Pickering and Chatto, 2009), p. 21.
18. Daniel Defoe, *Moll Flanders* (New York: Norton, 2004), p. 3.
19. William Kent, 'Remarks by way of Painting & Archit.', 1714-1717 (Bodleian Library, Oxford), ff. 1–36 (ff. 25-36).
20. De Man, p. 81.
21. Antonio Sant'Elia and Filippo Tomasso Marinetti, 'Manifesto of Futurist Architecture' in Ulrich Conrads, ed., *Programs and Manifestoes on 20th-Century Architecture* (Cambridge MA: MIT Press 1970), pp. 34–38 (p. 35).
22. Anthony Vidler, *Histories of the Immediate Present: Inventing Architectural Modernism* (Cambridge MA and London: MIT Press, 2008), pp. 4–5.
23. Le Corbusier, *Towards a New Architecture*, trans. by Frederick Etchells (London: Architectural Press, 1946). First published in English in 1927.
24. Walter Benjamin, *The Origin of German Tragic Drama*, trans. by John Osborne (London and New York: Verso, 1998), p. 178. Completed but unpublished in 1928.
25. Walter Benjamin, 'The Work of Art in the Age of Mechanical Production' in *Illuminations: Essays and Reflections*, ed. by Hannah Arendt, trans. by Harry Zohn (New York: Schocken Books, 1969), pp. 217–252 (p. 239).
26. Denys Lasdun, 'The Architecture of Urban Landscape', in Denys Lasdun, ed., *Architecture in an Age of Scepticism: A Practitioner's Anthology Compiled by Denys Lasdun* (London: Heinemann, 1984), pp. 134–159 (p. 137).
27. Denys Lasdun, in 'Interview with Denys Lasdun', revised draft, 13 June 1979, p. 9, Lasdun Archive, RIBA Library Drawings and Archives Collections, Victoria and Albert Museum, London; Denys Lasdun, 'The Architecture of Urban Landscape', p. 139.
28. Ernest N. Rogers, 'Continuità', *Casabella Continuità*, no. 199, December 1953–January 1954, p. 2.
29. T. S. Eliot, 'Tradition and the Individual Talent', in *Points of View* (London: Faber and Faber, 1941), pp. 23–34 (pp. 26–27).
30. Denys Lasdun, 'Draft, Suggested Theme–The Late Show, BBC', 8 July 1992, Lasdun Archive; Lasdun, in 'Interview with Denys Lasdun', agreed draft, 27 June 1979, p. 4, Lasdun Archive.
31. Vincent Scully, *American Architecture and Urbanism* (London: Thames & Hudson, 1969), p. 257.
32. Malcolm Bradbury, 'Author's Note', in *The History Man* (London: Secker and Warburg, 1975).
33. Paul Ricoeur, 'Objectivity and Subjectivity in History' in *History and Truth*, trans. by Charles A. Kelbley (Evanston: Northwestern University Press, 1965), pp. 21–40 (p. 22).

STUDIO INTRODUCTION

THE ARCHITECTURAL NARRATIVE

CONSTANCE LAU

Studio Design Methodology

The notion of multiple interpretations is approached by means of the architectural narrative. This is constructed as a design tool and employed to integrate the different facets of research material during the working process. Design authorship furthers this practice by means of precise decisions, which encourages user involvement, resulting in the creation of new meanings and multiple interpretations of the work. Inherent to this design process are issues of site and especially site-specificity, as well as the techniques of montage in relation to interpretation and appropriation. The working process involving inter-disciplinary research aspires towards the invention of a design language that contributes alternative and more potent ways to engage with works of architecture.

The creation of different readings begins with the composition of individual storylines within chosen subject matters. These include art and architecture movements, architectural writings, poetry and music. The argument that 'there is always a history of drawings, objects and buildings within and against which an architectural work can be seen' is important.[1] Hence the consideration of ideas outside the immediate field of architecture to generate design work is imperative. The integration of this research material addresses the notion of 'polyphony', which means 'many voices', and in design practice refers 'to a relational activity between different actions'.[2] Hence this collection of literary and theoretical design references informs aspects of working as well as thinking, and is used to structure the programme in conjunction with precise site investigative studies. The role of multiple interpretations and narratives includes material relating to the current and historical sites associated with the work. These include contextual issues of displacement and site-specificity, which can be used to formulate, identify and locate new sites for design proposals.

The key ideas are approached in a two-fold manner. Intensive research is used to establish a strategic architectural position through a collection of texts, drawings and images. The arguments raised initially will serve as a catalyst for the ensuing design project. The resulting architectural proposal reflects a fragment of the research and represents authorship decisions that have led to this precise and particular expression of the material. Hence the early body of research shapes the architectural narrative and, consequently, the eventual design work.

The qualities of design authorship are demonstrated in the projects discussed. Design authorship begins with the construction of individual design narratives in which assumed and/or general understandings of the chosen subjects are challenged. This is also the point in the design process in which the spatial articulation of the subject matter begins to take form. The clarity and complexity of the narrative is integral to the design work and the outcome further reflects the contribution of the working process which involves the techniques of montage. Hence each fragment of work produced informs a different aspect of the design proposal. These elements are evident in the design processes and outcomes, which similarly reflect the precise decisions garnered from meticulous research of the subject matter and architectural sites.

The wide-ranging programmatic themes - from the Russian Avant-Garde, Sir John Soane's House and Museum and the Arts and Crafts Movement to Mies van der Rohe's Barcelona Pavilion - are explored through individual design briefs. More importantly, the translation of these distinct ideas into works of architecture addresses the notion of multiple interpretations at the different stages of the design process. The architectural narrative is structured to express a range of readings and responses pertaining to different design sources. Hence the notion of multiple interpretations in this instance is explored through the architectural narrative, which is used to construct a dialogue with the audience and/or user.

By staging the works differently and questioning known conventions, different methods of engagement are encouraged. Consequently the experience of architecture is seen as ongoing theoretical and physical responses. Hence design practice is not a static course of action, but a continuous development through the project as new conditions and circumstances arise. More importantly, both the author and the user are intimately involved with the resulting work.

---

[1] Yeoryia Manolopoulou, *Architectures of Chance* (Surrey: Ashgate Publishing Ltd., 2013), p. 124. A further reference is noted as: Mikhail Bakhtin, *The Dialogic Imagination* (University of Texas Press, 1981)

[2] Manolopoulou, p. 124.

THE ARTS MARATHON PRODUCTION LINE

2011/2012

CONSTANCE LAU

The idea of art as a mass produced commodity will be explored through design and spatial principles concerning industrial architecture and the notion of a production line. Ideas of production are explored as both physical and theoretical responses to the urban fabric of the project sites in East London. These are Altab Ali Park opposite the Whitechapel Gallery, and the buildings which are collectively known as the Truman Brewery in Brick Lane, Spitalfields.

The significance of context and program started with the notion of prefabrication in relation to ideas explored in the works of the Russian Avant-Garde. Understanding the intent of the manifesto and especially the inventive and experimental attitudes towards design are crucial. Notions of construction and precision in relation to space, and the spatial elements are vital and these concepts will be manifested in the Art Factory. Hence this site-specific building simultaneously celebrates the role of every individual component during the process of assembly, to the final architecture.

Robin Evan's 'Translations from Drawing to Building' discusses the 'transmutation' that occurs during this transitional process, and the effects of the resulting gap.[1] This gap of ideas, production, use and presentation is precisely where the Tactile Studio will be located. Concepts concerning the practice of architecture, like design and thinking, as well as that of matter and making, are furthered with notions of site-specificity where the architectural constructs are used to articulate precise archaeological narratives. These are expressed through ideas of conservation, reuse and, more importantly, in relation to the tactile nature of the architectural proposals. The design proposals focused on engaging with the spatial, historical and material experiences of the site.

The design brief is also deliberately constructed to address the differences in scale between architectural readings associated with the idealistic ambitions of a 'factory' and those pertaining to the intimate experience of a 'studio'. From mass production to intimate and individual constructs, the resulting readings are able to fluidly reflect both the historical and future narratives of the sites.

The projects presented explored different concepts of making during the design development processes in order to inform the architecture of the final proposal. These are used to construct the design narratives and explore ideas of making in a wide range of scales. This included the making of the building to the making within the building.

The ideas of production in the projects by Loreta Lukoseviciene look to specific aspects of history, which are the works of the Russian Avant-Garde and Elizabethan tailoring techniques in this instance. From the making of pigment which led to the design of the Factory, to the making of the site as a costume to inform the construction of the Theatre in the Tailoring Academy, the sites are approached as a parallel supporting element through which the narratives are expressed and the design projects articulated within.

The projects by Larisa Bulibasa celebrate site-specificity and the physical properties of site. The different acts of making in these proposals happen within the site, and the idea of site operates as the key research focus, as a narrative as well as design generator.

---

[1] Robin Evans, 'Translations from Drawing to Building', *AA Files*, 12 (1986), p. 5.

THE PIGMENT PRODUCTION LINE

LORETA LUKOSEVICIENE

The Russian Avant-Garde is an art movement that flourished during the end of the eighteenth and beginning of the nineteenth-centuries in the Russia Empire. A group of artists and designers which included Kazimir Malevich, Wassily Kandinsky, Gustav Klutsis, El Lissitzky, Liubov Popova and Vladimir Tatlin spearheaded this art revolution by breaking conventions associated with culture and heritage.

The boundaries of traditional academic art training were broken by radical innovations like the introduction of eclectic aesthetics to painting. The application of pure and abstract geometrical compositions which simultaneously evoke stillness and movement was used in paintings, theatre performances and works of architecture.

This project recalls well known paintings associated with the Movement and researched the paints used, as this material was the main medium in the creation of revolutionary art. The artists used colour and form to symbolise ideas. The paint was produced from pigments and hence this Pigment Factory specialises in the production of natural pigments which will be used to restore Russian Avant-Garde paintings.

The proposal consists of a gallery and museum, and is designed in the form of a production line where small amounts of pigments will be produced for the required restoration work. Additional facilities include spaces for painting restorers and researchers, as well as studio spaces for artists.

The making of natural pigment traces back to the early ages when humans produced cave drawings by crushing rocks to make paint. This proposal can be read as a continuation of the well established English paint making industry, and an extension of Whitechapel's history of fabric dyeing and, the expertise of natural paint preparation. This intervention is seen as a response to the ongoing changes in the area with an increasing number of art galleries and related industries.

To date, the experimental nature of the pigments used in the Russian Avant-Garde paintings have made restoration difficult. This Factory will attempt to recreate specific palettes with the multicultural knowledge of people who form part of Whitechapel's heritage. Hence this project not only reintroduces the Russian Avant-Garde palettes but also attempts to bring communities together by the sharing of skills through the production of pigment.

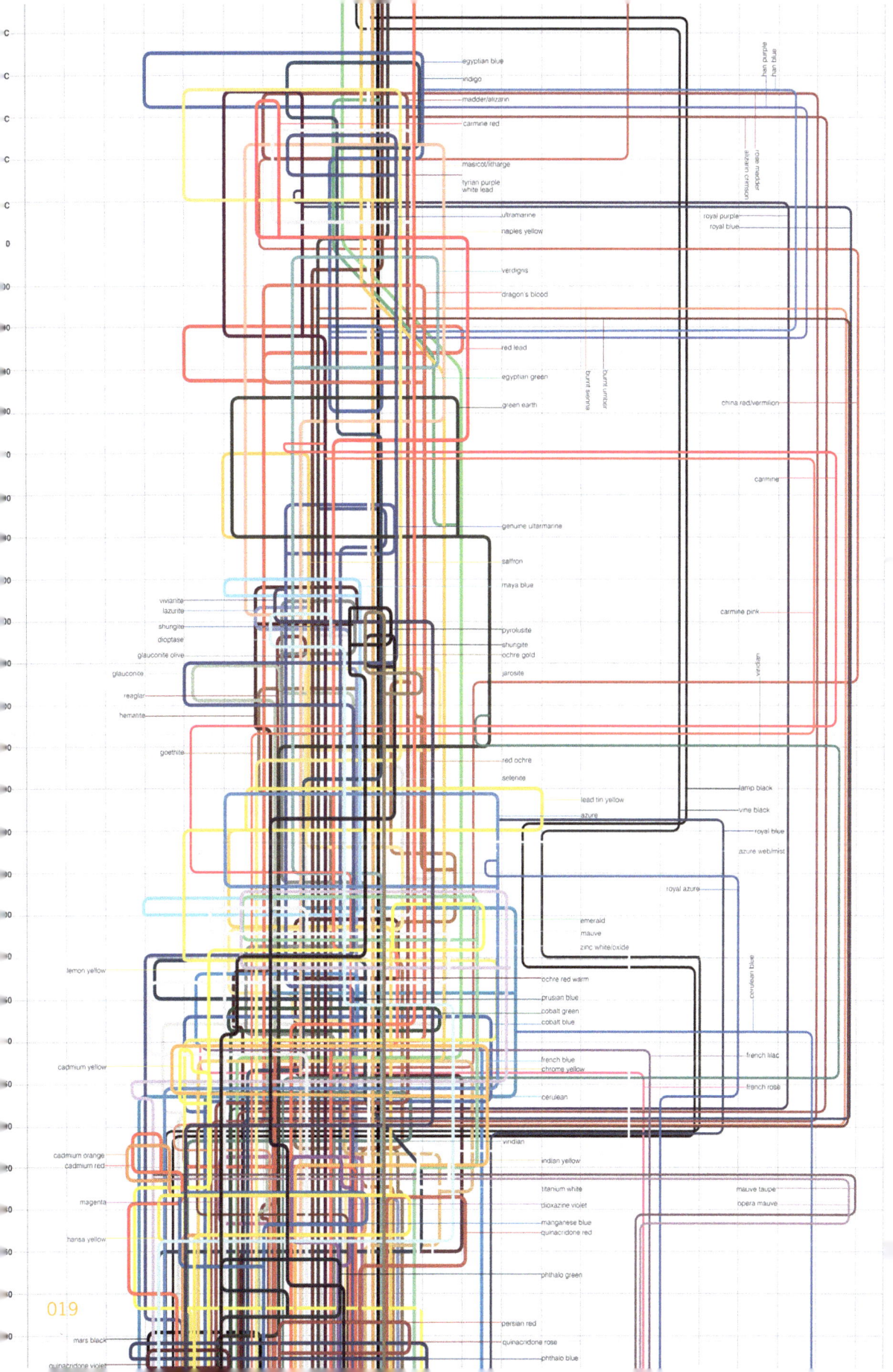

saffron	egyptgreen	umber	cobalt blue
R=25 G=193 B=5	R=110 G=159 B=153	R=132 G=95 B=53	R=44 G=64 B=187
Crocus sativus	[Ca, Cu]3Si3O9	$Fe_2O_3(*H_2O) + MnO_2*(n\ H_2O) + Al_2O_3$	$CoO*Al_2O_3$

carmine	lazurite	zinc white	shungite
R=167 G=29 B=38	R=71 G=78 B=133	R=255 G=255 B=255	R=18 G=21 B=26
$C_{22}H_{20}O_{13}$	$(Na, Ca)_8[(S,Cl,SO_4,OH)_2 1(Al_6Si_6O_{24})]$	ZnO	C_{60}

bone char	geothite	azurite	tyrian purp
R=18 G=21 B=262	R=113 G=70 B=53	R=35 G=62 B=84	R=79 G=54 B=84
$Ca_5(OH)(PO_4)_2$ and C	FeO(OH)	$2\ Cu\ CO_3*Cu(OH)_2$	$(Na, Ca)_8Al_6Si_6O_{24}(S,SO_4)$

madder	gamboge	indigo	glauconite
R=79 G=54 B=84	R=255 G=231 B=21	R=35 G=62 B=89	R=101 G=104 B=86
$C_{14}H_8O_4$	Garcinia Hanburyi	$C_{16}H_{10}N_2O_2$	$(K,Na)(Fe_3,Al,Mg)_2(Si, Al)_4O_{10}(OH)_2$

Paint making and natural pigments

The colour palettes of the artists during the Russian Avant-Garde movement were inspired by folkloric and Russian orthodox iconographic art. The latter is usually painted with tempera, one of the earliest known paints, and commonly used since the twelfth-century. This is prepared by mixing colour pigments with a water-based emulsion made with egg yolk. Other binding agents include glue, honey or milk that additionally serve as thickening agents to retard the effects of fading. Hence the vivid colours are well maintained and conservation works during the nineteenth-century have revealed the bright colours which have been obscured by the numerous repainting efforts over time.

The paints used in some of the Russian Avant-Garde works adhere to traditional preparation methods, which consist of mixing colour pigments and a water-based emulsion made with egg yolk. During the nineteenth-century however, tempera was increasingly replaced with industrialised oil paint. This was a combination of colour pigments, linseed oil and a small quantity of white spirit. As the advent of paints packaged in tubes became readily available, the artists stopped making their own paints.

However the colour pigments used in the paint production process remain crucial to identifying original Russian Avant-Garde paintings by means of tracing their origins. The analysis is possible due to the precise processes required to extract the resulting vibrant colours from the powdered raw ingredients. This knowledge has also influenced the decision to design a pigment, as opposed to a paint making factory in this instance.

The documentation of paint making (left) for the works shown (this page) are made by mixing natural pigments with linseed oil or water to create oil paint and *gouache* respectively. Both these mediums were used by the Russian Avant-Garde artists. The first line under the label indicates the full name of the colour as recognised by the art industry. The next line gives the proportions for digital replication where R G B represents red, green and blue respectively. The last line gives the chemical combinations or animal parts required to make the pigment. A sample of the paint, made with the pigment, made into paint, and tested on a white and black background, is also shown.

Experimenting with the making process has revealed the complexity and skill required for the precise colour of choice to emerge. Artists through the ages have experimented with colour creation by using pigments from all over, and especially remote parts of the world in order to create signature colours that will be associated with their work for years to come. More importantly, this intensive and manual process which encourages experimental creativity has no digital equivalent.

Axonometric drawing of the Pigment Factory presented within the urban context of Altab Ali Park. The formal arrangement of the volumes references the dynamism of the Russian Avant-Garde proposals, especially El Lissitzky's Wolkenbügel Skyscraper, 1924-25, Moscow, and Vladimir Tatlin's Monument to the Third International, 1919-20, St. Petersburg.

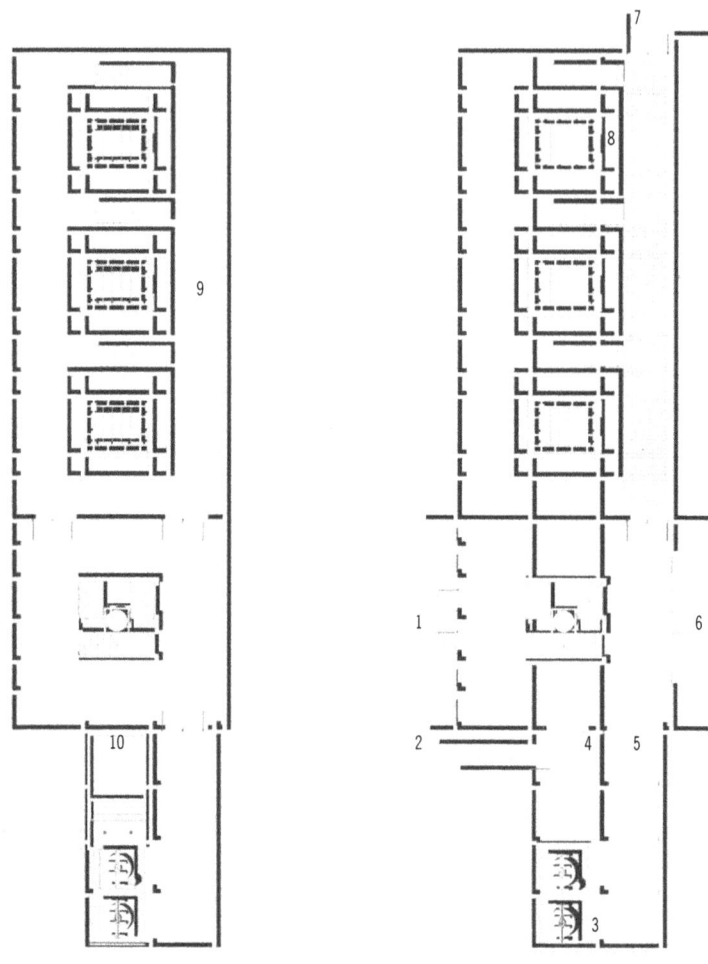

Basement

Ground Floor

Floor plans of the Pigment Factory:

(this page) The basement and ground floors of the Factory are occupied by pigment production activities and also used as storage spaces for raw materials.

(right) The spaces in the Tower are dedicated to painting restoration workshops, study rooms and the museum.

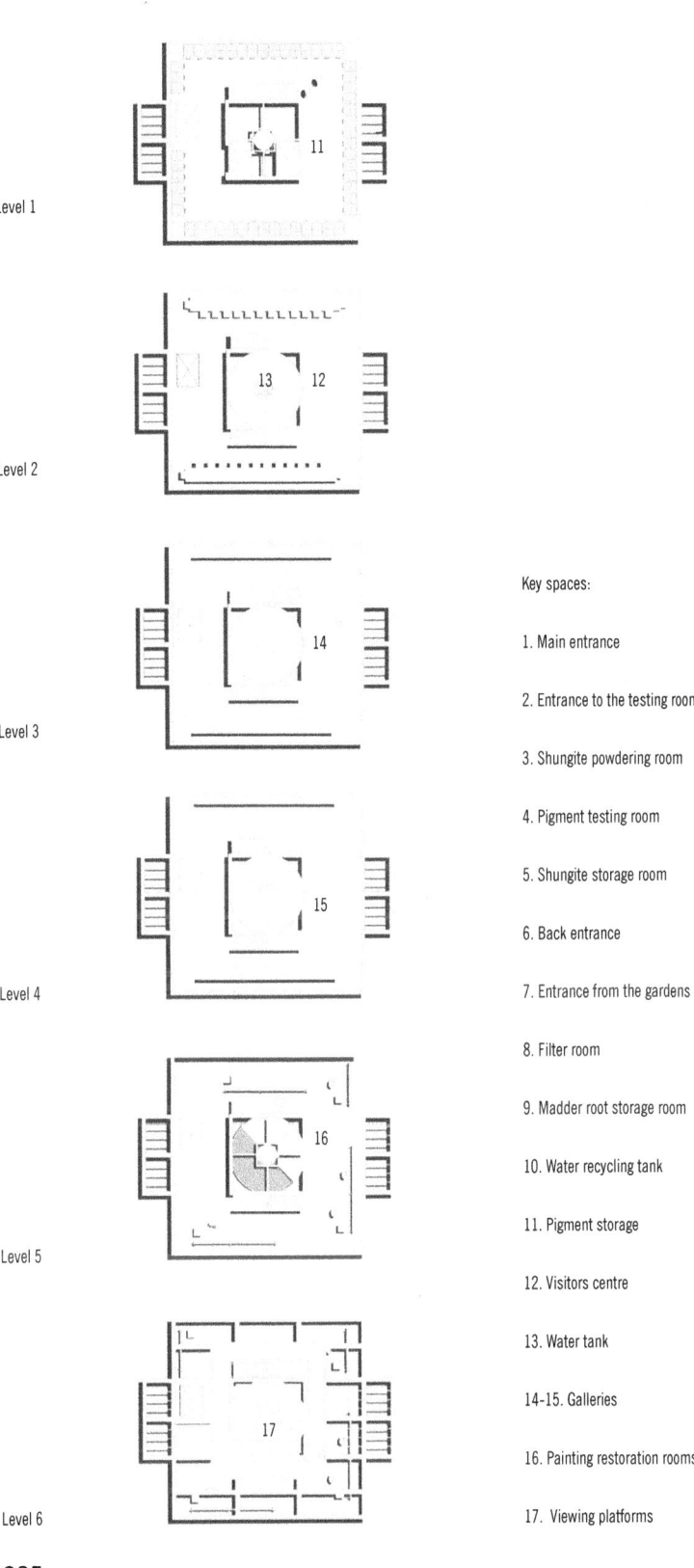

Key spaces:

1. Main entrance
2. Entrance to the testing room
3. Shungite powdering room
4. Pigment testing room
5. Shungite storage room
6. Back entrance
7. Entrance from the gardens
8. Filter room
9. Madder root storage room
10. Water recycling tank
11. Pigment storage
12. Visitors centre
13. Water tank
14-15. Galleries
16. Painting restoration rooms
17. Viewing platforms

View showing the filtration process during the production of natural pigments. The cloth is used to separate the fluids from the plant roots that have been soaking.

View showing the pigment production gallery.

THE ELIZABETHAN TAILORING ACADEMY

LORETA LUKOSEVICIENE

The Elizabethan Tailoring Academy is located at the heart of what used to be the Truman Brewery in Brick Lane. Spitalfields is favoured by the creative industries and tourists because of its trendy and quirky markets as well as shops which sell handmade crafts, clothes and antiques. The area is known for its once thriving silk weaving industry which was established by French immigrants, also known as the Huguenots. This community migrated to London with their weaving and tailoring skills, and hence made this area famous for the design and production of distinctive fabrics.

The design process started with a masterplan analysis of Spitalfields. This research presentation was likened to the making of garments and the masterplan was designed to unfold like a patchwork item. The form resembles a beautiful garment with emphasis on the history and mixed aesthetics of the local architecture. This piece is further 'embroidered' with streets and small alleys. The research also highlighted a distinctive feature of Spitalfieds in the form of craft and fashion shops, and street markets which are highly popular with visitors to the area. In this instance, the Old Truman Brewery at the junction of Brick Lane and Dray Walk are of particular interest as thousands of people go pass this junction every weekend, creating tight pockets. Hence careful interventions to the masterplan redirected this pedestrian flow and reused the surrounding buildings.

Dray Walk used to be a back entrance to the Old Truman Brewery. The latter is a complex of buildings which have since been transformed and filled with trendy restaurants, designer fashion shops and art galleries. Hence this existing context enables the seamless integration of the proposed Tailoring Academy. Site readings experiment with the condition of the Truman Brewery as a closed complex of numerous buildings that are tightly 'sewn' together to support the different processes of brewing.

The key idea for the design proposal argues that buildings can be tailored as three-dimensional garments. The reading of Brick Lane extends lengthways across the complexity of the Truman Brewery. This pattern is tested by means of weaving fabric over and under the site to form continuous supports for the structure of the existing building. The project focuses on the patterns created where this architectural garment is folded and unfolded in different places. The new building is used to house a tailoring school which specialises in recreating special garments for theatre performances.

The Tailoring Academy is a combination of different spaces like the Tailoring rooms, Library Balconies, Hanging Archive Gallery and especially the Folding Pattern Theatre. The Tailoring rooms are designed by following the various tailoring processes like shaping, cutting, seaming, and sewing. The costumes made by the students will be archived in the Gallery, acting as show pieces to fellow students and visitors. The same skills will be further applied to 'tailor' patterns for the buildings. The Academy also houses an open-air Theatre designed with the notion of the performance of learning.

Hence the Elizabethan Tailoring Academy can be read as a synthesis of the architectural fabric of Dray Walk and the structural grid of the surrounding buildings. This Academy is cut out and sewn together with trimmings to form fine pleats that encapsulates the existing patterns on site.

(right) The map of London, drawn to appear like a garment that has been constructed from different pieces of fabric.

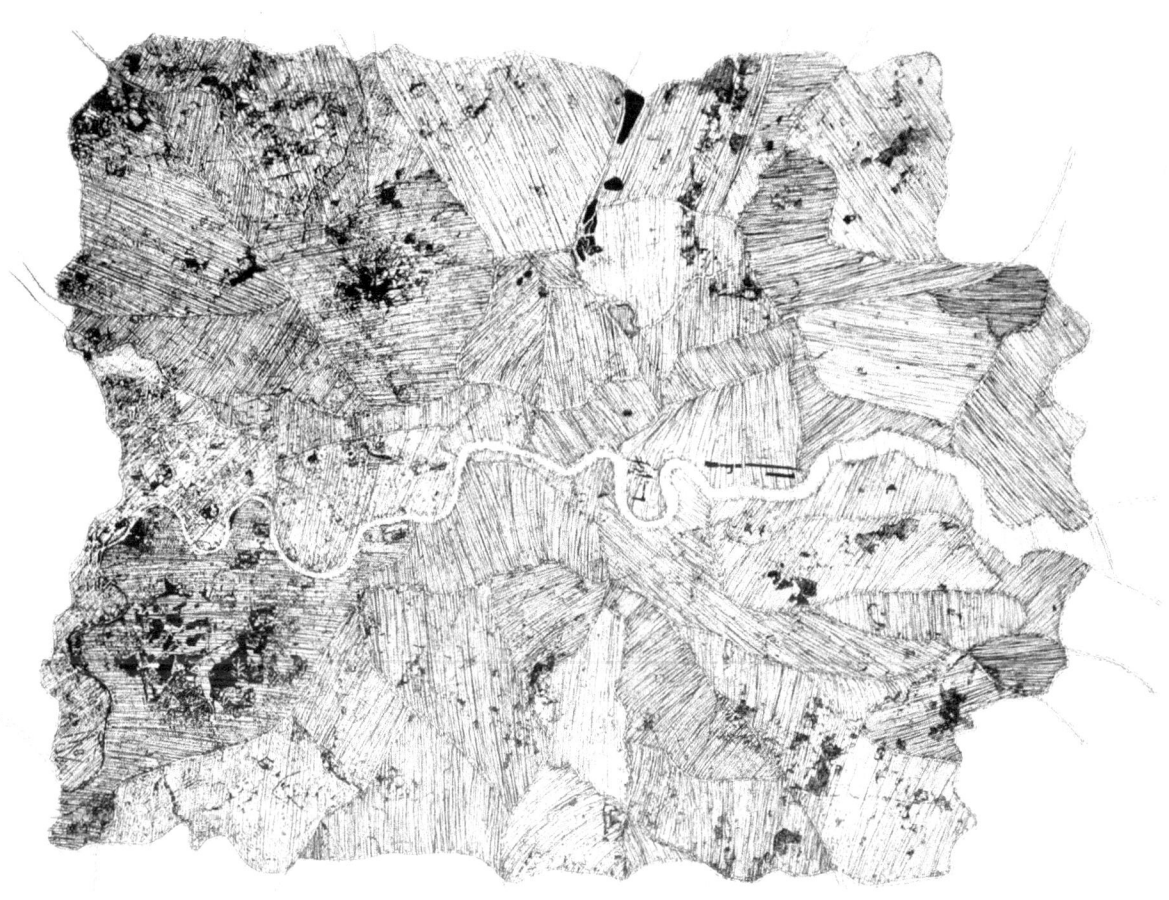

 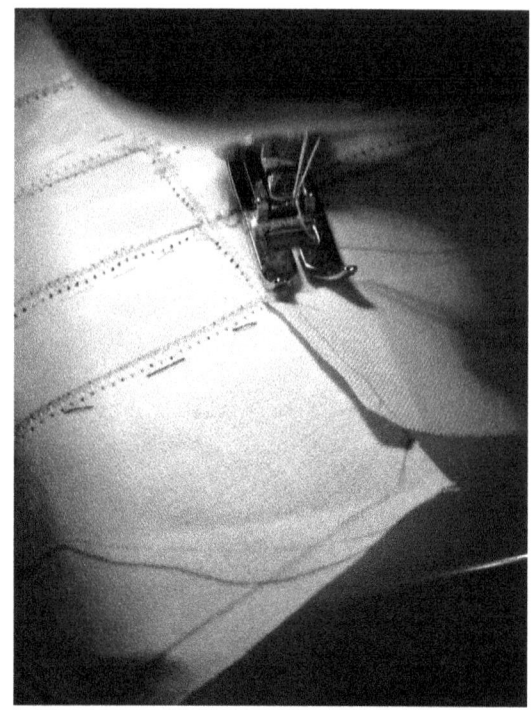

(this page) Exploring the use of cloth as a building fabric and 'making' experiments which investigate the site by means of different tailoring techniques.

(right) Textures and sewing techniques are key to the making of the masterplan, which is drawn to appear like it has been stitched together.

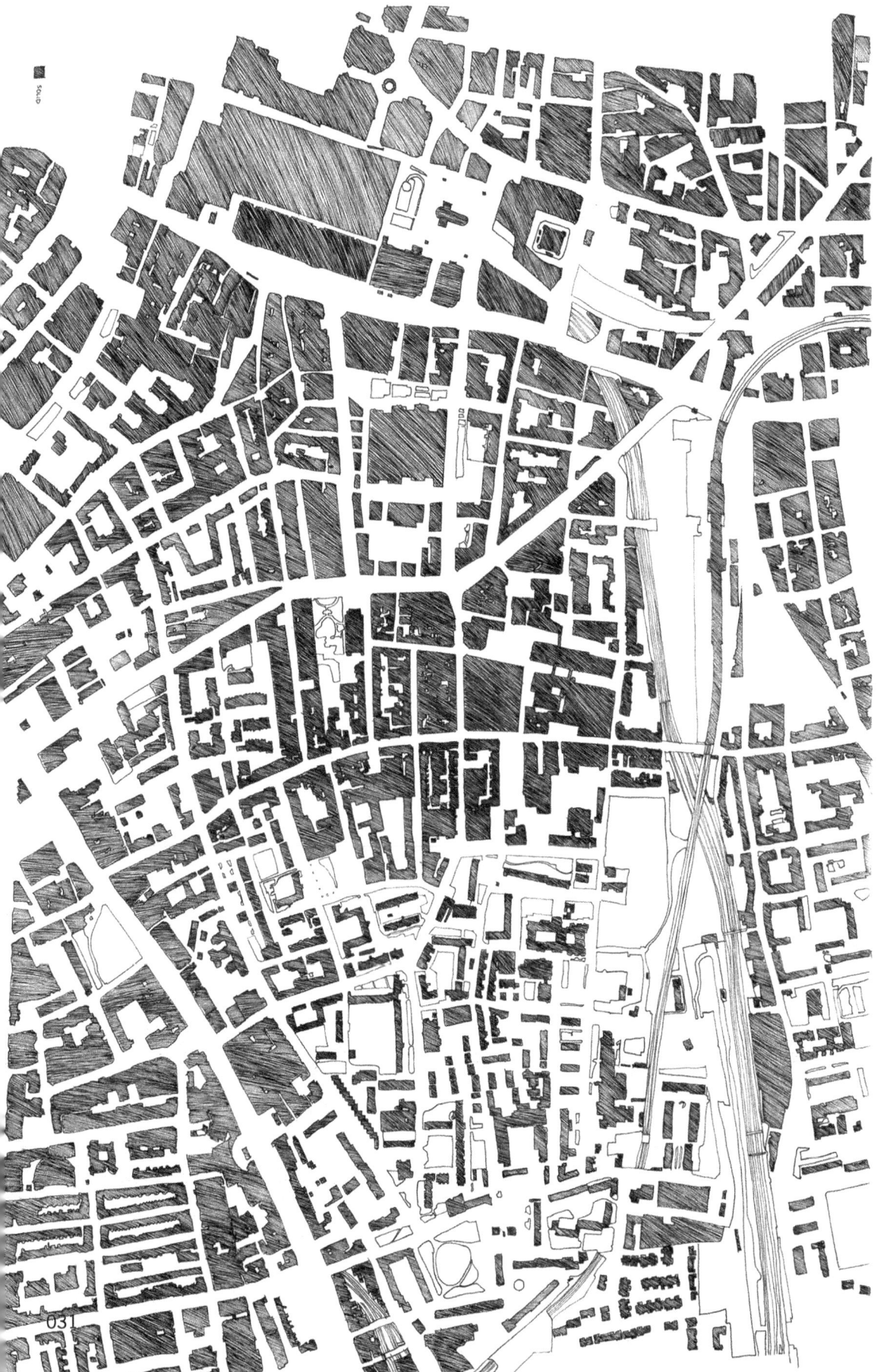

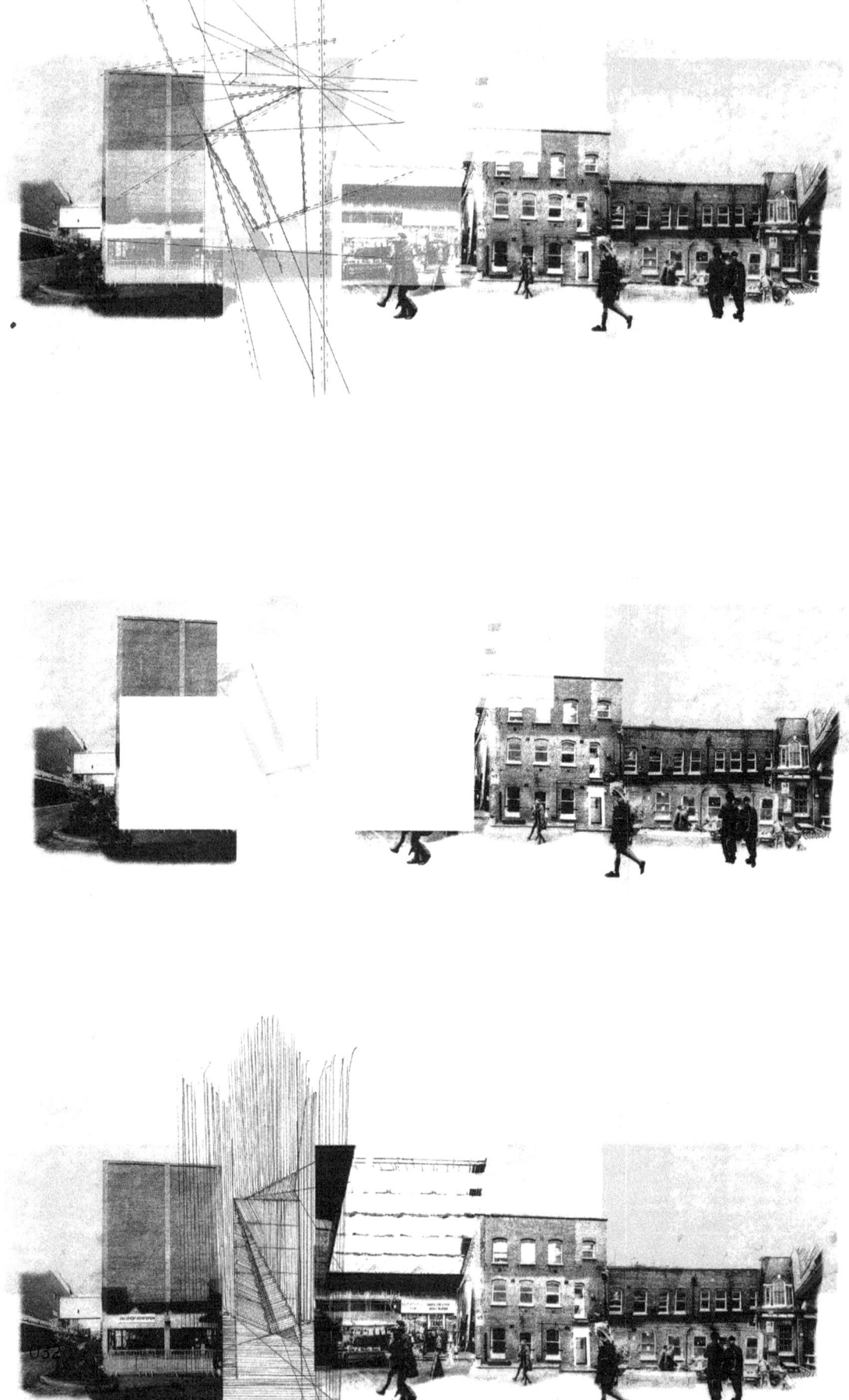

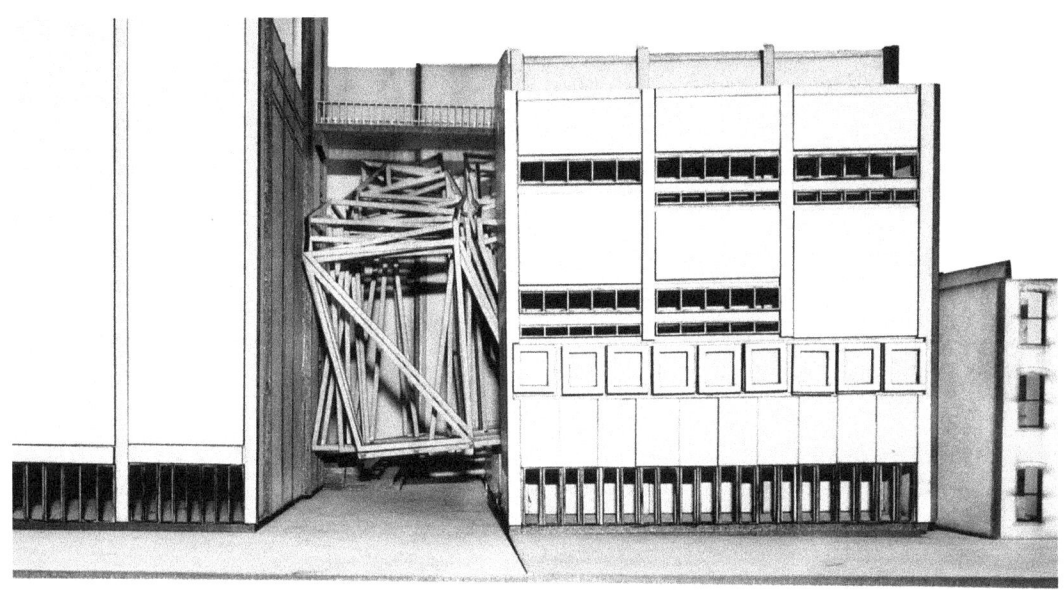

(left) Concept sketches exploring site readings by means of tailoring techniques, which are employed to 'cut' and 'fold' the proposed structure into the existing buildings.

(this page) Site model exploring the concept of structuring in relation to the construction of Elizabethan costumes on Dray Walk. Concepts of layering, geometry and habitation which are important to the tailoring of Elizabethan costumes are adopted in the design proposal.

The development of the structure as a means of enclosure for the Academy is further tested as a programmatically and contextually responsive architectural feature in the tight urban infill site.

Plans showing the spatial organisation of the Academy:

p. 35.
Roof plan showing the connection between the Academy and the immediate buildings on site.

p. 36.
(left) Ground floor plan showing the Galleries and Theatre space.

(right) Plan showing the suspended rooms for the different tailoring activities.

p. 37.
(left) Plan showing the suspended Seaming and Ironing rooms.

(right) Plan showing the suspended rooms for storage and display of the completed costumes.

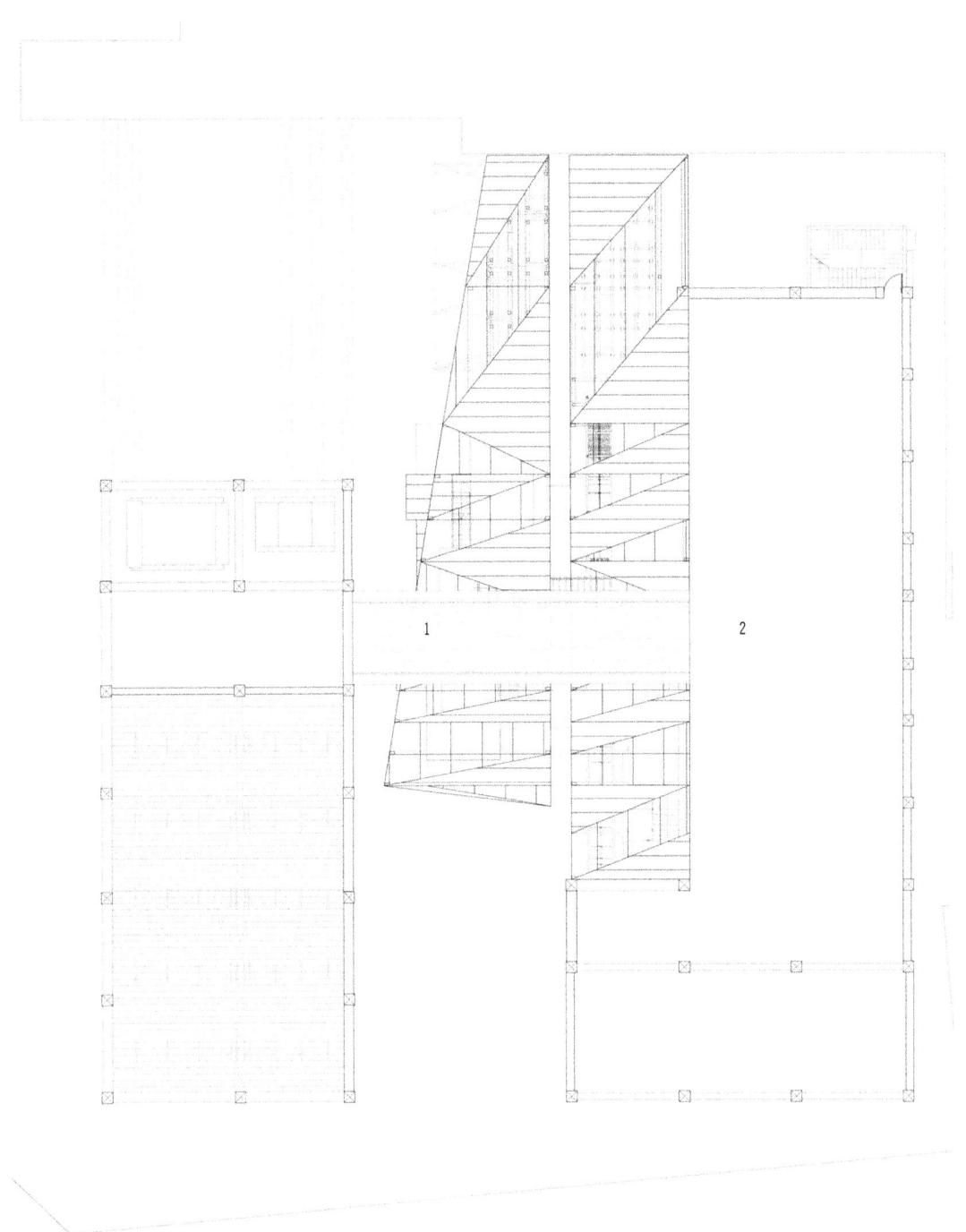

Key spaces:

1. Entrance
2. Bridge to Gallery

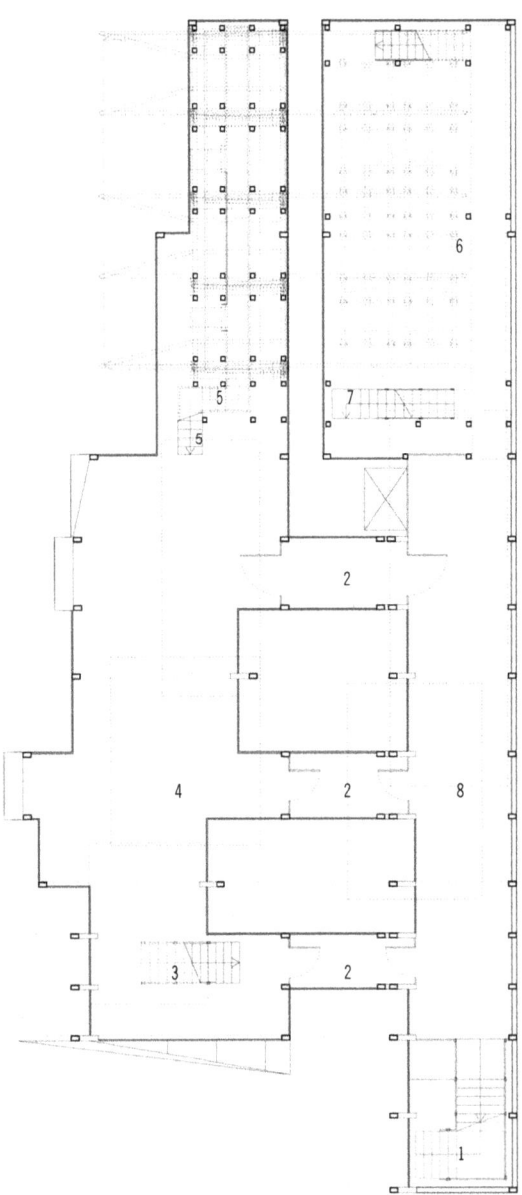
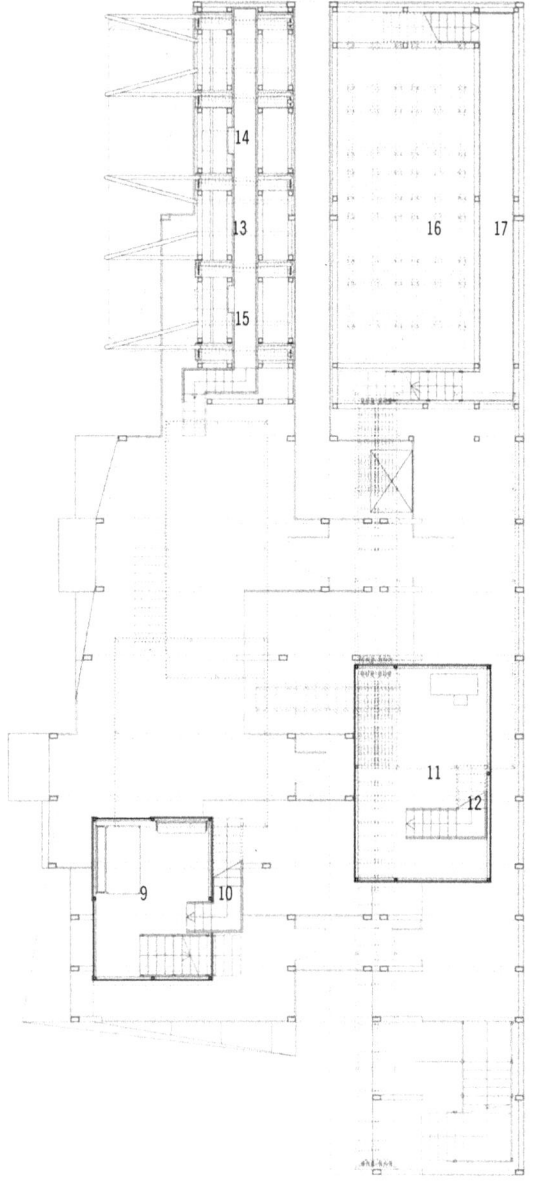

Key spaces:

1. Entrance
2. Bridge to Gallery
3. Entrance to Tailoring rooms
4. Gallery
5. Entrance to viewing platforms of Folding Theatre
6. Workshop
7. Entrance to Pattern Workshop
8. Exhibition Hall
9. Cutting room
10. Stairs to Shaping room
11. Fitting room
12. Stairs from Archives
13. Folding Theatre
14. Stage of Folding Theatre
15. Viewing platform of Folding Theatre
16. Platforms to Stage
17. Pattern Tailoring Workshop platforms

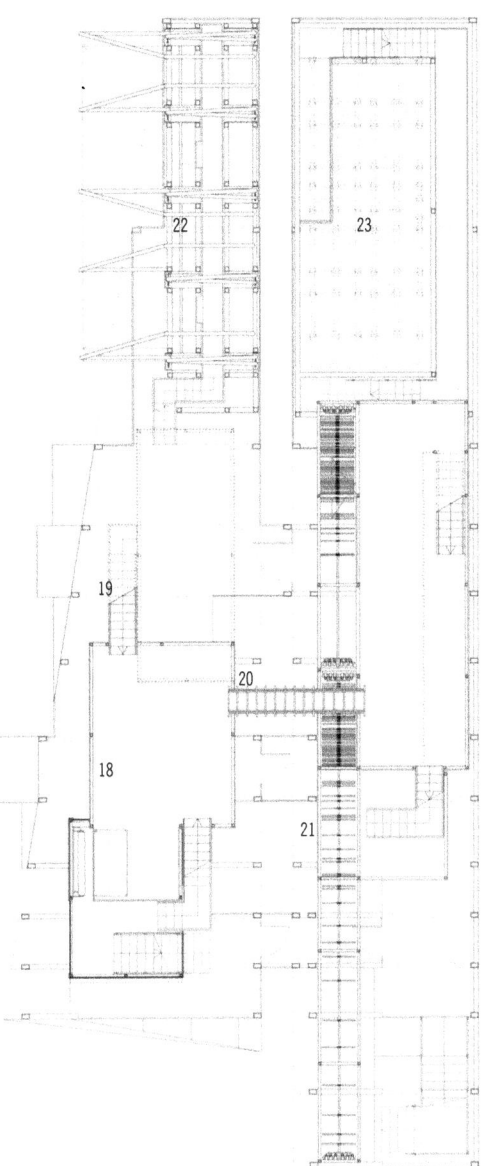
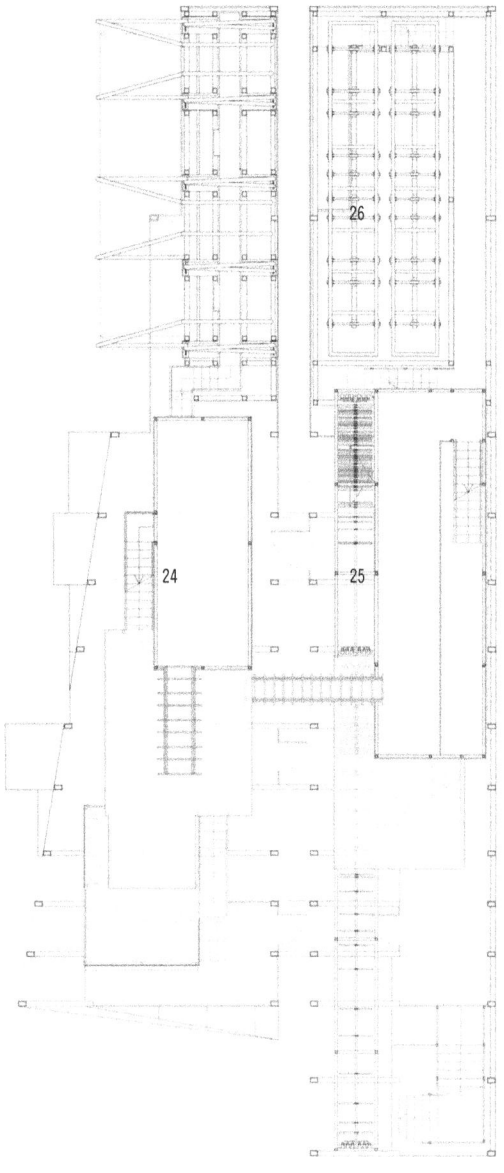

18. Shaping room
19. Stairs to Sewing room
20. Bridge to Archives and Fitting room
21. Floating Archives
22. Folding Theatre
23. Pattern Tailoring Workshop platforms

24. Sewing rooms
25. Fitting room and 'Floating' Archives
26. Structural 'hanging' frame of the Pattern Theatre

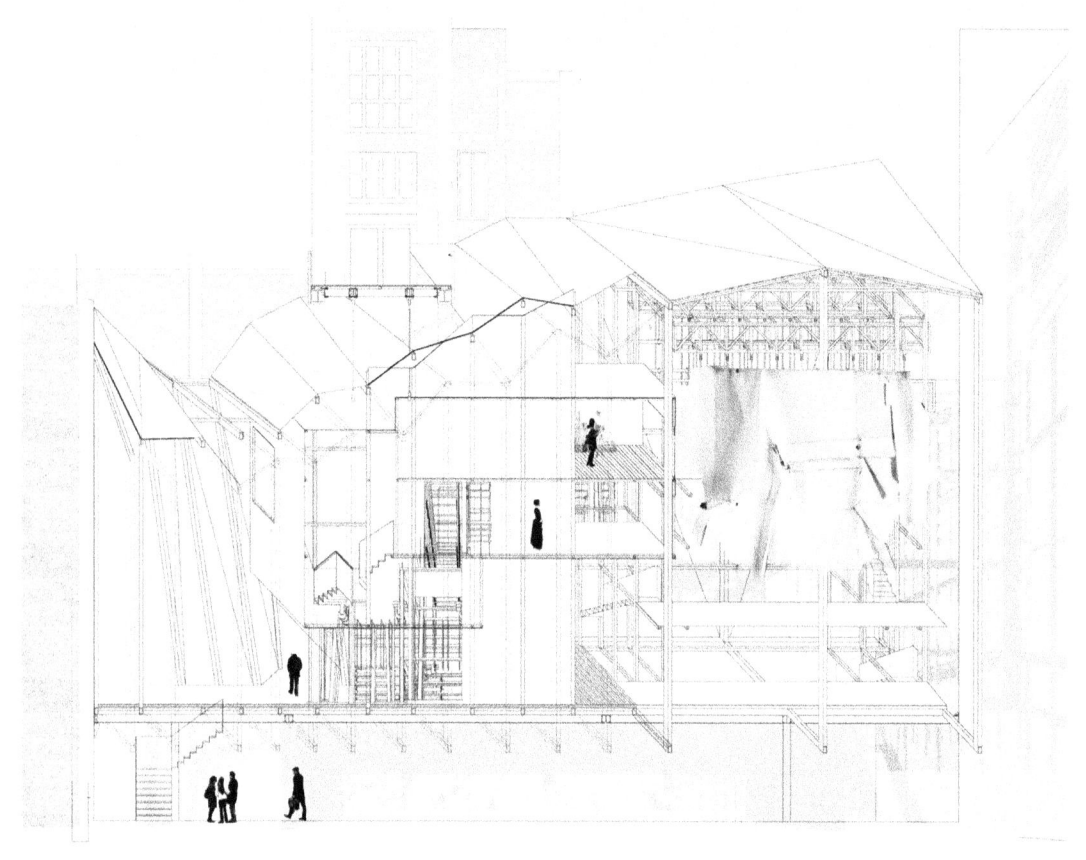

(this page) Long section showing the spatial relationships between the public Galleries, suspended rooms and the Pattern Theatre. The Theatre is so named as the design is 'cut' and 'shaped' to accommodate the form of the site.

(right) Concept model showing the components of the Pattern Theatre which were developed using techniques similar to the making of the site models.

The deployment of the Pattern Theatre's storage mechanism shows the folding process of the stage sets. The construction process and eventual forms further reference the patterns which were developed during the making of the site models.

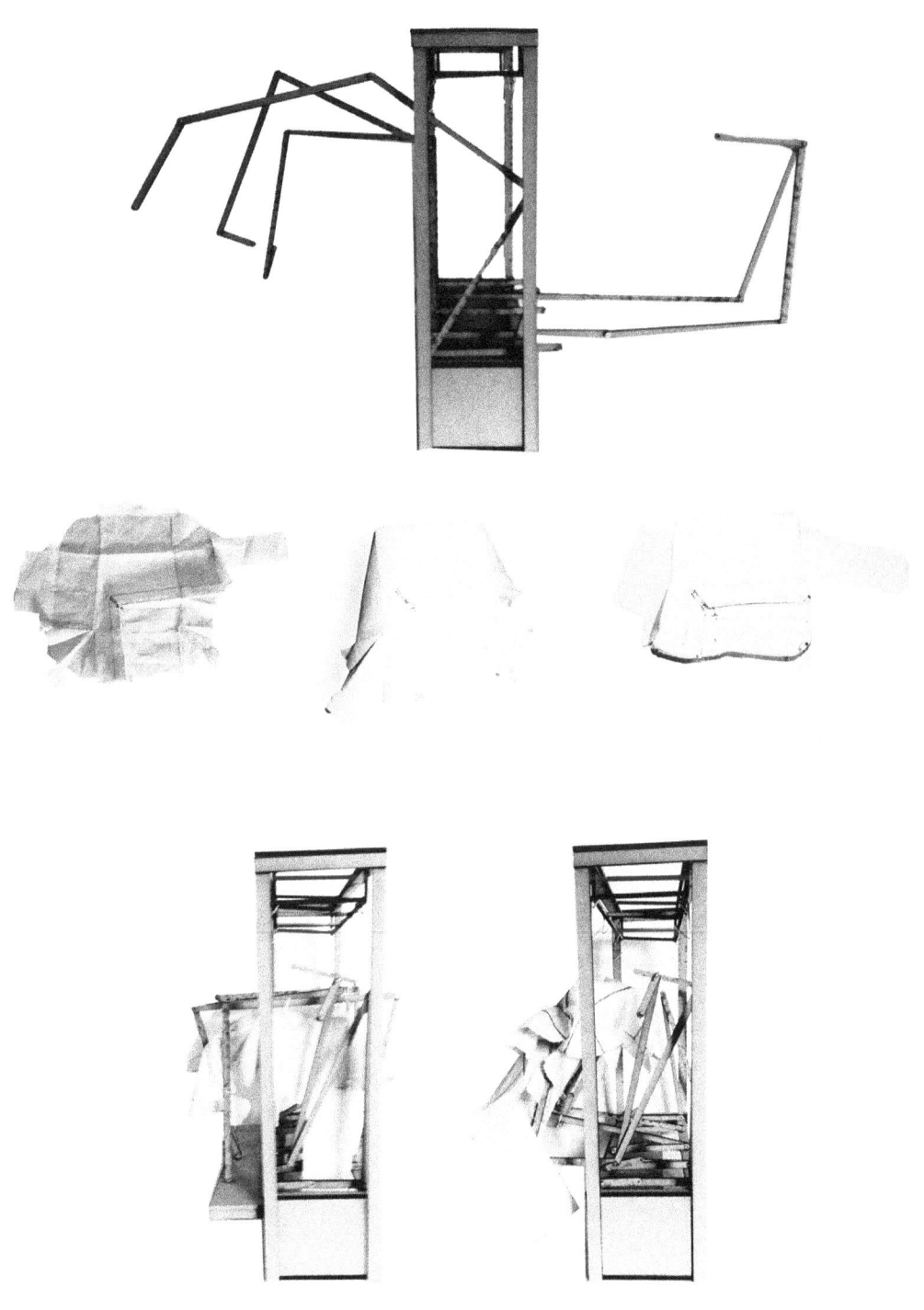

Performances inspired by the Elizabethan era and exhibiting the costumes produced by students of the Tailoring Academy. The elevated building simultaneously allows for through passage, as well as for an audience to gather and enjoy the shows.

Interior view of the Galleries suspended within the Tailoring Academy. The costumes produced by the students are further suspended to maximise the use of the space while enabling the work to be viewed from all angles.

View of the Academy from the street entrance, demonstrating the manner in which the structure and transparent 'skin' of the enclosure unfolds alongside the activities inside the building.

BIBLIOGRAPHY

Alcega, Juan de, *Tailor's Pattern Book, 1589* (New York: Costume & Fashion Press, 1999). First published in 1978.

Arnold, Janet, *Patterns of Fashion, volume 1: Englishwoman's Dresses and Their Construction: c.1660–1860* (London: Macmillan Publishers, 1989). First published in 1964.

Arnold, Janet, *Patterns of Fashion, volume 2: Englishwoman's Dresses and Their Construction: c.1860–1940* (London: Macmillan Publishers, 1982).

Arnold, Janet, *Patterns of Fashion, volume 3: The Cut and Construction of Clothes for Men and Women: c.1560–1620* (London: Macmillan Publishers, 1985).

Arnold, Janet, *Patterns of Fashion 4: The Cut and Construction of Linen Shirts, Smocks, Neckwear, Headwear and Accessories for Men and Women: c.1540–1660* (London: Macmillan Publishers, 2008).

Barnett, Vivian Endicott, Helmut Friedel, and Rudolf H. Wackernagel, *Vasily Kandinsky: A Colourful Life: The Collection of the Lenbachhaus, Munich* (New York: Harry N. Abrams and Dumont, 1996).

Bowlt, John E. and Olga Matich, *Laboratory of Dreams: Russian Avant-Garde and Cultural Experiment* (Stanford, Calif.: Stanford University Press, 1996).

Bowlt, John E., *Russian Art of The Avant-Garde: Theory and Criticism 1902–1934* (London: Thames and Hudson, 1988).

Bürger, Peter, *Theory of the Avant-Garde*, trans. by Michael Shaw (Minneapolis: University of Minnesota Press, 1984).

Cooke, Catherine, *Russian Avant-Garde: Theories of Art, Architecture and the City* (London: Academy Editions, 1995).

Douglas, Charlotte, 'Colours Without Objects. Russian Colour Theories, 1908–1932', *The Structurist*, vol. 13–14 (1973–74), p.30–41.

Finlay, Victoria, *Colour: Travels Through the Paintbox* (London: Sceptre, 2003).

Goodway, David, *London Chartism, 1838–1848* (Cambridge, UK: Cambridge University Press, 1982).

Gur'ianova, Nina. A., *Exploring Colour: Olga Rozanova and the Early Russian Avant-Garde 1910–1918*, trans. by Charles Rougle (Amsterdam, Netherlands: G&B Arts International, 2000).

Gurr, Andrew, *Playgoing in Shakespeare's London* (Cambridge, UK: Cambridge University Press, 1987).

Gurr, Andrew, *The Shakespearean Stage, 1574–1642* (Cambridge, UK: Cambridge University Press, 2009). First published in 1970.

Gwynn, Robin D., *Huguenot Heritage: The History and Contribution of the Huguenots in Britain* (London: Routledge & Kegan Paul, 1985).

Kelly, Francis Michael and Randolph Schwabe, *European Costume and Fashion, 1490 – 1790* (Mineola, New York: Dover Publications Inc., 2002). First published in 1929.

Murray, Natalia, *The Unsung Hero of The Russian Avant-Garde: The Life And Times of Nikolay Punin* (Netherlands: Brill, 2012).

Peacock, John, *The Stage Designs of Inigo Jones: The European Context* (Cambridge: Cambridge University Press, 1995).

Spira, Andrew, *The Avant-Garde Icon: Russian Avant-Garde Art and the Icon Painting Tradition* (Aldershot, Hampshire: Lund Humphries, 2008).

Steinberg, Marc W., *Fighting Words: Working Class Formation, Collective Action, and Discourse in Early Nineteenth-Century England* (Ithaca, N.Y.: Cornell University Press, 1999).

Thuer, Chantal-Helen, 'The Making and Meaning of Russian Avant-Garde', lecture at the Courtauld Institute of Art, 8 Nov. 2011.

Vincent, Susan J., *Dressing The Elite: Clothes in Early Modern England* (Oxford, UK: Berg Publishers, 2003).

White, Edmund, *The Flâneur: A Stroll Through the Paradoxes of Paris* (New York: Bloomsbury, 2001).

THE ART FACTORY: A VERTICAL PRODUCTION LINE

LARISA BULIBASA

The design proposal for the Art Factory explores the manufacturing of nature as art, and especially issues concerning temporality and transition.

The project site in Altab Ali Park takes on board the idea of an Arts Marathon Production Line, which references ideas introduced by art and architecture movements like the Russian Avant-Garde, Bauhaus and De Stijl. Hence the design translates readings of a production line into the production of architecture, which in this instance is the Art Factory.

The Art Factory produces three site-specific spatial experiences that introduces new ways of understanding and engaging with works of art. These consist of a microclimate, an archaeological environment and a series of flexible rooms which house display, discussion and studio spaces. This program further reinforces the idea of art as a form of contextual response.

Key to the architectural proposal is the concept of adaptability where the spatial environments are designed to respond and blend into the site. These differences result from the relationship between site conditions like weather and the programmatic intentions of the architecture, both of which are constantly shifting. Hence this idea of site response was translated into the main design feature of the Tower where the exaggerated verticality further responded to the archaeological history of the previous churches on site.

(right) Concept sketches showing the development of the Arts Marathon Production Line, and the stages during the 'making' of the Art Factory. These are explored in further detail in the following pages.

The Art Factory is designed to appear and function as a vertical production line that is always in flux, and never complete.

The layered cultural and historical identities are expressed by the presence of different monuments and memorials. The archaeological environment consists of the foundations of three churches. The Park was formerly known as St Mary's Gardens, named after the 13th-century 'White Chapel'. This medieval church was replaced by St Mary Matfelon in the 14th-century, which was subsequently replaced in the 19th-century. The foundations of the last church are marked by brick lines on the ground.

The Park was renamed Altab Ali in 1994, and the stance against racism was furthered by the design of the wrought-iron arch at the gateway which combines Bangladesh and Gothic motifs. In addition to a late-Georgian chest tomb and the Whitechapel drinking fountain, the Park also houses the Shaheed Minars Martyrs' Monument. This commemorates the struggle for Bangladesh's independence in 1952, and is a replica of the original in Dhaka. Hence the presence of the an Art Factory adds another reading and layer to the fabric of the Park.

The verticality of the Art Factory is also designed to respond to the depth of the archaeological site in the Park.

The Art Factory is designed to exist in a state of flux, where the process of reinvention and construction is continuous. This definition of 'making' which is site-specific reflects the cutting-edge art scene in East London.

RESTORE, REUSE AND REGENERATE: UP-CYCLING AND ARCHITECTURE CONSERVATION

LARISA BULIBASA

'London ... has always been rebuilt, and demolished, and vandalised. That ... is part of its history'.[1]

Since the creation of the Roman Wall, London has developed a complex landscape with a unique pattern of urban expansion and a close-knit network of alleyways. Over time, London became a layered city, brimming with sites of archaeological interests, one of which has been highlighted for restoration, reuse and regeneration in this design project.

The group of buildings collectively referred to as the Truman Brewery is located along Brick Lane, and more importantly, in the vicinity of the ancient City of London. In addition to its high archaeological potential, the area is also representative of the seventeenth to nineteenth-century brick making industry that was prevalent in London. This is most evident in the brickwork of the existing architecture.

This rich tradition of the site is revealed and continued in the design proposal through the process of architectural conservation. The design proposal reconsiders the notion of boundaries between private and public, as well as the idea of an assumed ground level and the underlying layers. These are explored through the processes of exhibition and education and simultaneously expressed by the architecture. The historically rich Vat House and an adjacent building function dually as exhibits and habitable spaces. The architectural language is influenced by the existing features on site, which are seen as markers for the new project boundaries. These are, an existing brick bridge, a triple volume brick wall and the Vat House, the last of which is the oldest building on the east side of Brick Lane.

The evoking of memories during the conservation process are contrasted and accentuated against the new architectural interventions. The peeling back of historical layers reveals the 'hidden treasures' of Brick Lane, articulates archaeological narratives, and more importantly allows the existing buildings to be appreciated and experienced differently, as well as appropriately reused.

By enhancing the apparent layered and multi-faceted qualities, the proposal puts a positive spin on the area and strengthens its spatial, historical and material experience. The design program addresses the differences in scale between the large public spaces of a Bridge Gallery, an existing archaeological site and the intimate private spaces of a Studio and Workshop. These spaces are bridged by means of the building program, activities and architectural language. Most of all, the design concept celebrates ideas of change. The proposed structure is continuously shifting and adapting to new conditions, and the potential for new spaces and different ways of using the building are integral to the architecture.

This project was nominated for the 2012 RIBA President's Bronze Medal.

[1] Peter Ackroyd, *London: The Biography* (London: Chatto and Windus, 2000), p. 760.

(right) Masterplan depicting East London's archaeological sites. This drawing attempts to highlight and reveal potential 'hidden treasures'.

1: Former stables that were later converted into a Boiler House

This drawing documents the elevations of the former Stables and Vat House which form part of the Truman Brewery complex. They are both Grade II Listed and constructed with stock brick.

1: The former Stables, dated 1831-6 was subsequently adapted to fulfil a variety of functions which included offices and a Music Hall. The building eventually became a Boiler House, and a chimney was added in 1929-30.
2: The Vat House is dated c.1800.
3: The elevation of this building is of special interest and will be flanked by the Bridge Gallery which is designed to connect Woodseer street to the Vat House.

2: Vat House 3: Proposed site for the Bridge Gallery

Aerial view of the Truman Brewery complex showing the Bridge Gallery entrance and Vat House to the east, and the Director's House to the west of Brick Lane.

Aerial view of the Truman Brewery complex showing the proposed Vat House Archaeological Site, Workshop and Bridge Gallery.

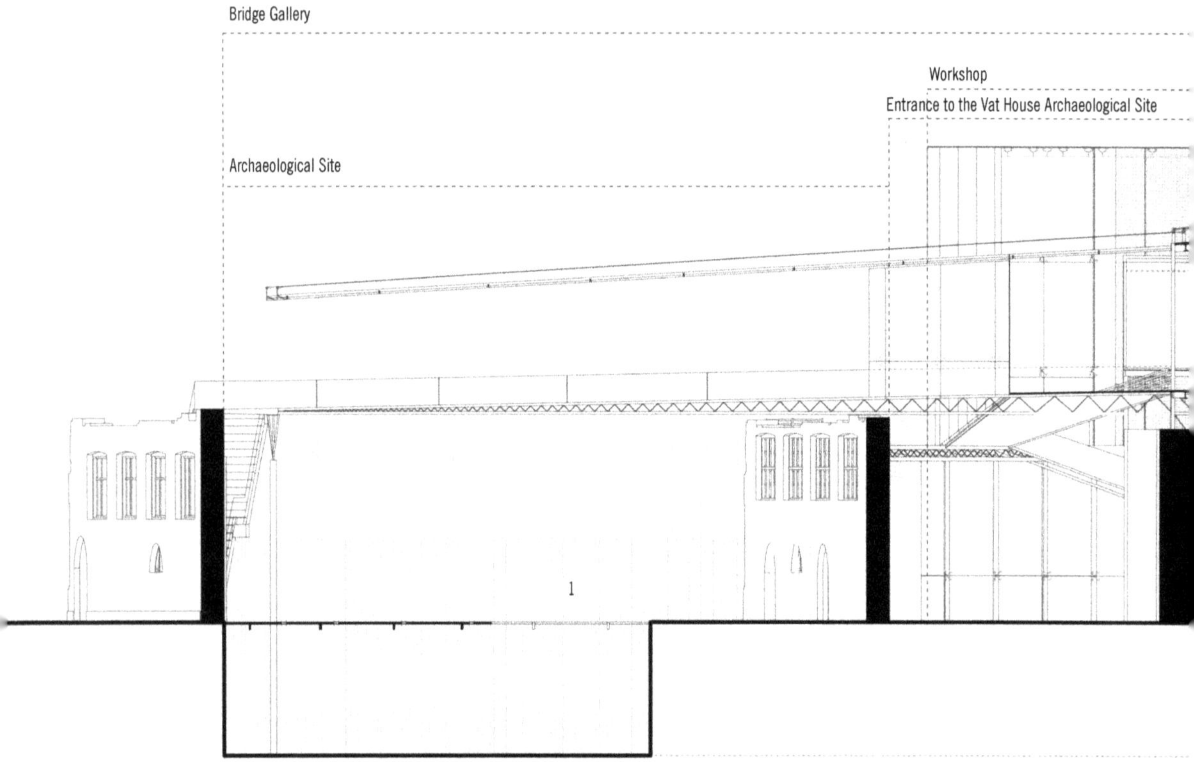

Bridge Gallery

Workshop
Entrance to the Vat House Archaeological Site

Archaeological Site

1

6
7
9
8

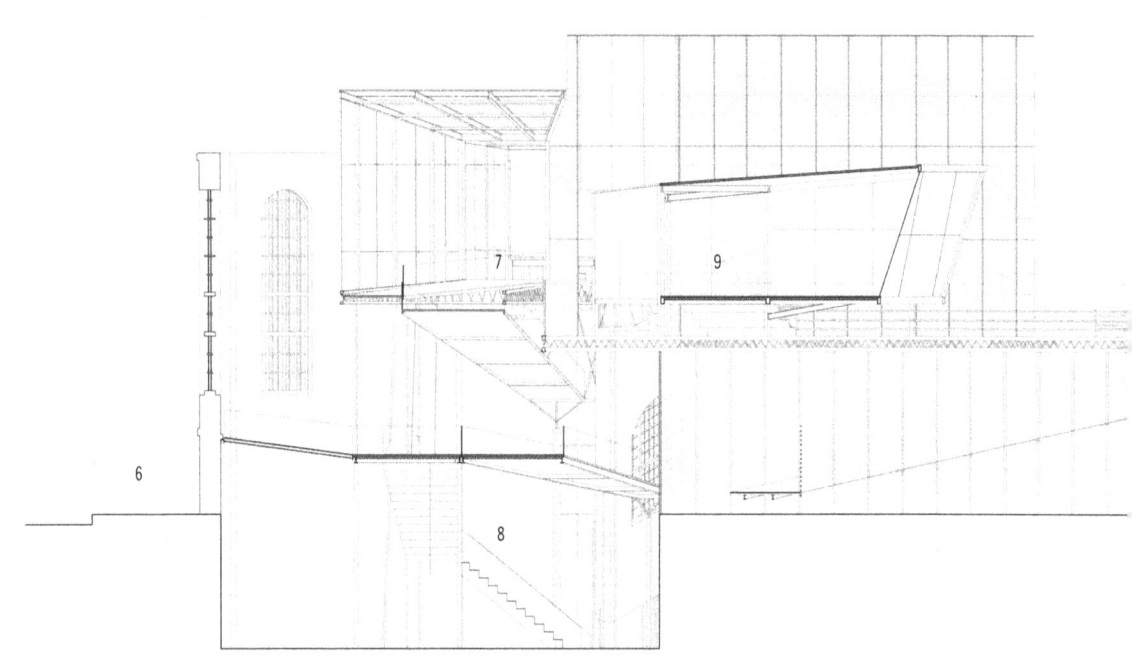

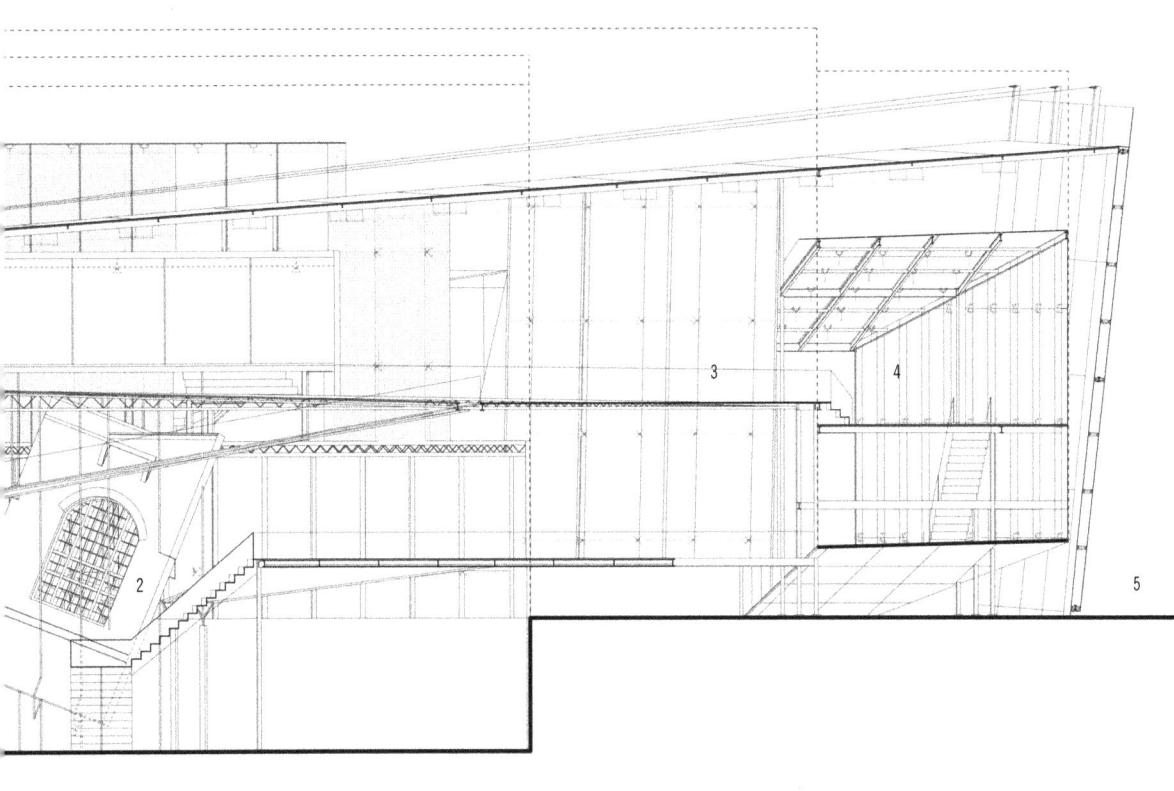

KEY:

(top) **Long Section**
1: Vat House Archaeological Site
2: Workshop
3: Bridge Gallery
4: Bridge Gallery entrance
5: Woodseer street

(left) **Short Section**
6: Brick Lane
7: Bridge Gallery
8: Workshop
9: Studio
10: Courtyard

Interior view of the Bridge Gallery showing the tactile quality of the spaces, with glimpses of the Workshop in the background.

Interior view from the entrance of the Bridge Gallery showing the Studios and more importantly, the integration of public and private spaces within the building.

Perspective view from the courtyard showing the physical and visual connections between the existing Vat House and the Bridge Gallery.

Perspective view of the Vat House Archaeological Site and the Bridge Gallery.

BIBLIOGRAPHY

Ackroyd, Peter, *London: The Biography* (London: Chatto and Windus, 2000).

Benjamin, Walter, *The Work of Art in the Age of Mechanical Reproduction*, trans. by J. A. Underwood (London: Penguin Books, 2008). First English edition of the essay was published in 1968.

Building the Revolution: Soviet Art and Architecture 1915–1935 (London: Royal Academy of Arts, 2011).

Coles, Alex and Mark Dion, *Archaeology*, ed. by Mark Dion (London: Black Dog Publishing, 1999).

Cook, Peter, *Drawings: The Motive Force of Architecture* (West Sussex: Wiley, 2012).

Crimp, Douglas, *On the Museum's Ruins* (Cambridge: MIT Press, 1995).

Evans, Robin 'Translations from Drawings to Buildings', *AA Files*, 12 (1986), pp. 3–17.

Forty, Adrian, *Words and Buildings: A Vocabulary of Modern Architecture* (London: Thames and Hudson, 2000).

Gordon Matta-Clark, ed. by Corinne Diserens (London: Phaidon Press Limited, 1993).

Gropius, Walter, *Bauhaus, Dessau* (London: Phaidon Press Limited, 1993).

Pallasmaa, Juhani, *The Eyes of the Skin: Architecture and the Senses* (London: Academy Editions, 1996).

Tanizaki, Junichiro, *In Praise of Shadows*, trans. by Thomas J. Harper and Edward G. Seidensticker (London: Vintage, 2001).

Weinstein, Richard, *Morphosis: Buildings and Projects, 1989–1992* (New York: Rizzoli, 1994).

PORTS OF CALL:
THE 'DANDELION' FOLLY
AND
THE ROYAL BOTANICAL AUCTION HOUSE

2012/2013

CONSTANCE LAU

In response to the key concepts of nature, exchange and trade, design research started with the 'seed cathedral' or UK Pavilion, which was designed by Thomas Heatherwick for the Shanghai EXPO in 2010. The fact that the structure has been dismantled and can only be experienced through the working drawings, images and accounts from people who visited the Pavilion is of interest and will form a key aspect of the design development process.

The ideas concerning concepts of displacement and temporality are furthered in the design explorations to facilitate alternative readings and interpretations of architecture, which is usually associated with ideas of stability and permanence. In this instance, issues concerning site-specificity and context can be extended beyond considerations that are merely material. Hence the piers between Westminster and Kew Gardens serve as ports of call for a series of follies where site-specific narratives can be constructed, presented and more importantly, experienced.

The narrative for Heatherwick's project also expanded upon ideas concerning Kew Garden's Millennium Seed Bank, and its Royal Botanical Gardens being the world's first major botanical institution. The design development revolves around a thorough and comprehensive study of the Gardens, as well as redefining the understanding and function of an auction. The meaning of an auction extends beyond the bidding for material goods to Include the trading of information and skills. This in part references the history of colonisation as well as the position and current role of Kew Gardens in the field of botanical research.

Hence the earlier idea of a seed being a fragment of a displaced environment will be expanded in the design proposal for the Auction House and a 'Pop-up' Garden. The manner of reading and understanding issues concerning context at Kew Gardens will further discussions of displacement and temporality. More importantly, this work will allow previous architectural arguments concerning intellectual, spatial, internal and external boundaries to be seamlessly integrated and furthered.

Panagiota Kotsovinou's design process begins with precise explorations of site, and especially that of the ephemeral qualities, including viewpoints and lines of sight. This body of site-specific research is subsequently used to generate, construct and control the physical attributes of the eventual architecture. Issues concerning displacement and temporality are exaggerated in the Rowing Observatory as the experience of the architecture is completely dependent and subjected to the event taking place, tide levels and weather conditions. The interest in history, tradition and displacement is furthered in the Folly at Kew Gardens where the auction revolves around three objects, all of which are historically significant for different reasons at specific points during their existence. Hence the reading and meaning of these objects are now reconstructed in relation to notions of physical and chronological displacement.

THE RHYTHMICAL FOLLY: A ROWING OBSERVATORY

PANAGIOTA KOTSOVINOU

The Rhythmical Folly is a monument dedicated to rowing. Located in Putney, the Folly aims at offering visitors the best view to the start of the Cambridge-Oxford Boat Race. The rest of the year, the Folly is a monument to this British national sport and to the prestigious regattas and races. For the local rowing community and clubs, the Folly is a symbol of excellence and virtuosity. During the year the Folly can also be used as a learning platform to conduct training sessions on rowing.

The project explores principal characteristics of rowing which are movement, temporality and displacement, and translates them into an architectural language for the design of the Observatory. The Folly is constructed around the observer's field of vision. Hence the observers' view cones become the architectural tool which sculpts the Folly. The material selection is inspired by traditional as well as contemporary boat-building techniques.

Rowing is further analysed and broken down into 'architectural elements'. While studying its inherent rhythm and repetition, parallels are drawn between the athletes' constantly changing viewpoints and the visitors' more static points of view. Level changes inside the folly are carefully choreographed and staged to simulate the athletes' sequential fields of vision. To accommodate a greater range of viewpoints, the Folly is further split into two levels to exploit the vertical extents. Hence a complex of two intertwined Follies is created. The lower folly focuses on the experience of rowing and imitates its conditions. This space is exposed and floats on the water, and more importantly, places the visitor directly into the race to become a distant participant as opposed to a mere observer.

The architectural construct is lightweight and transparent enabling this lower space to dissolve into the site. The upper folly places emphasis on a detached but more comfortable experience of the race. This space is enclosed and protected from the elements. The ellipsoidal form and polished mirror exterior are specifically designed to reflect the surroundings, the cheering crowds and the athletes. In essence, this work of architecture simultaneously becomes a temporary canvas celebrating the Boat Race.

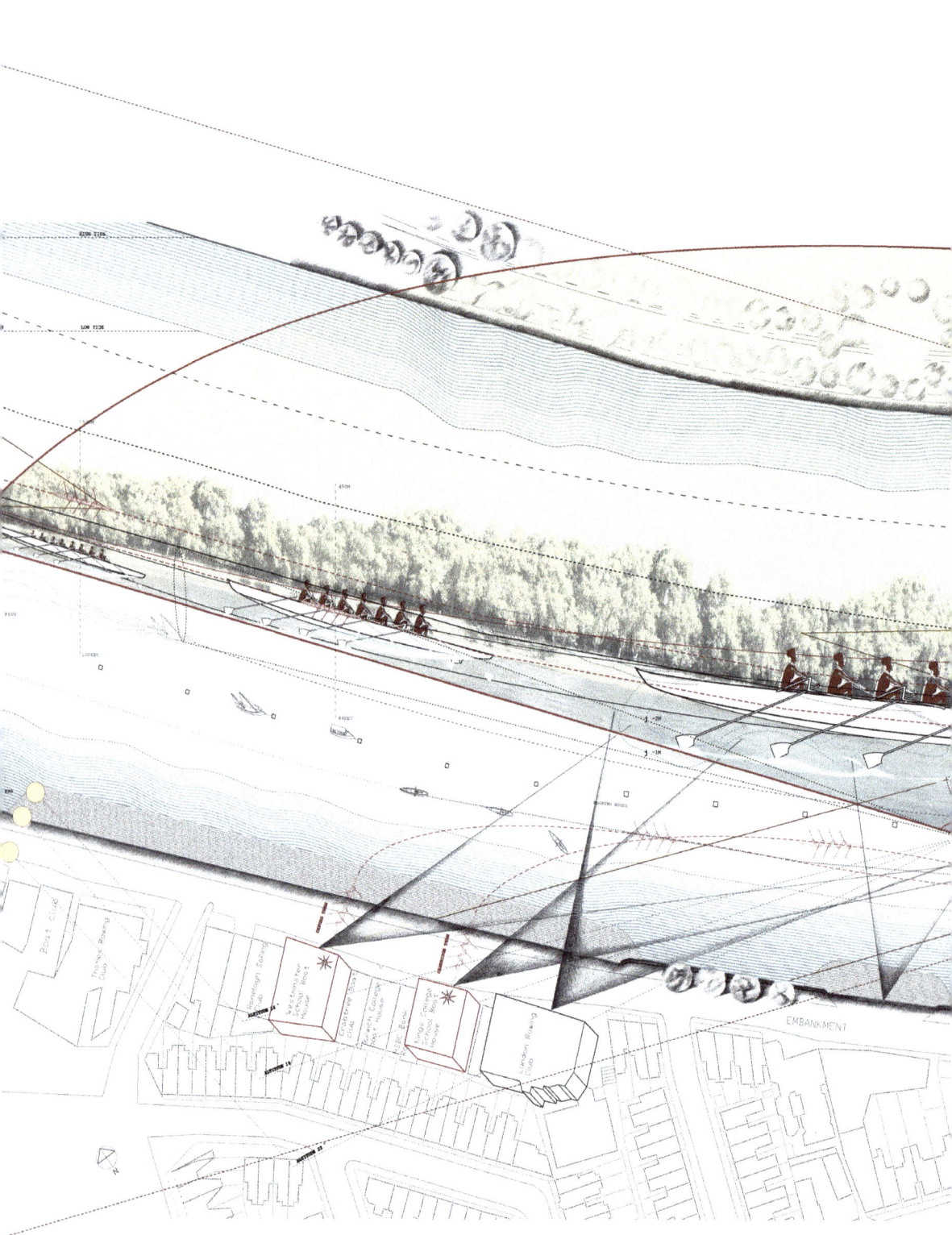

Contextual analysis and multiple mappings of the site highlighting the river traffic, important viewpoints, the boathouses and the race.

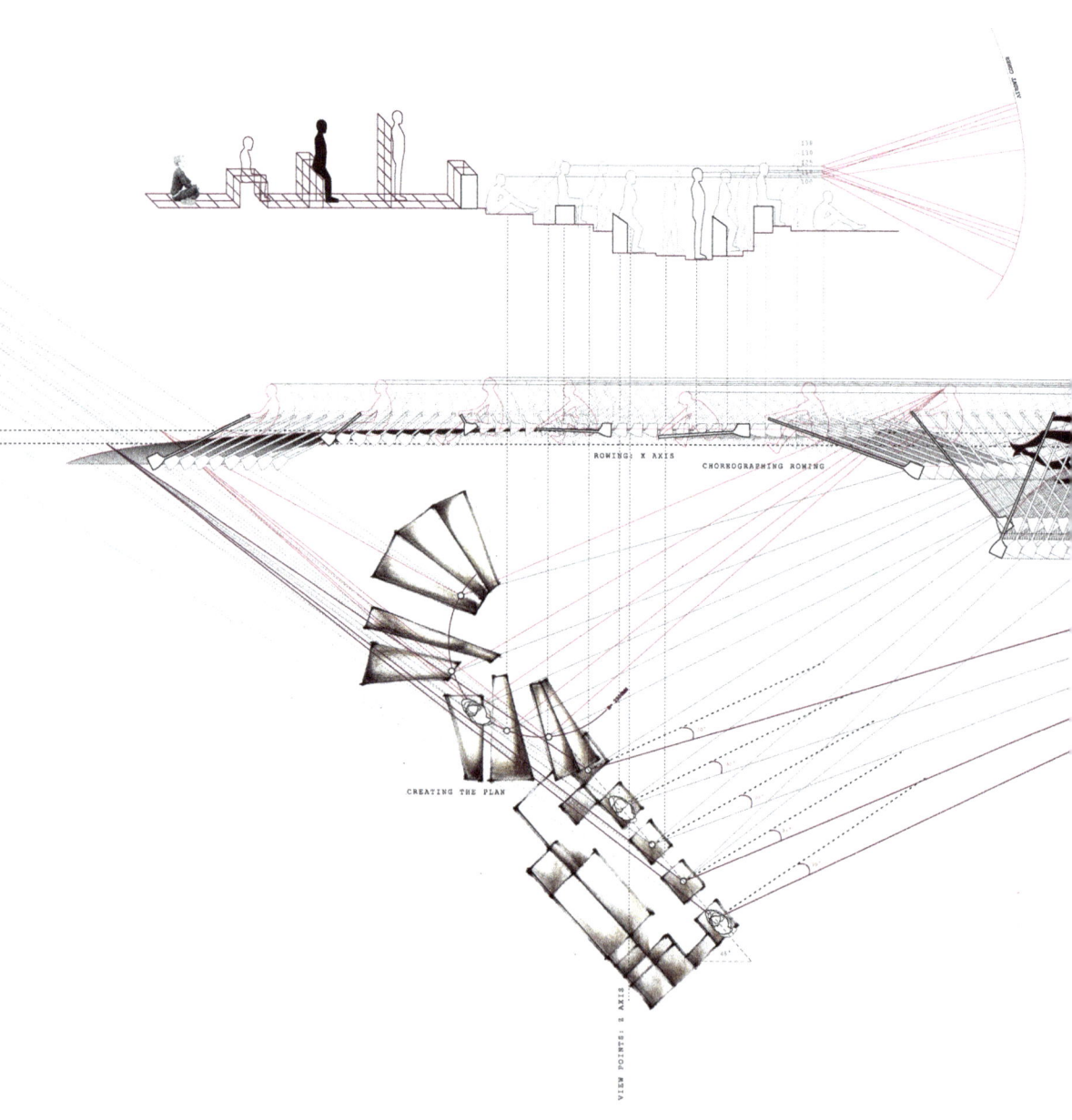

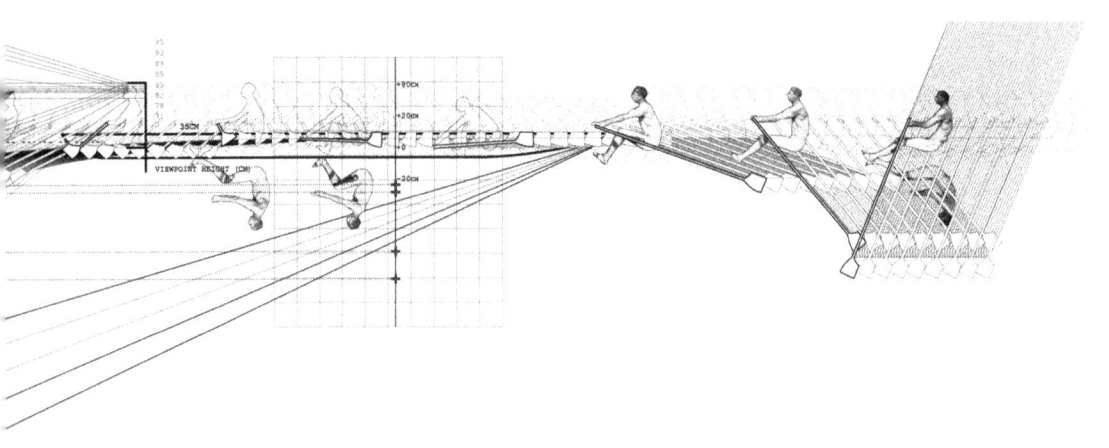

Choreography of rowing showing the athlete's rhythmic change of viewpoints, which is echoed in the eventual Folly's sequential level changes.

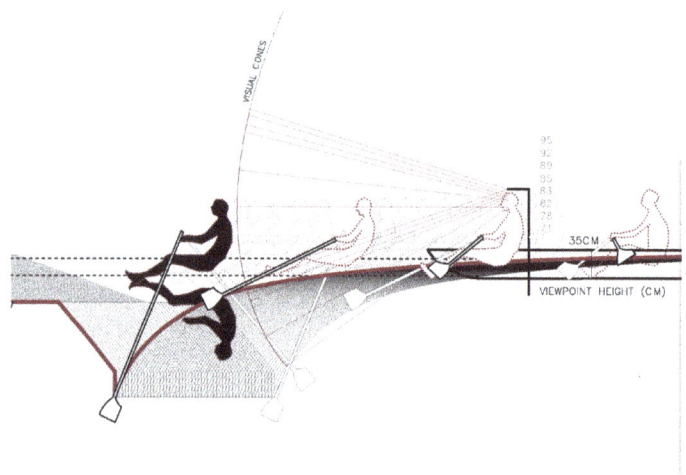

(top) Concept render showing the reflective qualities of the upper folly in relation to the physical and ephemeral qualities of the site.

(bottom) The Folly engages with British rowing history and its traces on site. Deconstructing the rowing sequence enables the design to precisely place the observer in the river, and the race, in order to experience rowing from a unique point of view.

The Folly dually functions as an architectural viewing device. Openings are carved out of a solid box to create circulation space and more importantly, provide uninterrupted visual links to the race.

Exploring the experiential qualities through material selection. Nautical materials are selected for their durability under exposure to the elements, as well as to commemorate the boat-building tradition.

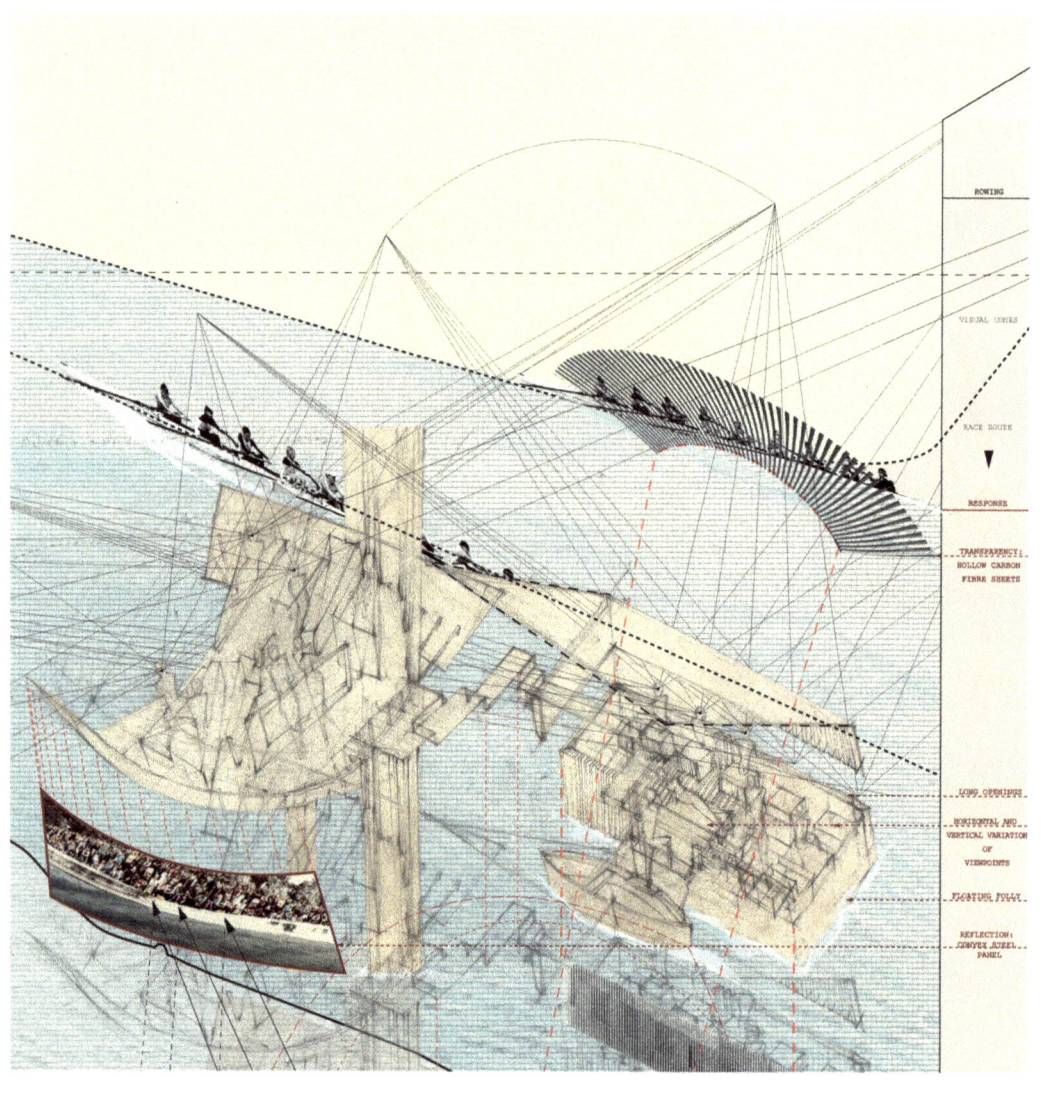

This image is a detail from the strategic design response drawing (right) addressing the site constraints. Key decisions include the placement of the Folly, site approach by boat and viewpoints from the riverbank, as well as the race.

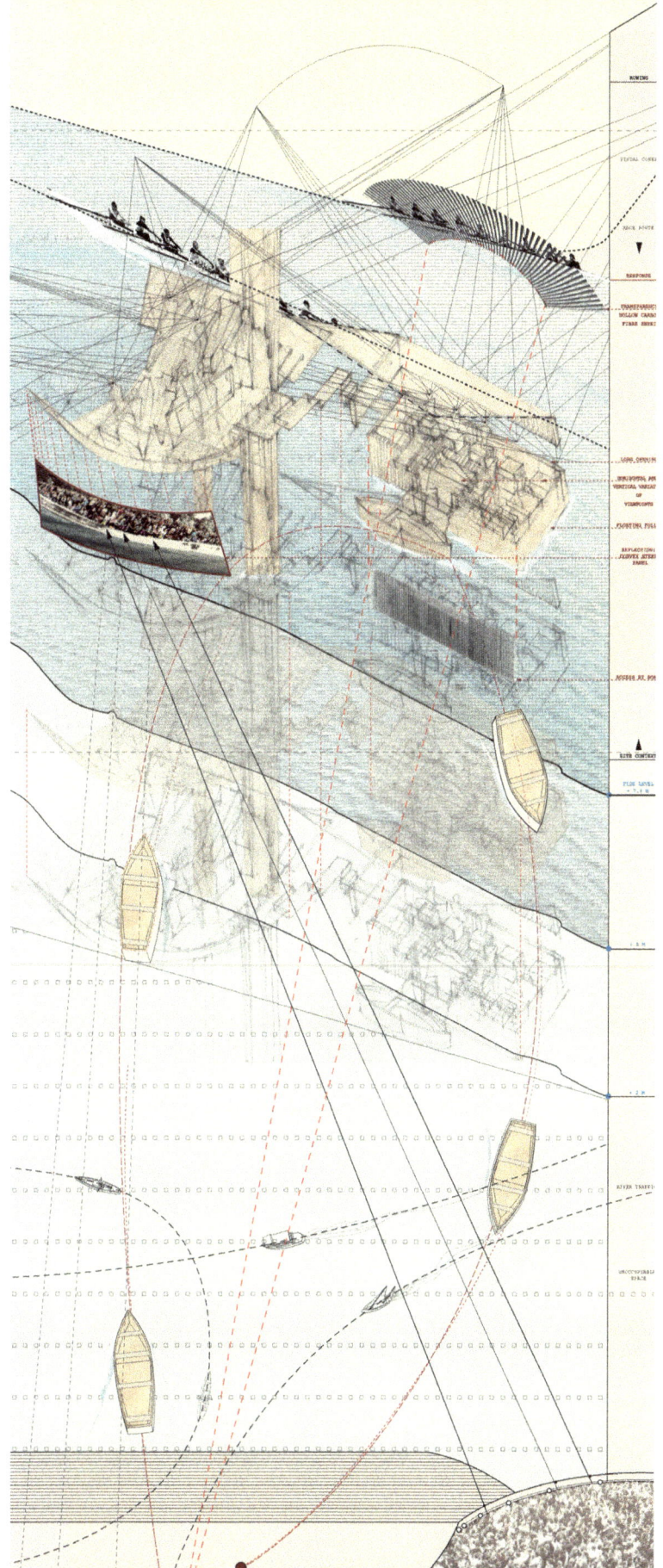

(top) The approach:
(left to right) 1. View from the riverbank 2. Approach by boat
3. Entering the lower folly 4. The lower folly 5. The upper folly

(bottom) The user experience:
(left to right) 1. Water-level view of the race from the lower folly
2. Formal celebrations in the upper folly 3. The polished-mirror exterior reflects the cheering crowd and the race

THE JOHN SOANE FOLLY AT KEW: A COLLECTION OF FOUND, BORROWED AND RECONSTRUCTED ITEMS

PANAGIOTA KOTSOVINOU

The John Soane Folly is an Auction House in Kew Gardens. The proposal aims for contextual and visual integration within the existing historical fabric and landscape, while simultaneously providing for precision and adaptability. The narrative of this Auction House explores specific visual and spatial connections at the Sir John Soane House and Museum, 1812, London and translates them into architectural explorations responding to precise site conditions and constraints at Kew Gardens. The building revolves around the notions of found, borrowed and reconstructed, three key principles which are evident from the auction lots' display, to the eventual layout and choice of materials for the proposal.

Emphasis is placed on analysing the history of the Gardens and mostly that of the ornamental buildings and follies. Most influential was the work of Sir William Chambers who designed numerous follies at Kew as well as the Kew Observatory, 1769, located in close proximity to the site.

The spatial qualities of the exhibition spaces are explored through the study of Soane's hybrid House and Museum. The promenade through the House, the visual cones, the hierarchy of views and spaces, as well as the use of light are rigorously analysed. An astronomical clock borrowed from Soane's House, a hidden folly found on site and a since demolished folly, Temple of Victory, 1759, by Chambers, which is reconstructed based on his original drawings, trigger an imaginary auction and establish the building's key axes and inner skeleton.

The Auction House's design is characterised by the existence of a focal point around which the functions and activities of a building are established. Hence this building is developed as a series of counter-balancing galleries cantilevering over a structural core. The auditorium is gently submerged into the ground to further ensure transparency and minimal intervention at ground level.

As the exhibition galleries house constantly changing auction lots, the careful control of light becomes crucial to both function and experience. A range of materials and devices are curated in precise combinations to provide theatrical settings which are designed to adapt to the constantly changing demands of the ongoing auctions.

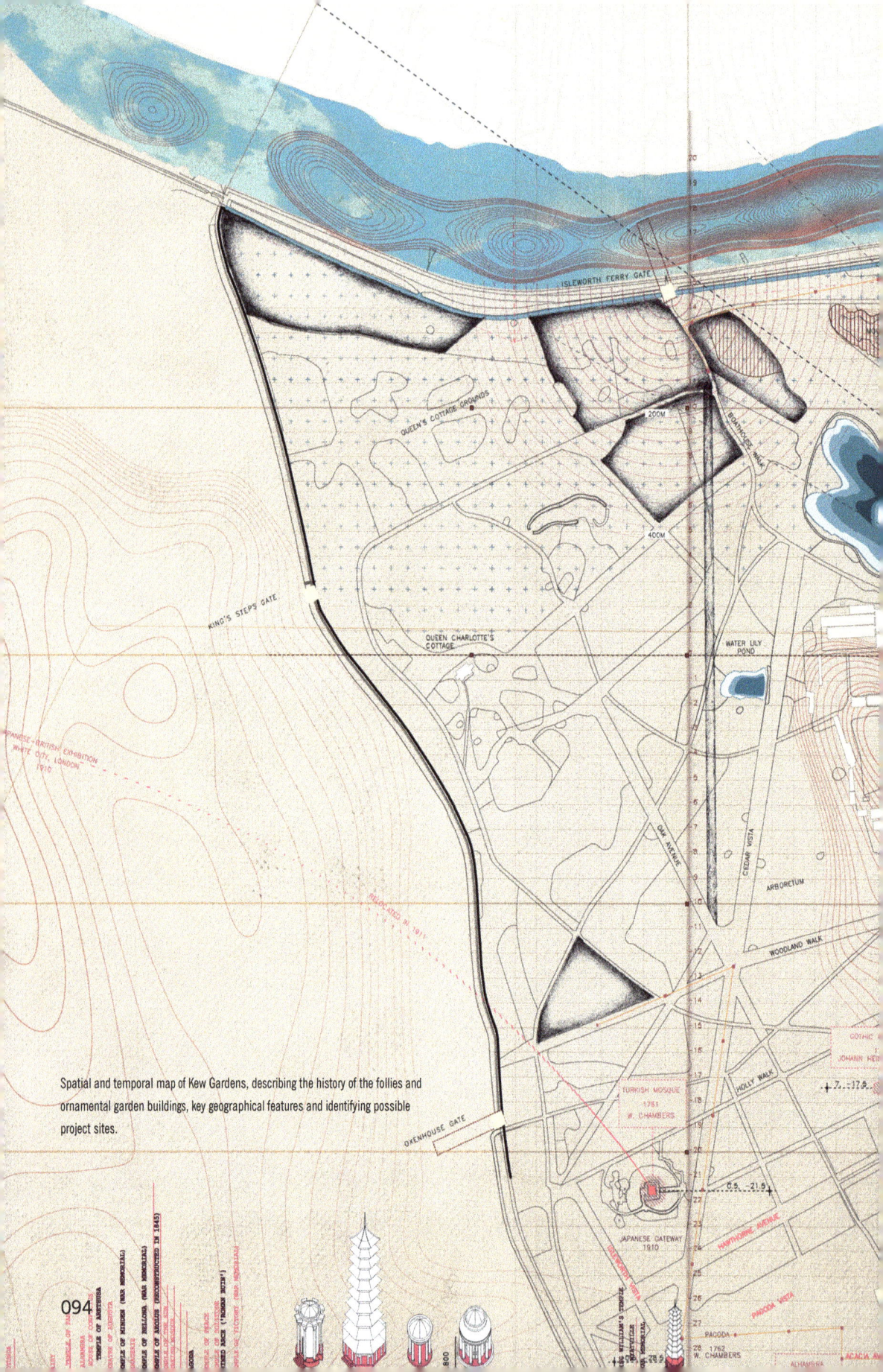

Spatial and temporal map of Kew Gardens, describing the history of the follies and ornamental garden buildings, key geographical features and identifying possible project sites.

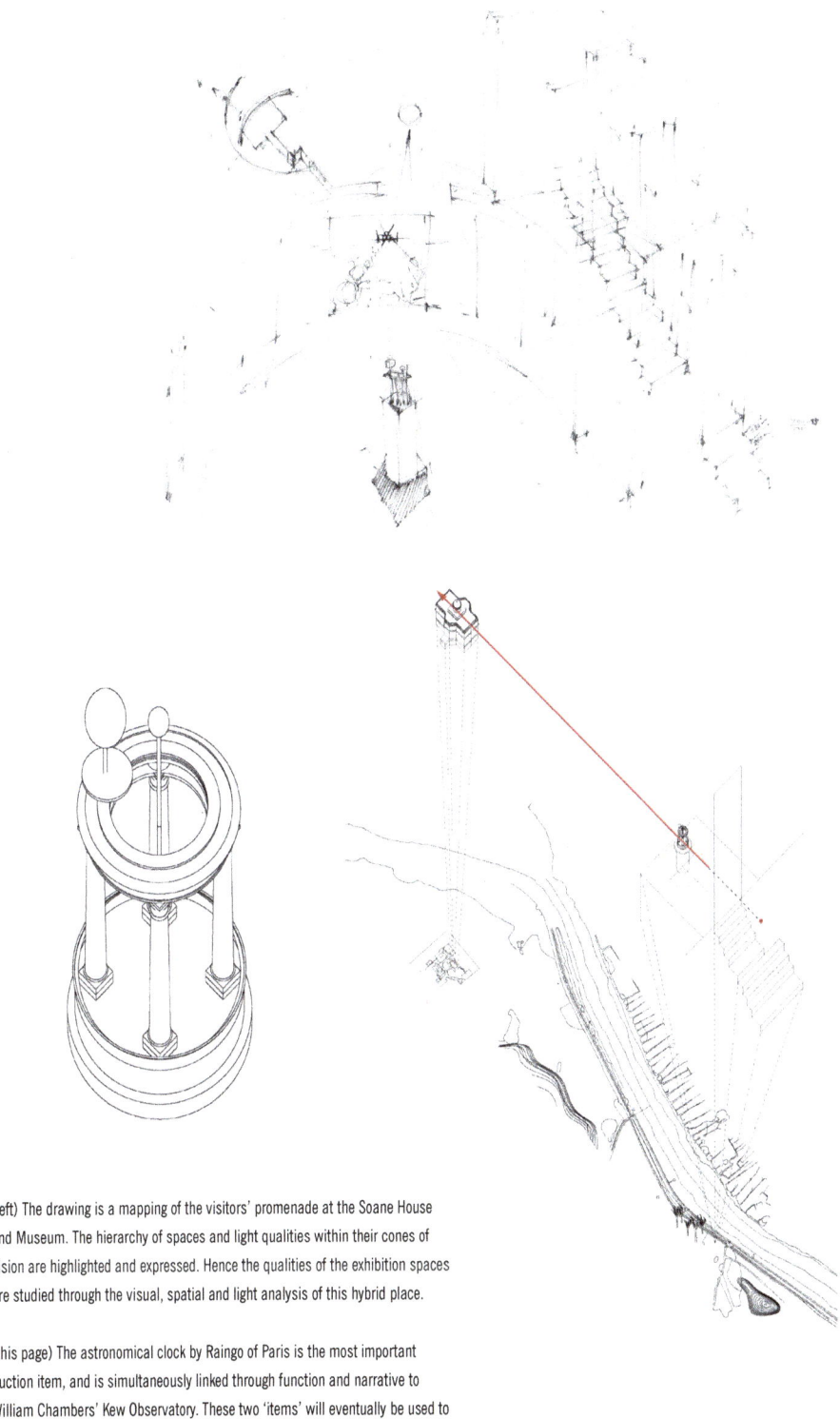

(left) The drawing is a mapping of the visitors' promenade at the Soane House and Museum. The hierarchy of spaces and light qualities within their cones of vision are highlighted and expressed. Hence the qualities of the exhibition spaces are studied through the visual, spatial and light analysis of this hybrid place.

(this page) The astronomical clock by Raingo of Paris is the most important auction item, and is simultaneously linked through function and narrative to William Chambers' Kew Observatory. These two 'items' will eventually be used to establish the main axes of the building.

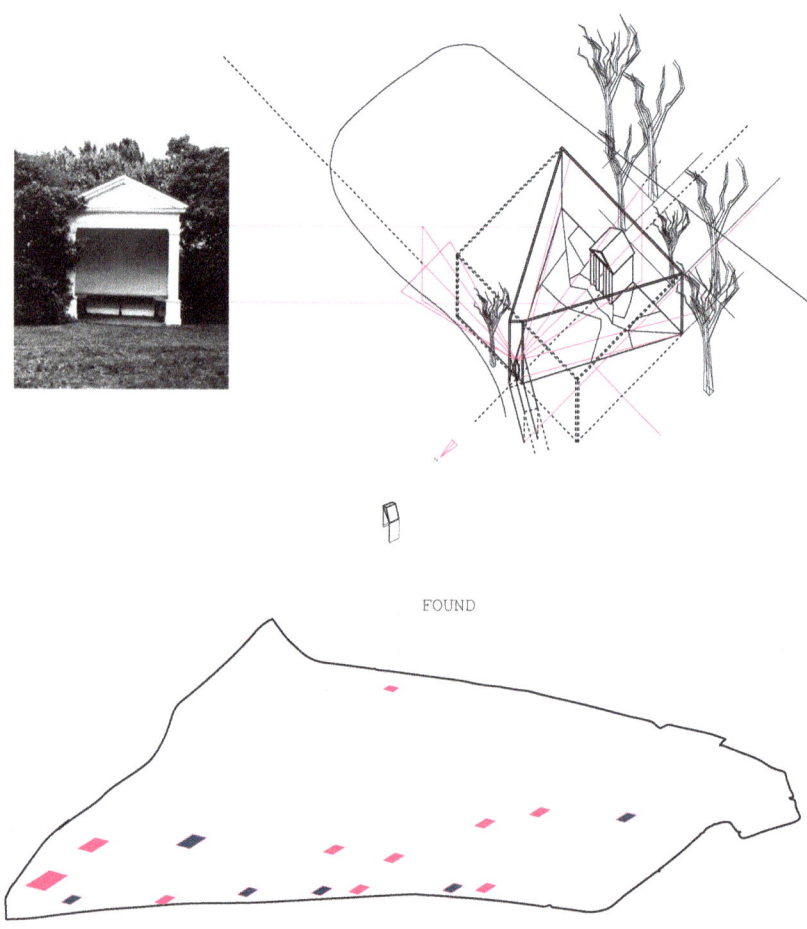

Item in the auction catalogue: The folly found near the north-west boundary of the Gardens.

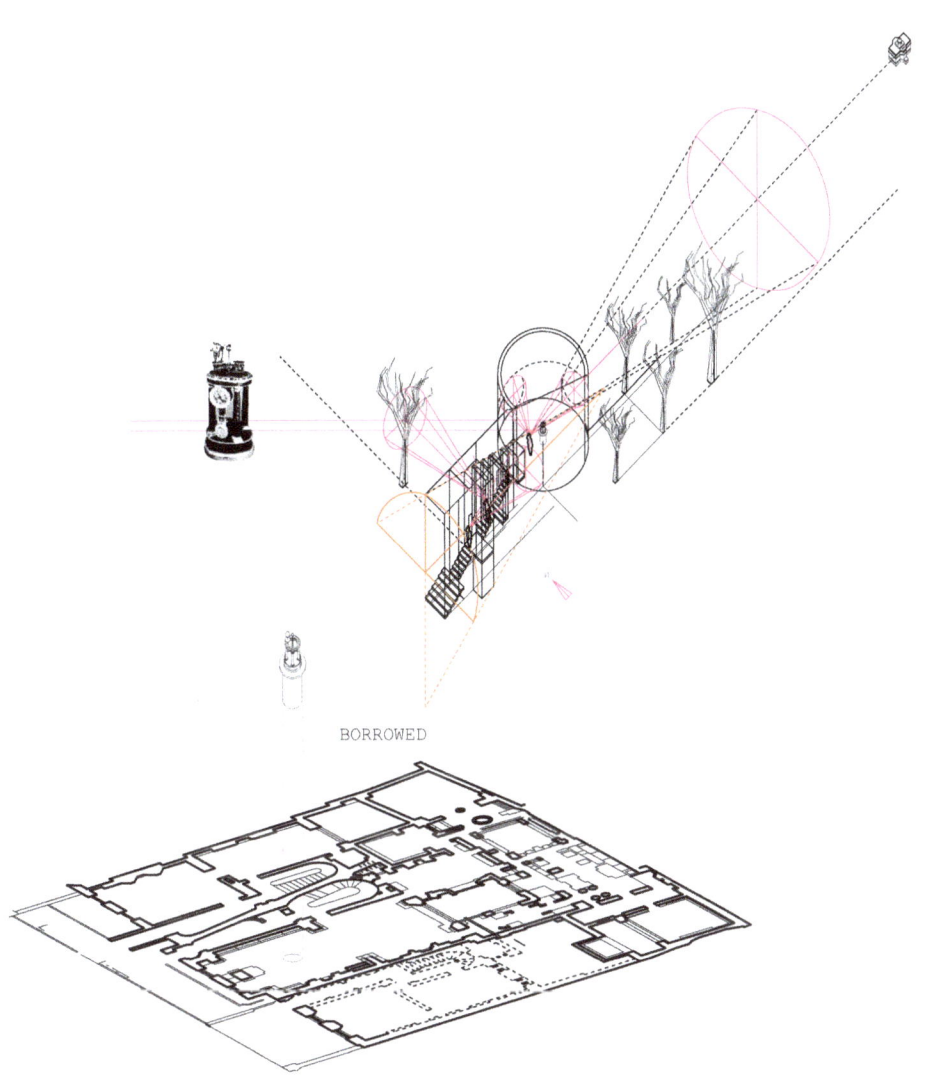

BORROWED

Item in the auction catalogue: The astronomical clock, borrowed from the Soane House and Museum.

Item in the auction catalogue: William Chamber's reconstructed Temple of Victory.

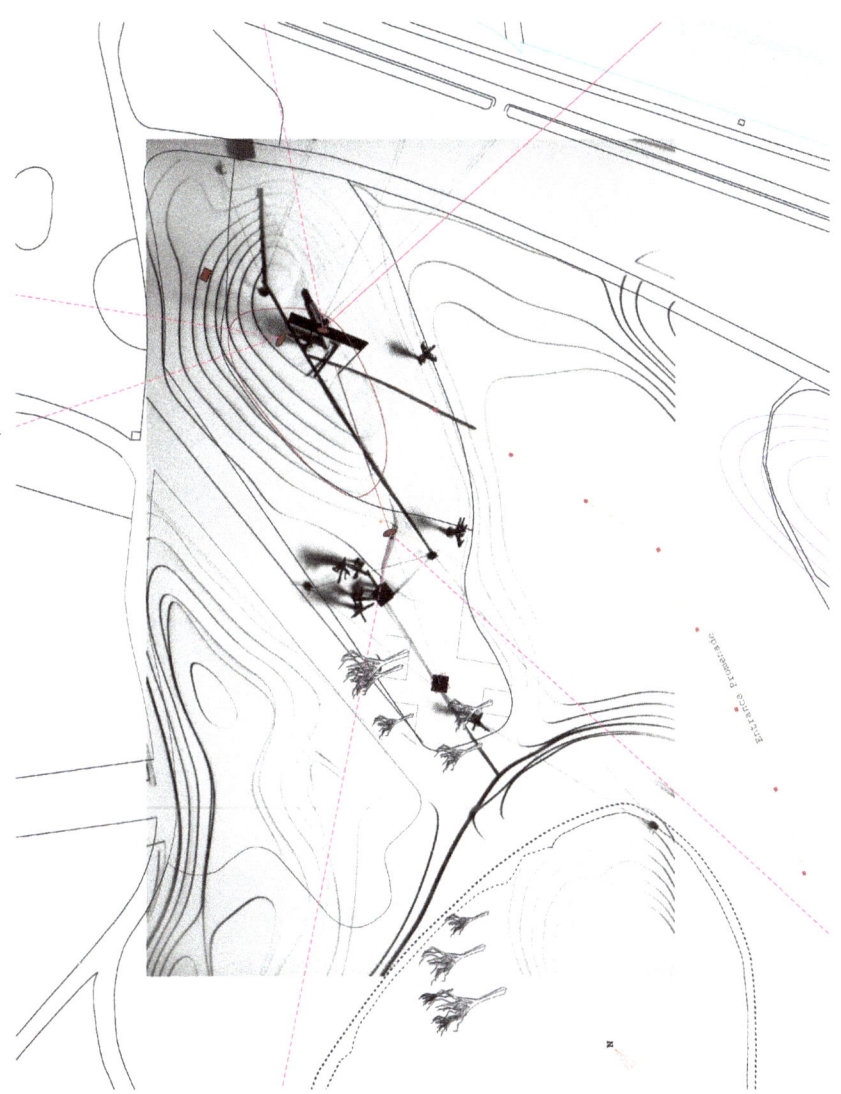

The conceptual model acts as a location plan, identifying the important 'auction items' on site and the visual connections between them. The astronomical clock borrowed from Soane's House and Museum, a hidden folly found on site, and the since demolished Temple of Victory by William Chambers, which is reconstructed based on drawings, are the key auction items and will trigger the first auction.

The choice of site was also determined by sunlight, orientation and visual connections to the river, the Kew Observatory, the lake, special features like the hidden folly, proximity to a gate, and the end of the Syon vista.

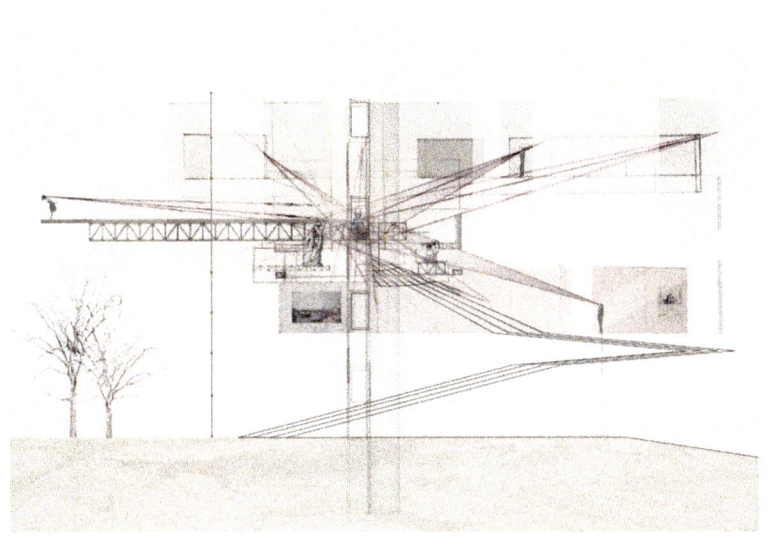

Conceptual section introducing the idea of counter-balancing galleries, which are cantilevered from a central core.

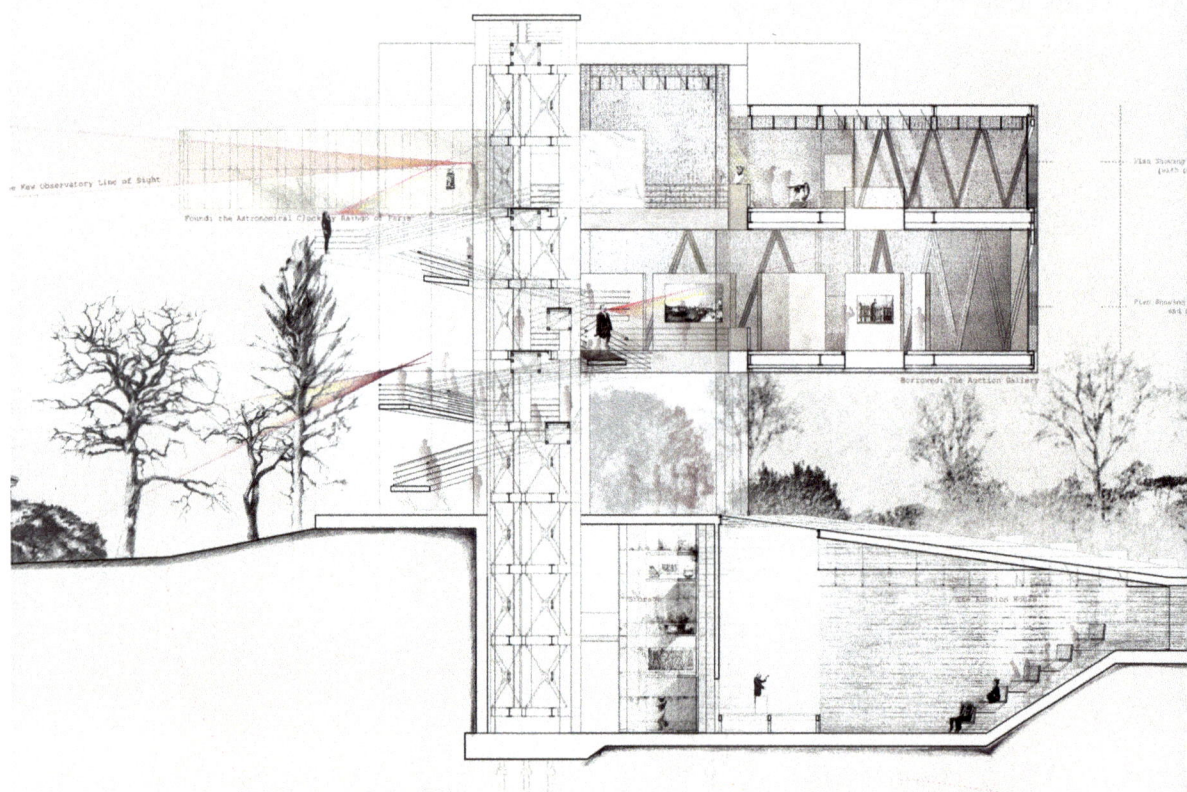

Section through the Permanent Collection Gallery, the central core, the Auction Galleries and the Auction Auditorium.

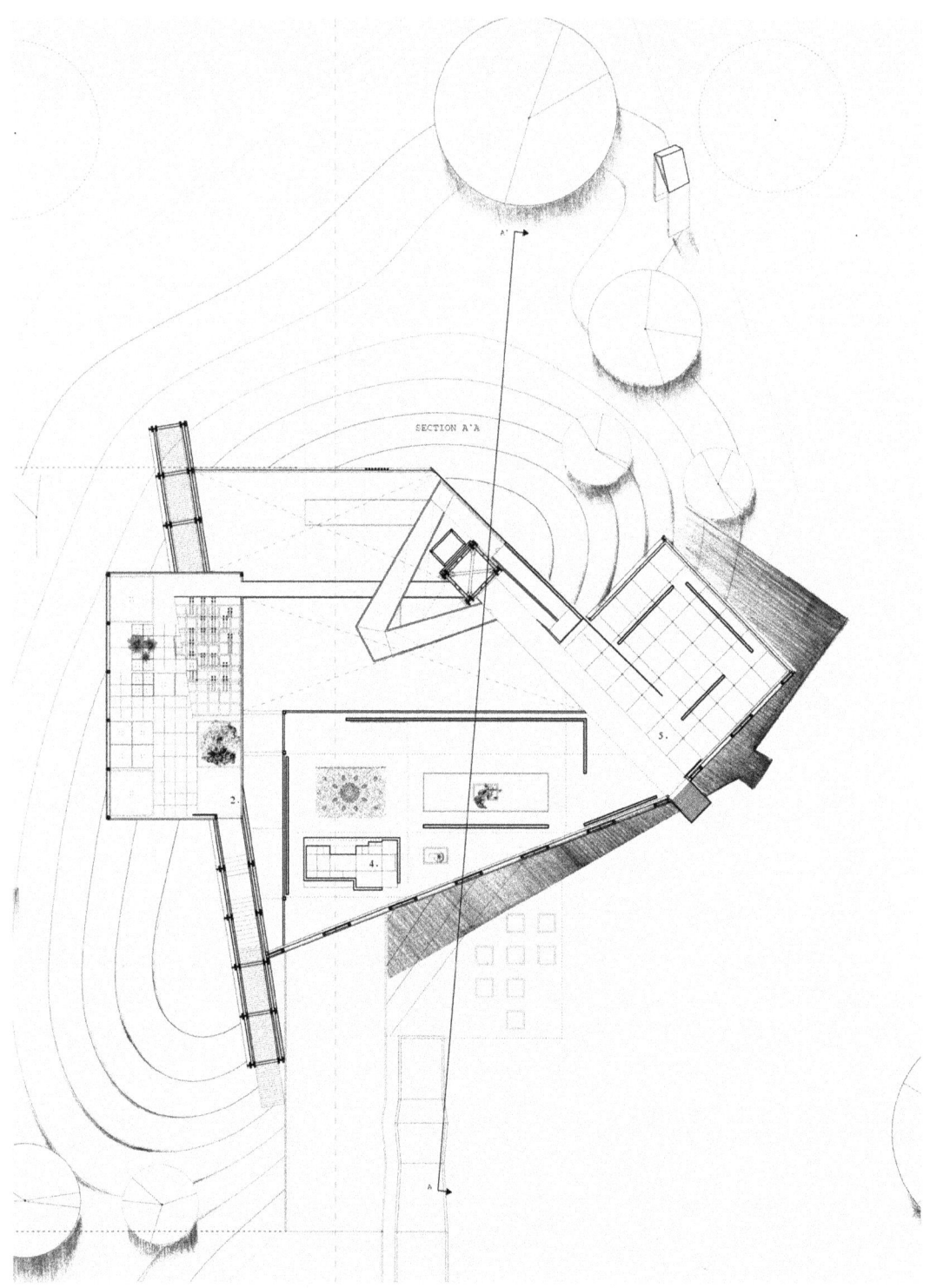

First floor plan, showing the Auction Galleries and the Plant Exhibition Gallery.

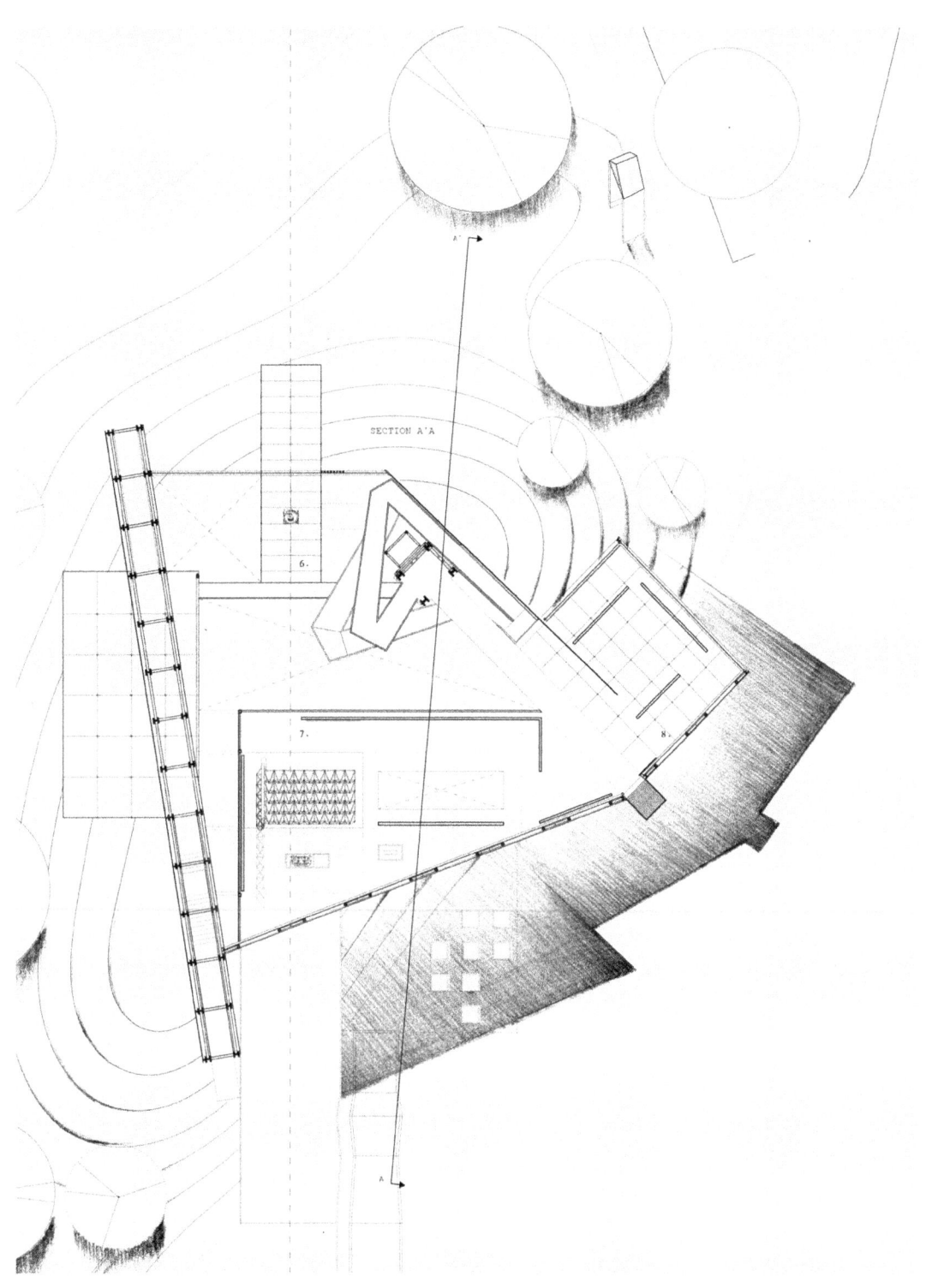

Second floor plan, showing the Upper Auction Galleries.

Interior view of the vertical visual promenade.

(right) Interior view showing the collection of Borrowed items.

pp. 112—113.
View of the Permanent Collection Gallery and the 'Pop-up' Garden.

pp. 114—115.
View of the Entrance Promenade at the end of the Syon Vista.

BIBLIOGRAPHY

Blake, John, *The sea chart: the illustrated history of nautical maps and navigational charts* (London : Conway Maritime Press, 2004).

Chambers, William, Michael Snodin, and John Harris, *Sir William Chambers* (London: V & A Publications, 1996).

Corner, James and Alex S. MacLean, *Taking Measures Across The American Landscape* (New Haven: Yale University Press, 1996).

Evans, Robin, *The Projective Cast* (Cambridge, Mass.: MIT Press, 1995).

Evans, Robin, *Translations From Drawing To Building and Other Essays* (Cambridge, Mass.: MIT Press, 1997).

Frampton, Kenneth, R. B Kitaj, and Martin Richardson, *Colin St John Wilson* ([London]: Royal Institute of British Architects, 1997).

Goodwin, Kate, *Dandelion* (Manchester: British Council, 2011).

Heatherwick, Thomas, *Thomas Heatherwick* (New York: The Monacelli Press, 2012).

Hendricks, Gordon, *Eadweard Muybridge: the father of the motion picture* (London: Secker and Warburg, 1975).

Kapoor, Anish and Nicholas Baume, *Anish Kapoor* (Boston, MA: Institute of Contemporary Art, 2008).

Levene, Richard C., and Fernando Marquez Cecilia, *Herzog & De Meuron* (Madrid: El Croquis Editorial, 2002).

Mayne Thom, and Val K. Warke, *Morphosis* (London: Phaidon, 2003).

McCarter, Robert, *Louis I. Khan* (London: Phaidon, 2005).

Pallasmaa, Juhani, *The Eyes Of The Skin* (Chichester: Wiley-Academy, 2005). First published in 1996.

Scarpa, Carlo, Francesco Dal Co, and Giuseppe Mazzariol, *Carlo Scarpa* (New York: Electa/Rizzoli, 1985).

Richardson, Margaret and Mary Anne Stevens, *John Soane, Architect* (London: Royal Academy of Arts, 2000).

Ursprung, Philip, *Herzog & De Meuron* (Montreal: Canadian Centre for Architecture, 2002).

Watkin, David, *Sir John Soane* (Cambridge: Cambridge University Press, 2000).

UNTO THIS LAST : THE CAMDEN WORKSHOP AND SCHOOL OF DESIGN

2013/2014

CONSTANCE LAU

This year's theme focuses on the British Arts and Crafts Movement which is credited to John Ruskin and William Morris. Of special interest is Ruskin's 1860 essay *Unto This Last* which serves to advocate a return to the principles of 'hand craftsmanship' and the notion of the local craftsman.[1]

The project site of Camden Town dates back to the 1790s, and the markets were historically known for their culture of 'making'. Hence the individual design narratives explore arguments, concepts and thought processes surrounding this Movement, and are developed as ongoing dialogues between these readings and ideas of site.

'A History of Camden in 10 Objects' references the British Museum's manner of narrating the history of the world through 100 objects, and looks to telling the story of Camden Town and its surroundings with 10.[2] The reading of history as a 'kaleidoscope', 'shifting and interconnected' will be layered over particular qualities of the chosen site.[3] The fact that the curated objects from the British Museum were first presented on radio is highly significant as the audience would have had to imagine the artefact being discussed, and during this process of engagement make it their own, and consequently make their own history.[4]

Taking on board this idea of reading and making history, the Arts and Crafts Workshop in which these objects will be made, housed and studied continues into the design proposal concerning Arts and Crafts architecture. This is where the notion of 'hand craftsmanship' and making also extends to ideas of building.

The design proposal and construction of The Camden School of Design seeks to address and redefine key concepts of the Movement. More importantly, this body of work serves to demonstrate the relevance of the local craftsman and notions of making in this present industrial and technological era of mass production. Key to the design proposals are also spatial interpretations of the terms 'school' as well as 'design'. Hence the narrative and manner of reading, understanding and presenting the physical context simultaneously with the context of the argument will serve to reveal multiple architectural definitions and design approaches concerning the Arts and Crafts Movement. Significantly, the relationship of history and/or historical material and design practice is understood as an ongoing dialogue.

The work of Ioana Vierita explores the writings of John Ruskin through the design narrative and demonstrates the use of site-specific knowledge to produce architecture. The understanding of Renaissance perspective is redefined and reinterpreted to inform and construct the School. Significantly, the design proposal exploits and expresses the qualities of creating three-dimensional forms through a drawing technique invented for the representation of spatial qualities on a two-dimensional surface.

The work by Sear Nee Ng looks to the material finds of the Arts and Crafts Movement. The work of William Morris' and the architecture of the Red House in Bexleyheath are analysed to construct the design narratives. The contribution to architectural history with regards to these existing pieces of work are subsequently highlighted. More importantly, the work is given new readings which are simultaneously historically meaningful and contextually current.

---

[1] John Ruskin, *"Unto This Last": Four Essays on the First Principles of Political Economy,* ed. by Lloyd J. Hubenka (Lincoln: University of Nebraska Press, 1967).
[2] Neil MacGregor, *A History of the World in 100 Objects* (London: Penguin Books Ltd., 2010). This book was produced in conjunction with the British Broadcasting Corporation (BBC) Radio 4 series.
[3] MacGregor, unpaginated.
[4] MacGregor, p. xiv.

THE ARTS AND CRAFTS WOOD WORKSHOP

IOANA VIERITA

The Arts and Crafts Wood Workshop in Camden investigates different ways of translating the reading of a poem by Stéphane Mallarmé.[1] This especially concerns the issue of freedom of interpretation with regards to the reading of space. Hence the project speculates on the possibility of designing a building which offers multiple ways of composing and interpreting space.

Mallarmé explored the relationship between text, the arrangement of words and their gaps on a blank page. An analysis of his poem *Un Coup de Dés Jamais N'Abolira Le Hasard* established three main ways of reading his text.[2] These are linear and/or non-linear, tabular and transparent. The Arts and Crafts Movement was based on honesty during the stages of design, stating that the craftsmen should be allowed to get involved with the process. However, freedom of design did not necessarily mean freedom of interpretation. Inspired by Gothic architecture, the Arts and Crafts Holy Trinity Church, has only one meaning, that of the fear of God. Hence by attempting to apply Mallarmé's theory on the spaces within the church, the possibility for it to have several interpretations emerges.

Through a series of experiments with a physical model of the church in various light conditions, a series of images based on Mallarmé's methods of reading were constructed. In this instance, darkness represented the blank page of the poem and the lit elements, the words. This allowed the development of corresponding design principles which were, compose, disperse and cohere.

The Arts and Crafts Wood Workshop in Camden represents the first step in re-establishing the Arts and Crafts community which has been lost due to the development of mass production. The building celebrates the construction and architectural elements of the Holy Trinity Church, housing fragments from the stained glass, wooden altar, angel lectern and other smaller elements.

In designing the Wood Workshop, the design principles of compose, disperse and cohere are used to create three specific moments, at three times of the day to enable the space to be interpreted in different ways. The linear, tabular and transparent moments are carefully constructed configurations of space which consist of either spatial links, objects or panels. The steps, walls and floors of the Workshop are inserted into the structure of an existing building next to the market. The east façade is completely open during the day, bringing more sunlight into the area of the market. This encourages the public to engage with the activities of the wood workers and catch glimpses of the Arts and Crafts objects displayed within the building.

---

[1] Stéphane Mallarmé was a major French poet and critic during the second half of the nineteenth-century, along with Charles Baudelaire, Paul Verlaine and Arthur Rimbaud.

[2] Stéphane Mallarmé, *Un Coup de Dés Jamais N'Abolira Le Hasard* (Paris: La Table Ronde, 2007). The poem was written in 1897, and was published in the magazine *Cosmopolis: A Literary Review* the same year. The book was first published posthumously in 1914.

(right) The design principles of disperse, cohere and compose are explored through the spaces, as well as spatial qualities of the Arts and Crafts Wood Workshop in Camden.

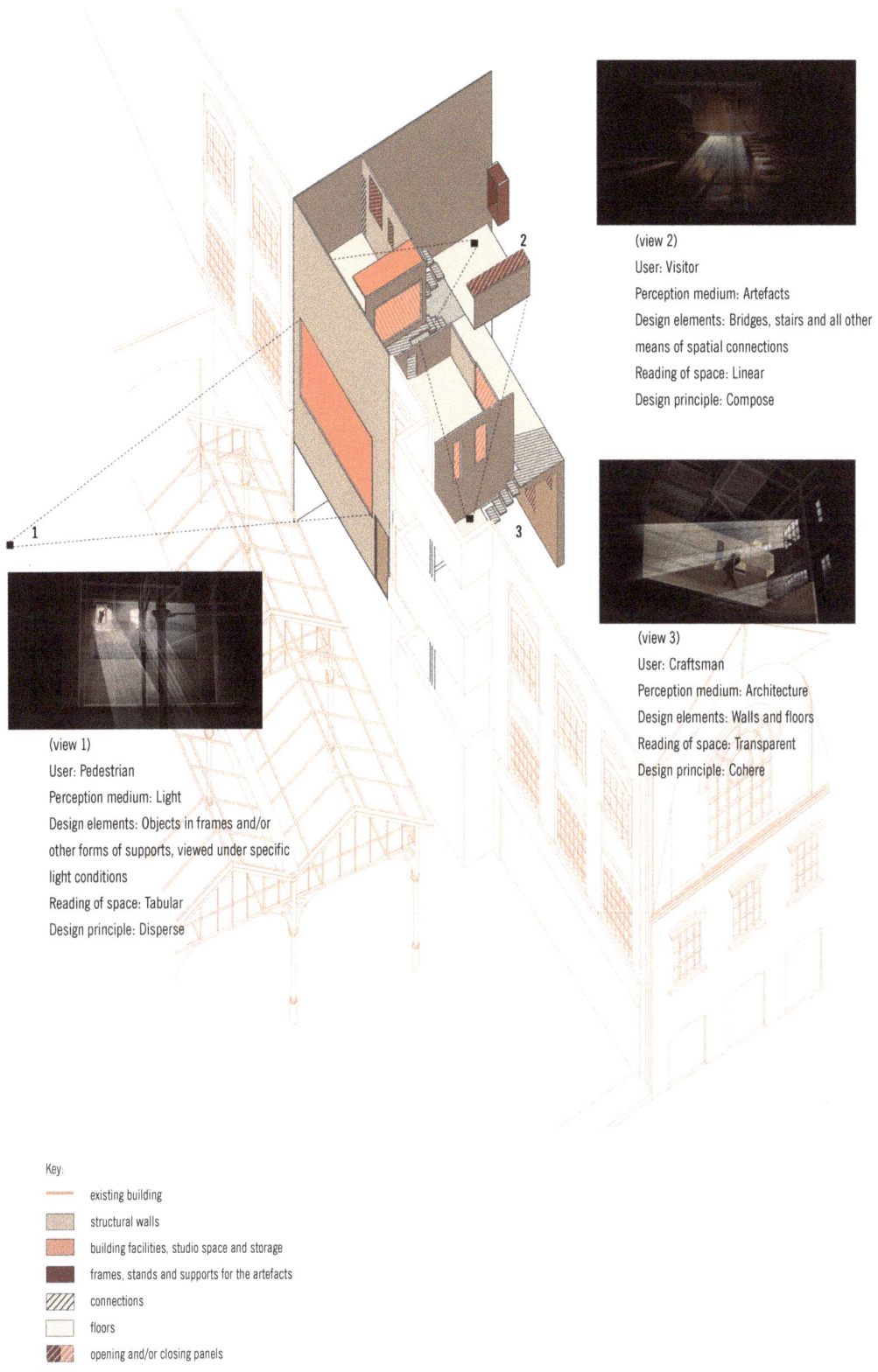

(view 2)
User: Visitor
Perception medium: Artefacts
Design elements: Bridges, stairs and all other means of spatial connections
Reading of space: Linear
Design principle: Compose

(view 3)
User: Craftsman
Perception medium: Architecture
Design elements: Walls and floors
Reading of space: Transparent
Design principle: Cohere

(view 1)
User: Pedestrian
Perception medium: Light
Design elements: Objects in frames and/or other forms of supports, viewed under specific light conditions
Reading of space: Tabular
Design principle: Disperse

Key:
- existing building
- structural walls
- building facilities, studio space and storage
- frames, stands and supports for the artefacts
- connections
- floors
- opening and/or closing panels

The Arts and Crafts Movement valued the idea of different opinions in design, and the craftsmen were encouraged to be part of of this process though the act of making. However there is very little proof that this actually happened. For instance, in the case of the Holy Trinity, Cathedral of the Arts and Crafts, 1890, London, there are very few drawings of this Gothic Cathedral to show that they were actually left unfinished for the craftsmen to interpret during the building process.

Hence the argument regarding different approaches to design can be extended to the interpretation of space. People use space in many different ways. Yet, general ideas of how certain buildings are perceived and understood are apparent, and designers have tendencies to subscribe to these assumptions. For instance, it is suggested that the Gothic Cathedral alludes to one interpretation, which is that of fear, of God.

In Mallarmé's quest for the perfect book, he created one poem in which the relationship between content and form was explored through the arrangement of words and spaces on the page. He developed several techniques to translate the sound, and especially intonation of words into visible elements. His poem, Un Coup de Dés, can be considered an architectural poem as Mallarmé used the scale, position and shape of words to generate sensations, and express the sound of the words.

Hence Mallarmé created the possibility of multiple interpretations of the text which emerged from different ways of reading the poem.

In these spatial experiments, the one permitted meaning and reading of the Cathedral is altered by applying Mallarme's theory in an attempt to create the possibility of several interpretations.

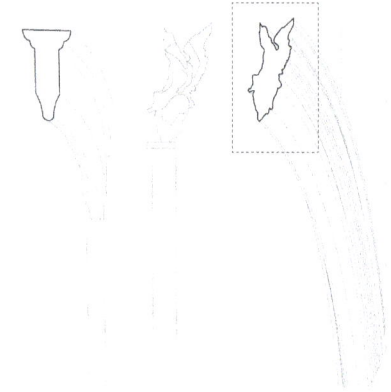

(this page and right) These studies of the Cathedral explore some of the spatial, structural and ornamental elements. Further analysis have revealed arches that are ornamental, as opposed to being structural. Hence in reverse logic, the question concerning the possibility of ornaments playing structural roles is raised.

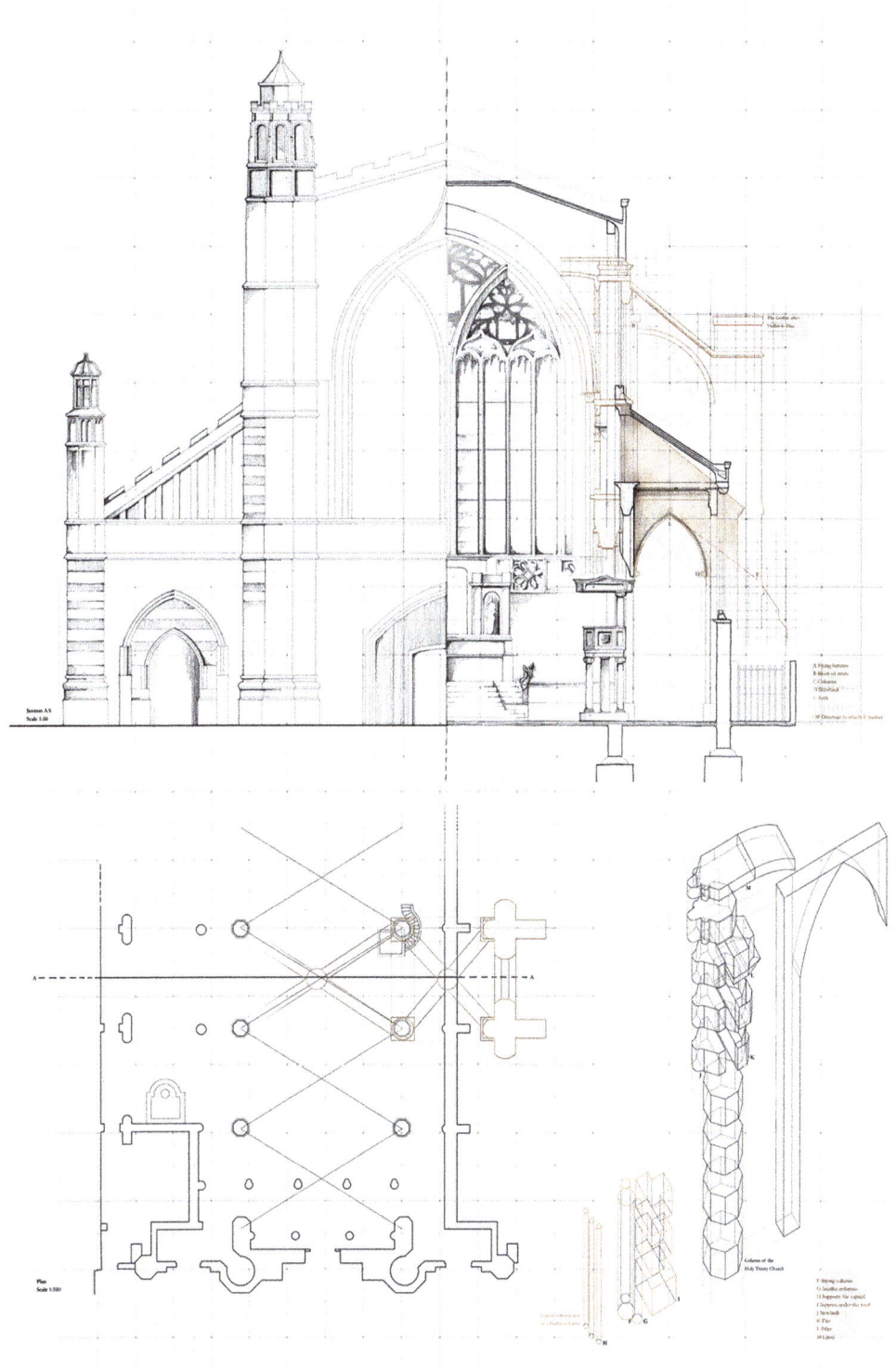

Un Coup de Dés Jamais N'Abolira Le Hasard

p. 125.
Reading 1: Tabular
The Poem's invisible architecture is implied by the distance between words. This is read as equal to that which separates the flashes that the idea summons up in the mind.

p. 126.
Reading 2: Analytical and Linear
The Poem is read from left to right.

Reading 3: Synthetic
The surface of the writing (the page) is considered the place of 'taking' place'. The white marks allude to the return of the poem to silence, a determined silence.

Hence the text and the page create the movement of the poem. This movement is designed in relation to the context of the work, revealing different meanings and combinations.

p. 127.
Reading 4: Transparent
The poem is made such that it is read and re-read several times without the need to adhere to a specific page order. By creating different combinations of pages, one has a different impression of the text at every reading. This suggests that the text has a flexible structure and can bend to the desires and instincts of the reader.

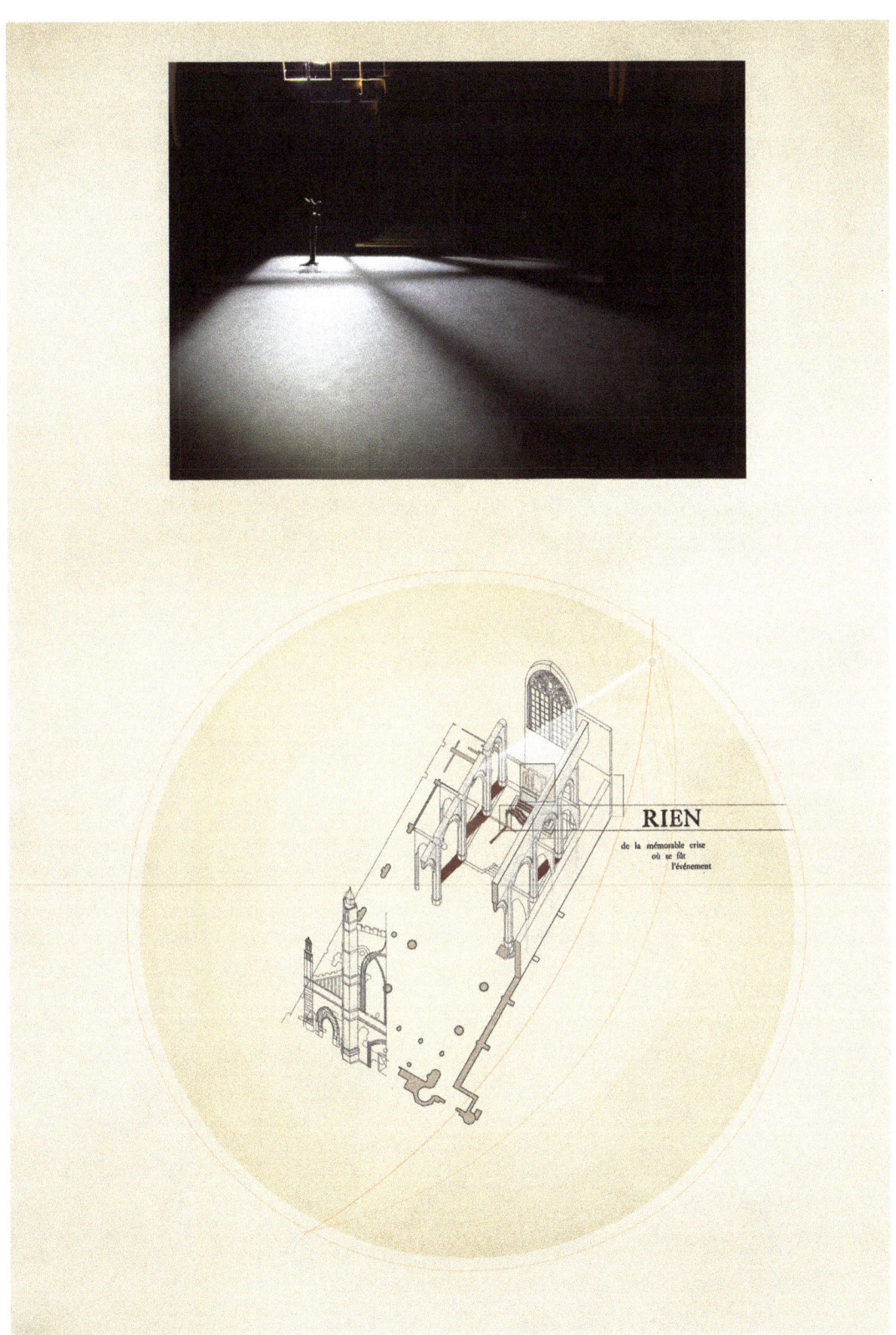

Tabular Reading

Linear Reading

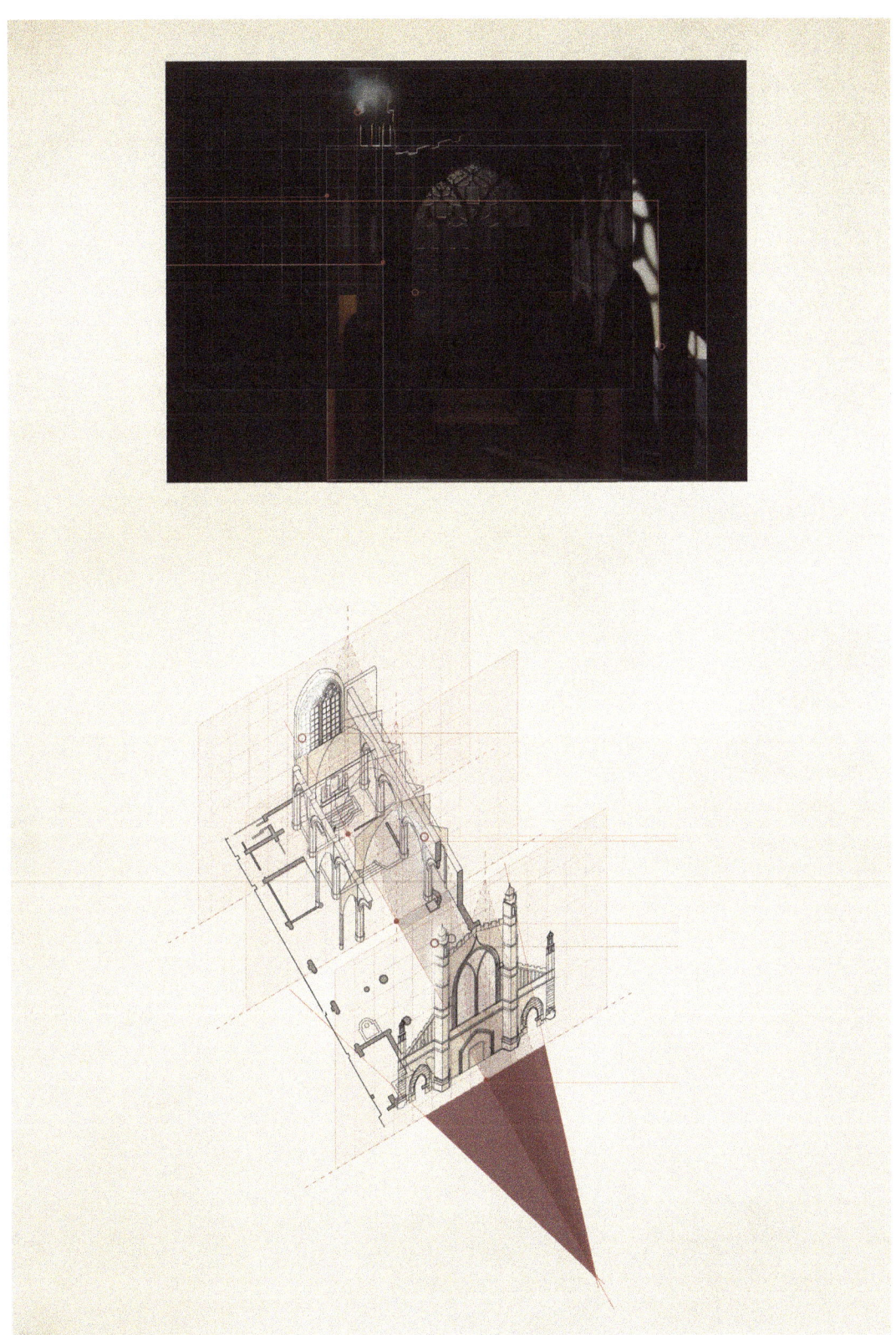

Transparent Reading

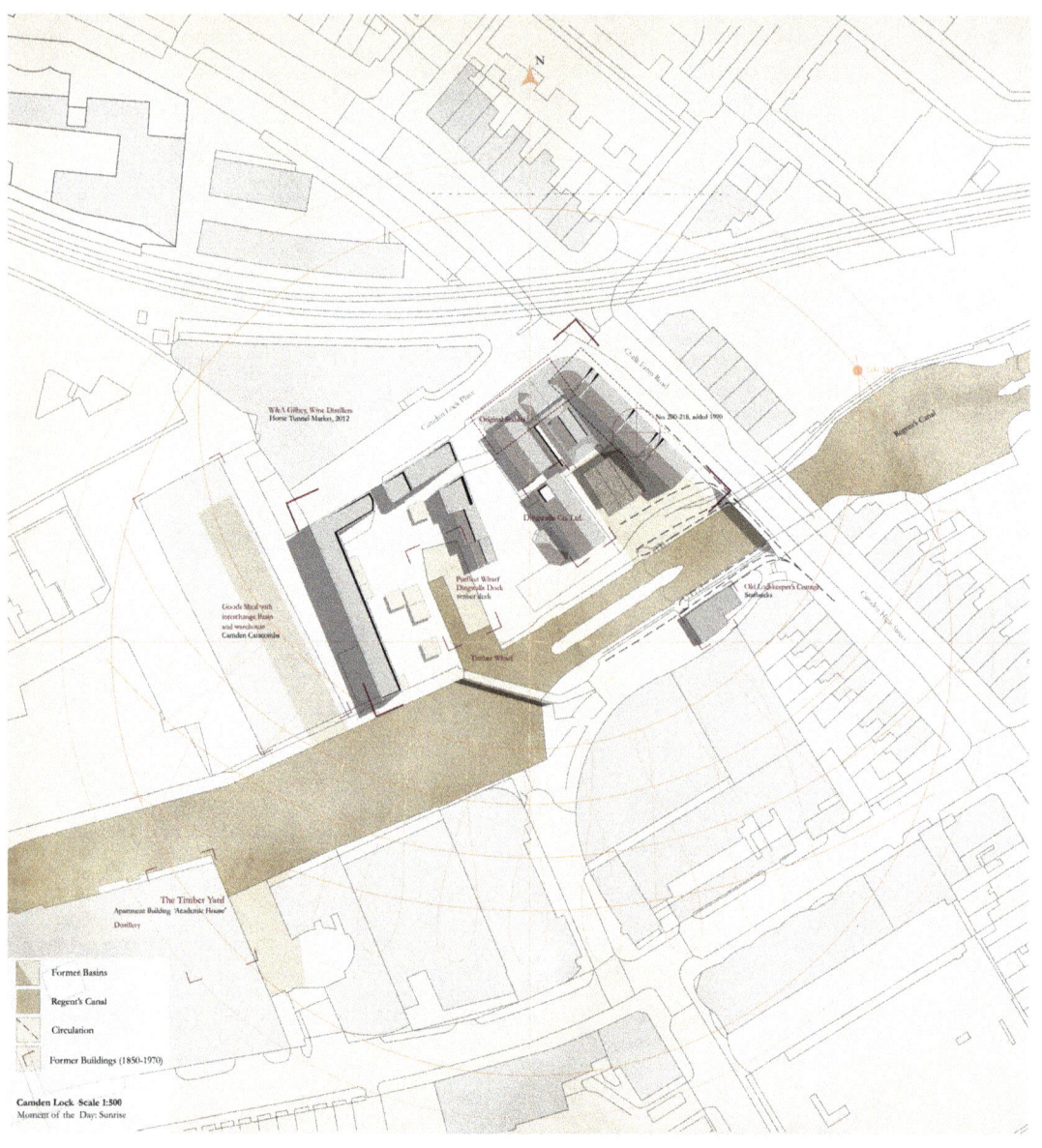

Site plan showing the key buildings within the immediate context of the project site on
no. 280-218 Chalk Farm road.

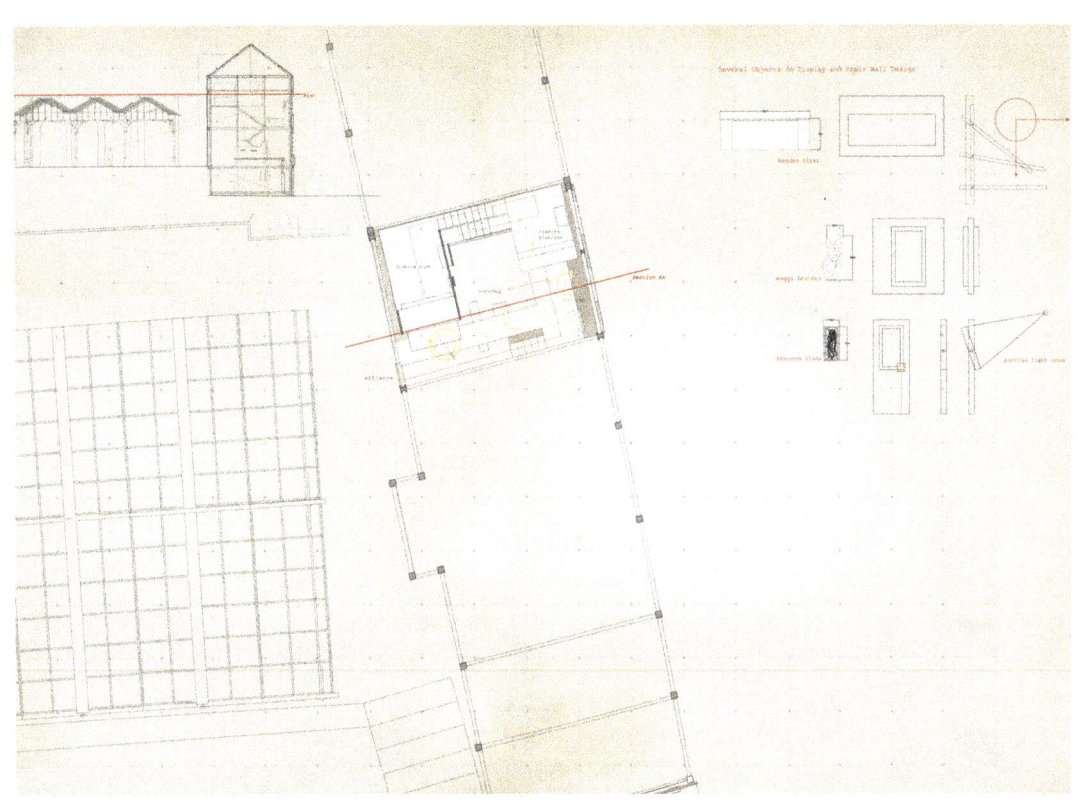

First floor plan of the Workshop with the Arts and Crafts objects displayed on specially designed stands, and precise openings located on and within the walls.

A module of the existing building is cut out to allow light into the adjacent square. The light and shadow analysis of the building which in this instance also adopts the role of 'The Book', is focused around the month of November, between 7am - 12pm. This intervention further enables light to enter Camden Lock Place and Market Square before 12pm.

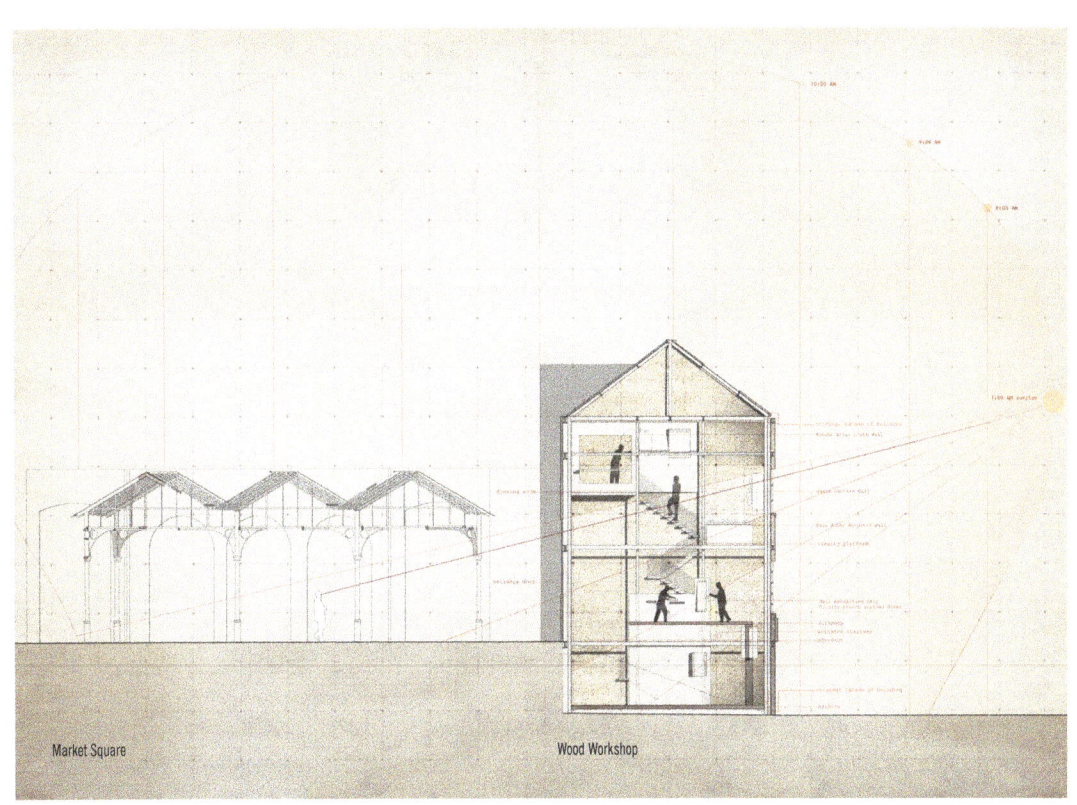

Market Square　　　　　　　　　　　　　　　　Wood Workshop

The spatial arrangement of the Workshop was designed around the light cone of the rising sun, to enable this ray of light to shine, precisely onto Market Square.

The viewer captures this moment in which the Angel Lectern from the Holy Trinity Church is lit by the rising sun, in a moment that is similar to sunrise at the Church.

The section drawing shows the different light configurations through the Workshop.

Each object that tells a story about the history of the Arts and Crafts is displayed on specially designed walls, which reconfigure to form some of the partitions in the Workshop and further unfold into tabletops and storage spaces. This division of the spaces further alter the quality of light in the Workshop.

(this page) These moments for three different viewers are composed of fixed views in different light conditions, hence creating three specific ways to perceive space.

(right, top) The Tabular moment expressing the qualities of 'disperse'. This is an exterior view of the Angel Lectern at sunrise.

(right, bottom) The Transparent moment expressing the qualities of 'cohere'. This is an overview of the moving walls and panels in the Workshop.

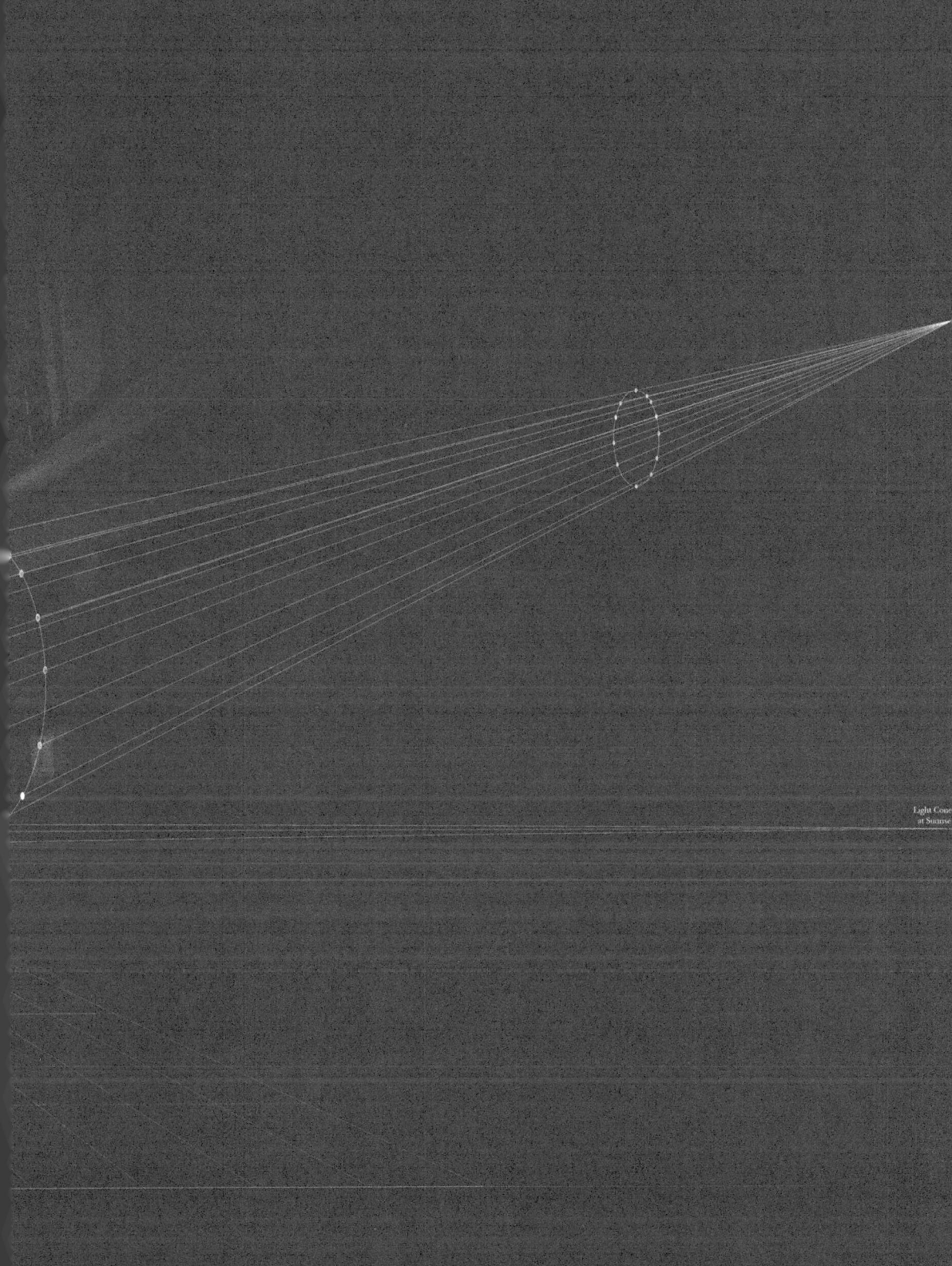

Light Cone at Sunrise

THE SCHOOL OF ELEMENTAL DRAWING

IOANA VIERITA

The Camden School of Elemental Drawing examines the nature of seeing, through the acts of measuring and drawing. Located next to a former Arts and Crafts hub, now the Camden Lock Market, the School aims to highlight the overlooked qualities of 'site' to the students and public by means of surveying, measuring and drawing.

Based on John Ruskin's writings concerning *The Elements of Drawing* (1857), the School creates a journey from drawing 'what one sees, to drawing what is in one's head'.[1] The latter refers to the notion of drawing from the imagination and is represented as a route consisting of both immateriality and physicality. The first is the journey from light to darkness, and the latter takes place from the suspended Drawing Rooms to the underground Drawing Chamber.

'Drawing what one sees': The main fragment of the building spans as a bridge on top of the site and includes a series of one-point perspective spaces, where students prepare their own drawing materials as well as attend drawing classes and lectures. The height, form and orientation of these suspended drawing spaces are defined by very specific sight lines to key elements of the site which include the railway viaduct, the Old Lockkeeper's Cottage, Holy Trinity Church, and Market Hall amongst others. The circulation between these spaces offers the public the opportunity to explore the site at different heights and more importantly, engage with the crafted aspects of the architecture.

'Drawing what is in one's head': The Drawing Chamber is a hidden, meditative space, located on the darkest part of the site, which is an area in complete shadow from morning to late afternoon.

The design of the School explores the relationship between perspective, measurement and the grid discovered during the Italian Renaissance, all of which are essential to drawing. The design is primarily set up from the basic measurements of the material panels and structural elements. The individual drawing spaces which are shaped by the opportunities of the site interrupt and interfere with these measurements. The small footprint of the building creates the opportunity for a new public plaza which additionally provides access to the recently developed Camden Lock Market.

The School forms a pilgrimage towards unfolding one's creativity through its stimulating sequence of spaces and multiple shifts in height and orientation. This pilgrimage further extends beyond the boundaries of the School, offering residents and visitors an alternative journey through the site, from the Holy Trinity Church, through Castlehaven Park all the way up to the busy Chalk Farm road. These connections and the resulting new viewpoints further serve to reinforce the notion of 'seeing'.

---

[1] The quote is taken from a video recording of a talk given by a director of the Ruskin School of Art, who discusses 'the elements of drawing' and explains that this is how Ruskin used to teach his students. The meaning of the quote is suggested in the way the book *The Elements of Drawing* is organised. John Ruskin, *The Elements of Drawing* (New York: Dover Publications Inc., 2012). First published in 1857.

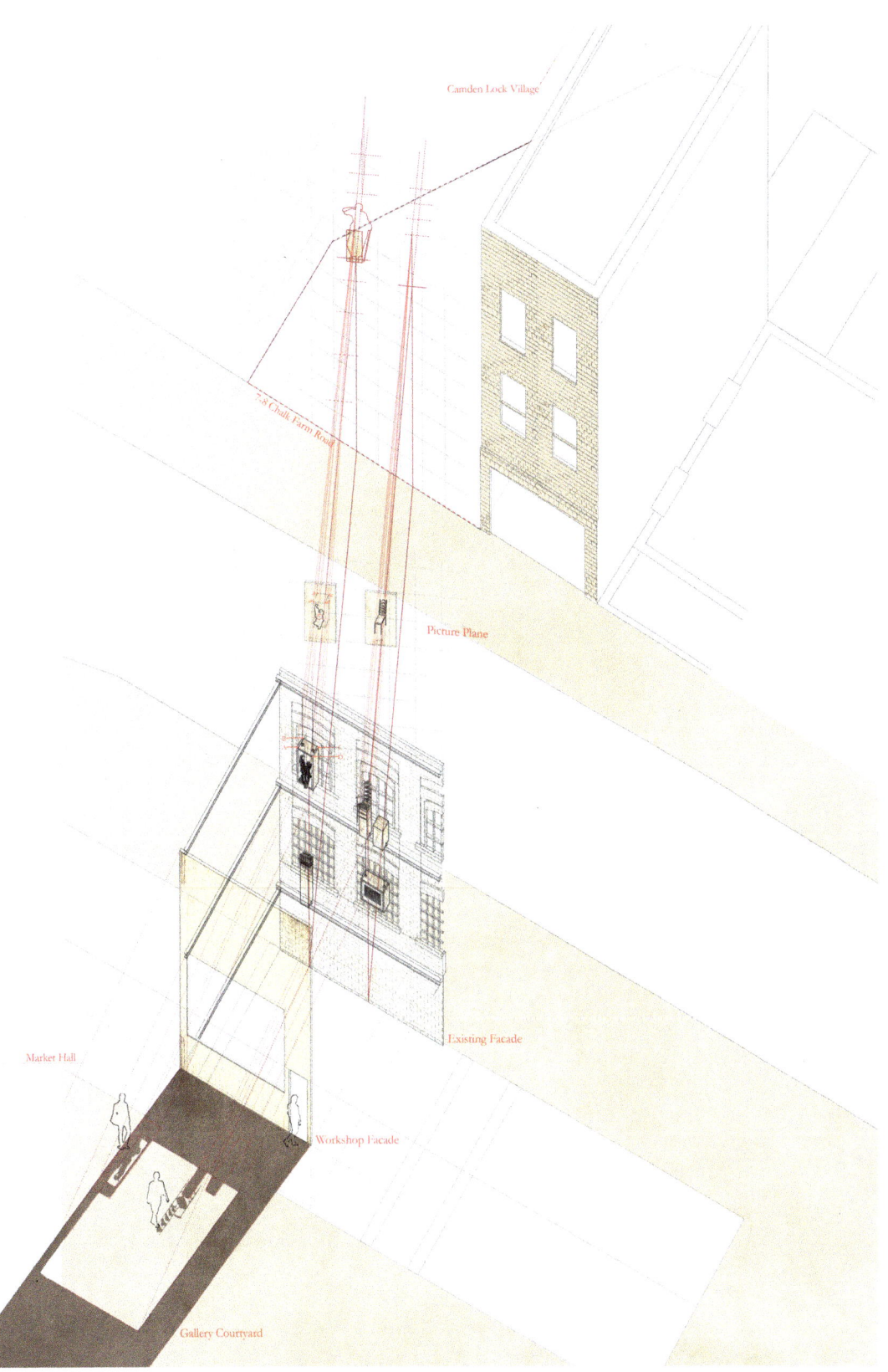

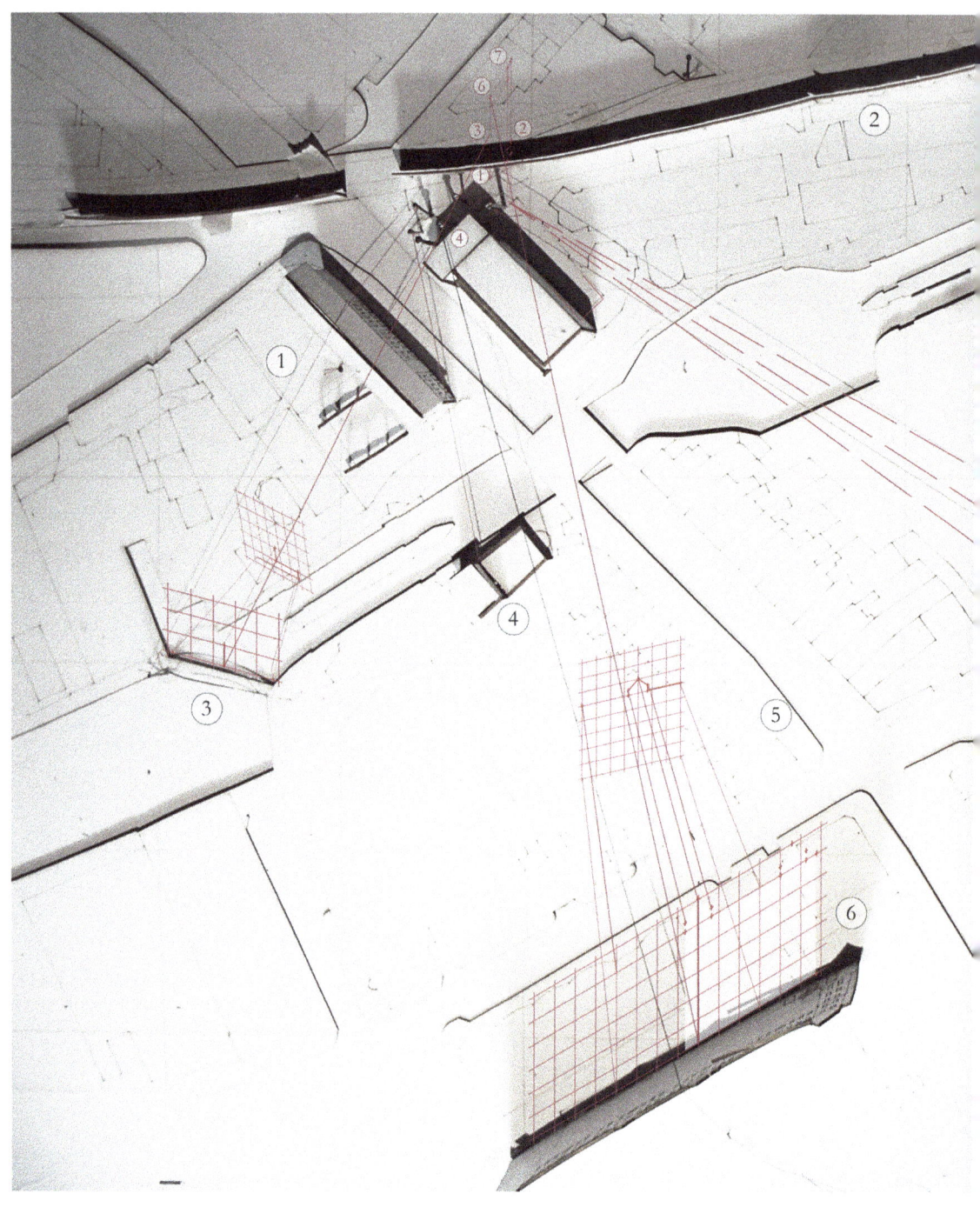

Perspective construction and drawing techniques were employed to locate the best positions from which to observe and potentially draw buildings of architectural merit in Camden.

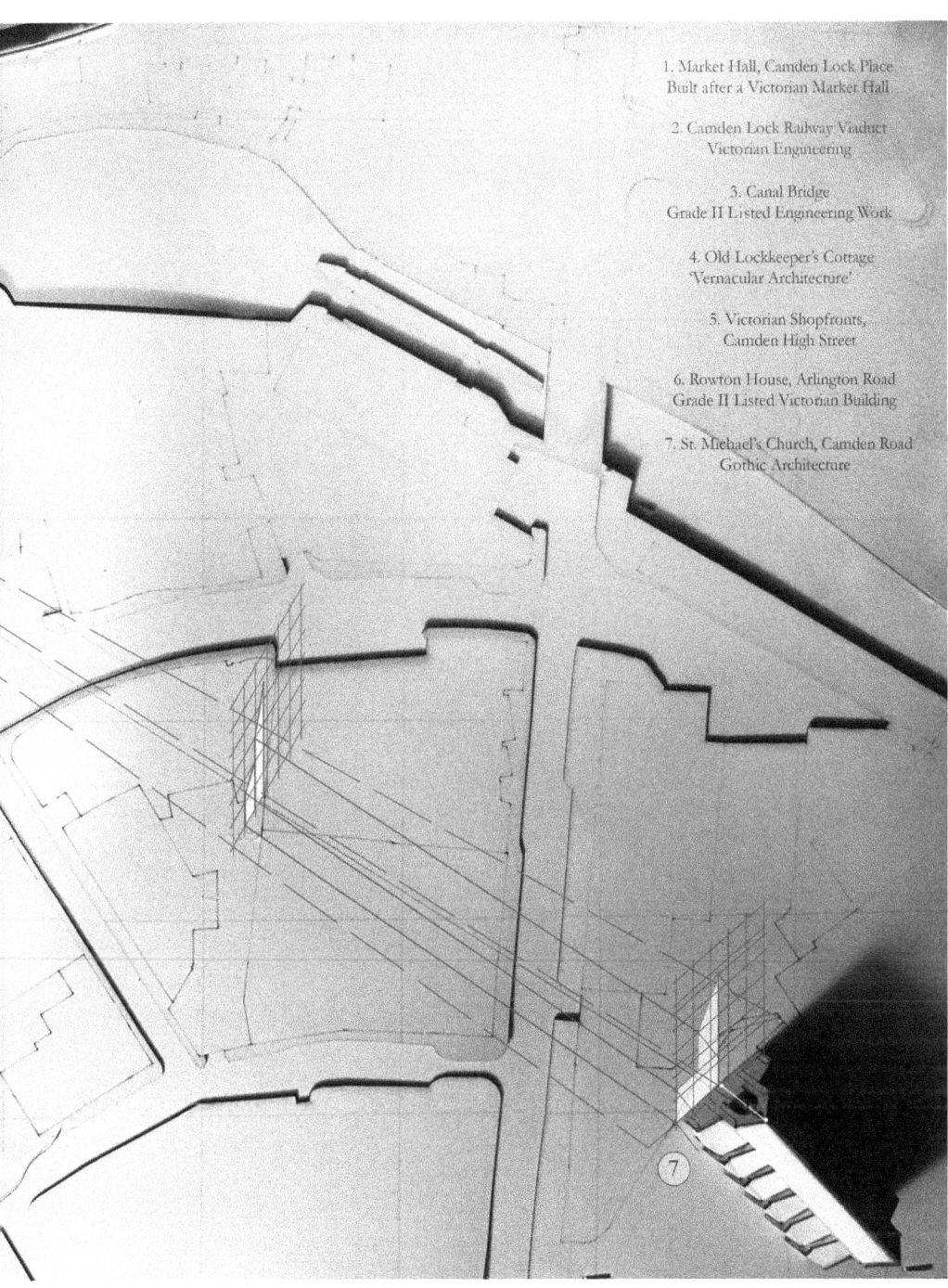

1. Market Hall, Camden Lock Place
Built after a Victorian Market Hall

2. Camden Lock Railway Viaduct
Victorian Engineering

3. Canal Bridge
Grade II Listed Engineering Work

4. Old Lockkeeper's Cottage
'Vernacular Architecture'

5. Victorian Shopfronts,
Camden High Street

6. Rowton House, Arlington Road
Grade II Listed Victorian Building

7. St. Michael's Church, Camden Road
Gothic Architecture

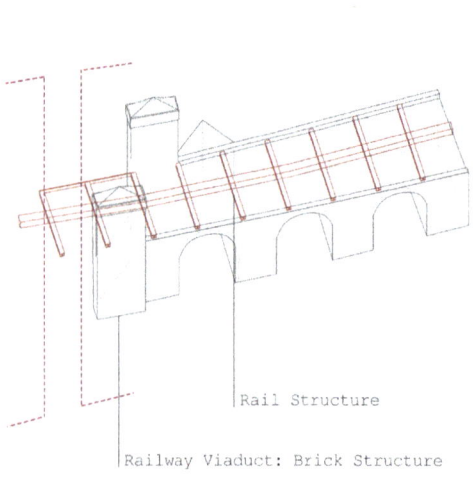

Rail Structure

Railway Viaduct: Brick Structure

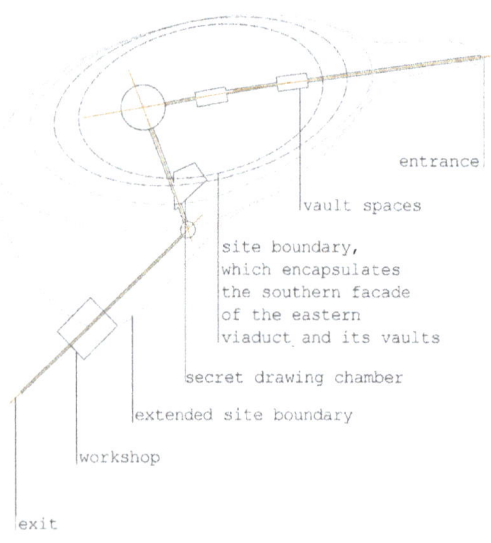

entrance

vault spaces

site boundary, which encapsulates the southern facade of the eastern viaduct and its vaults

secret drawing chamber

extended site boundary

workshop

exit

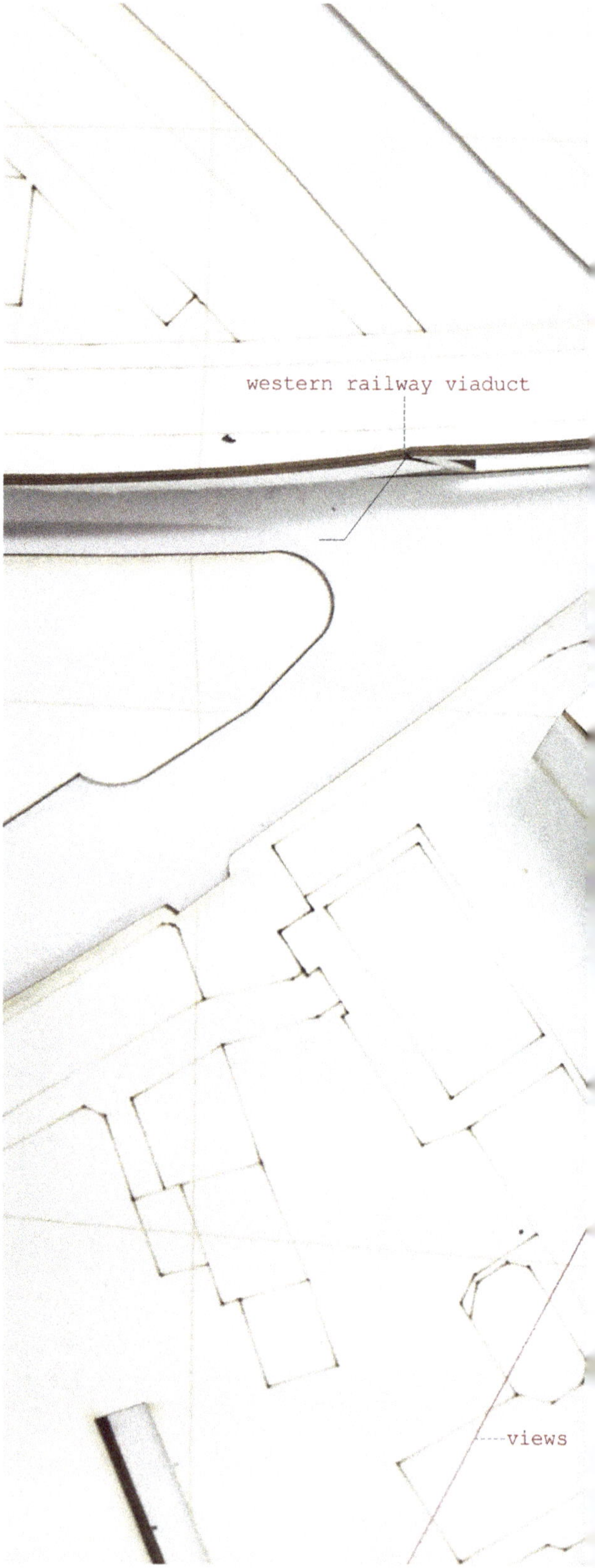

western railway viaduct

views

These site strategy studies were used to determine the physical and visual attributes of the site with the railway viaduct serving as a key defining feature of the design proposal. The experiments were further accompanied by a series of diagrams which explored the site boundaries against programmatic variations and possible routes to and through the site.

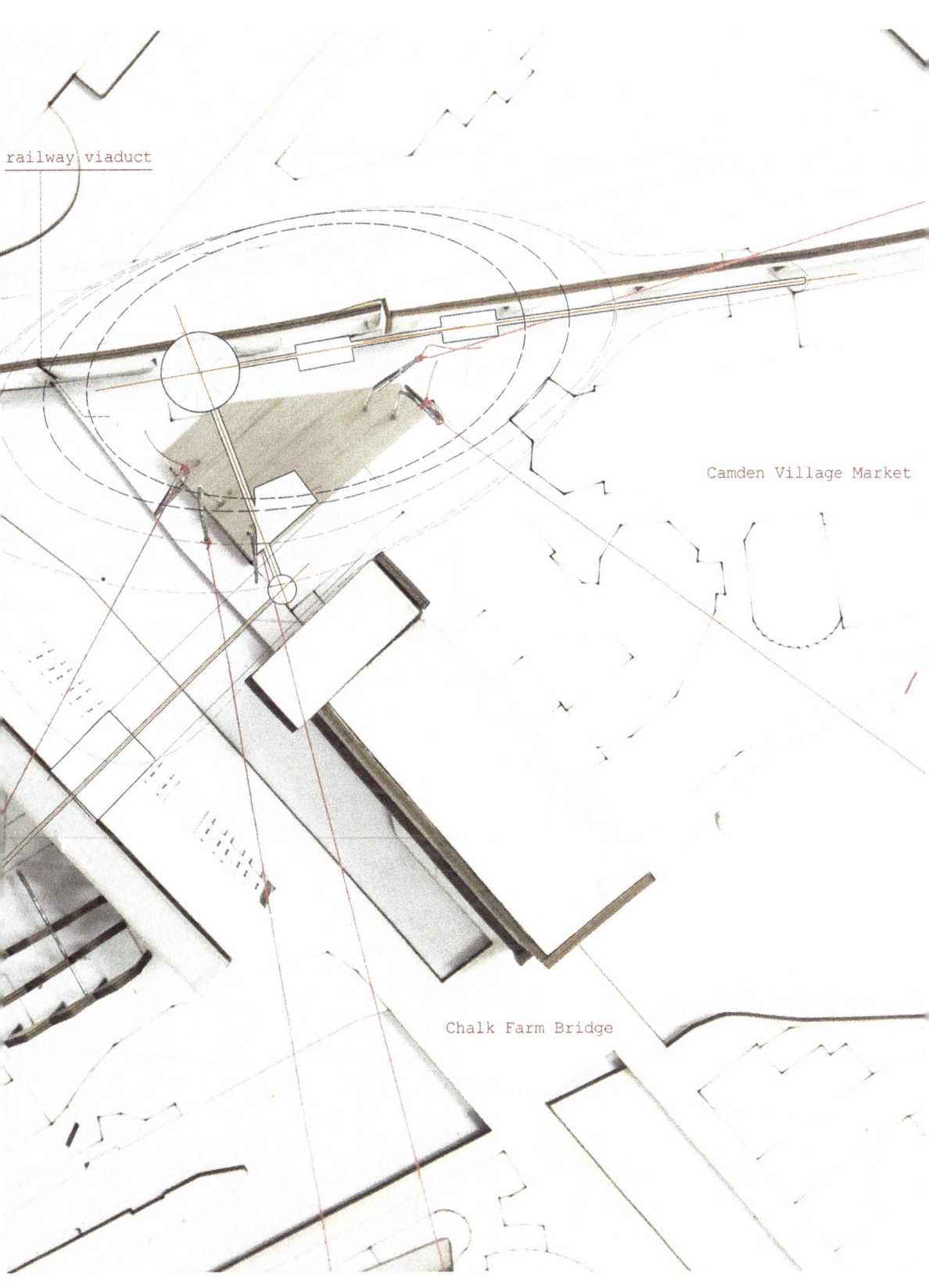

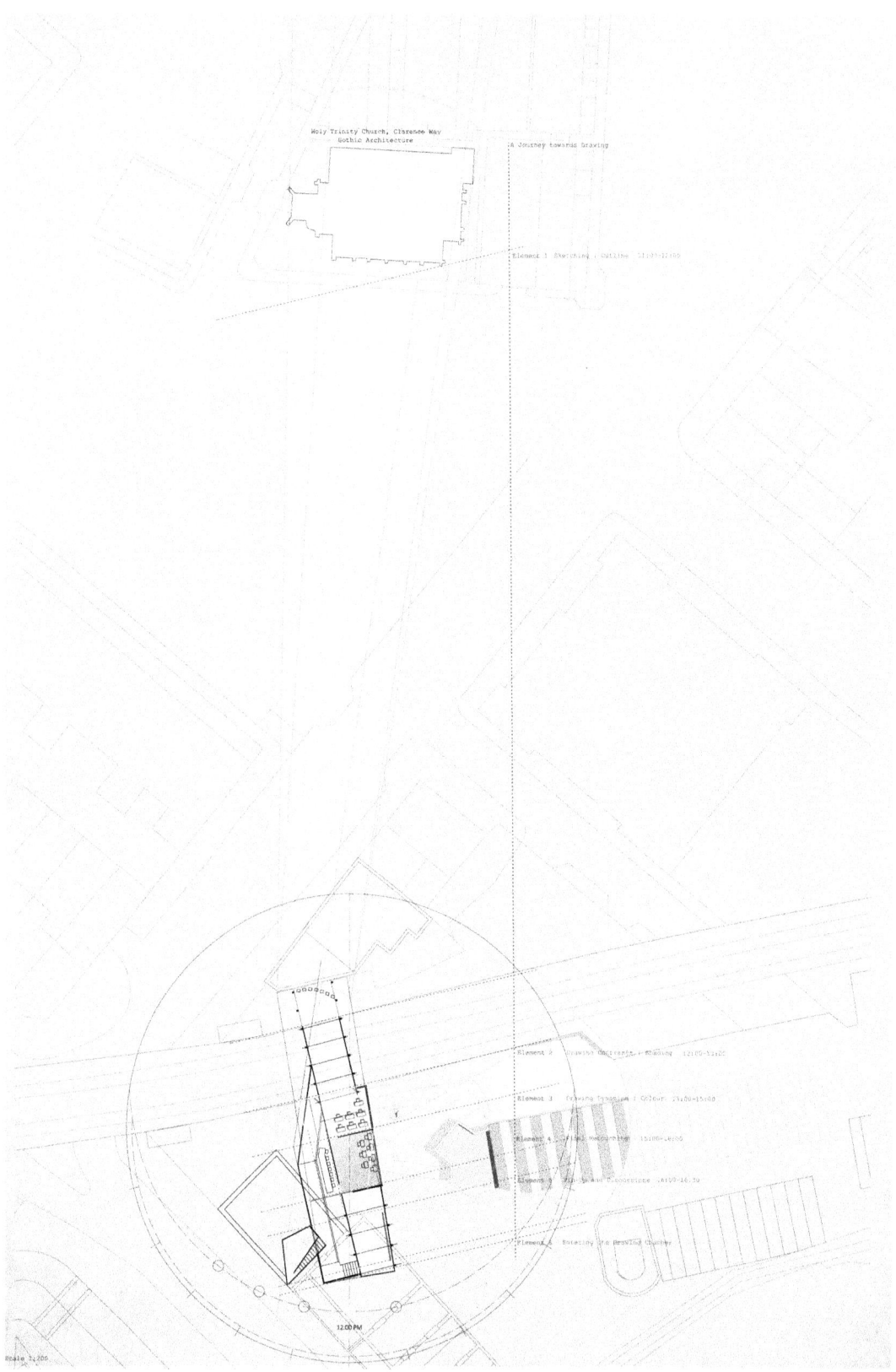

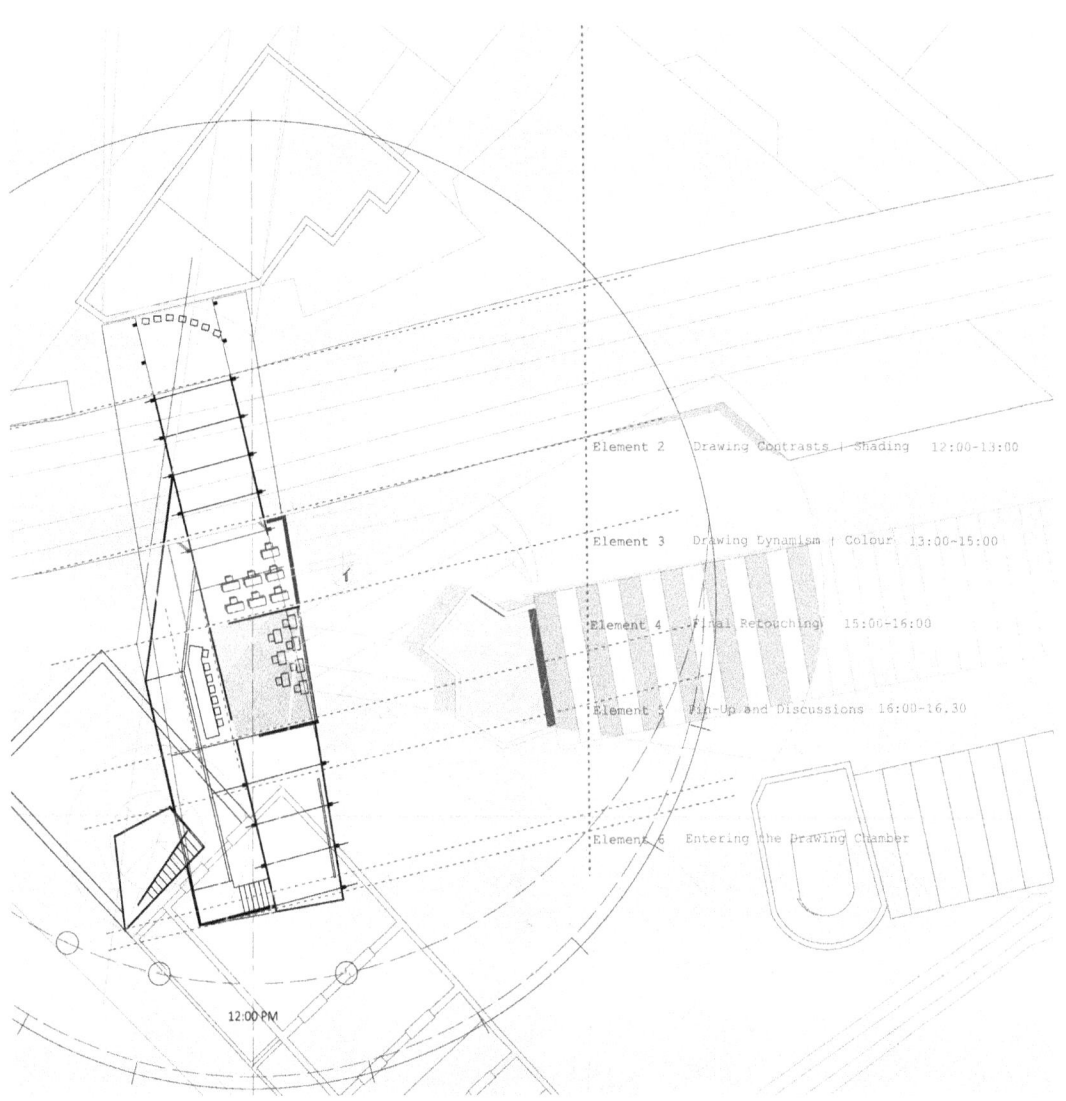

(left) Design development showing the specific site elements which have been used to set up the forms and main axes of the building.

(this page) Detailed light studies in relation to the design of the spaces and route through the School.

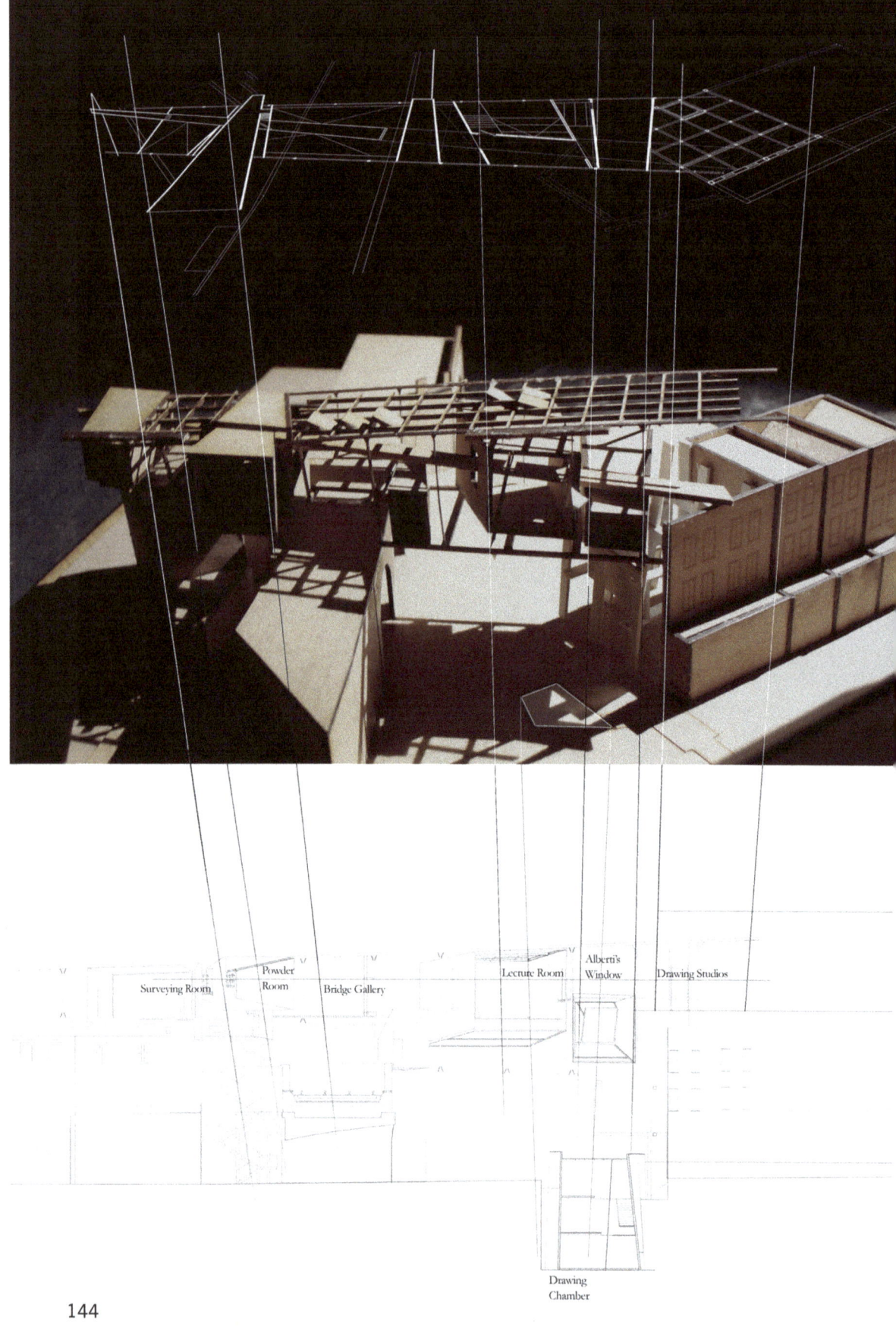

Public

A bridge in the direction of the residential area of Camden	Experiencing the site in the open spaces of the School and on the viaduct terrace	A different experience for the pedestrians

Drawing through observation and measurement	Drawing through meditation and seclusion	Gradually re-entering the site

Students

Experience: A transformative journey from drawing 'what one sees' to drawing 'what is in ones head', from reproduction to imagination, from lightness to darkness.	Practice: Engaging with the context through drawing and analysing. The Drawing Chamber is a retreat from the urban environment.

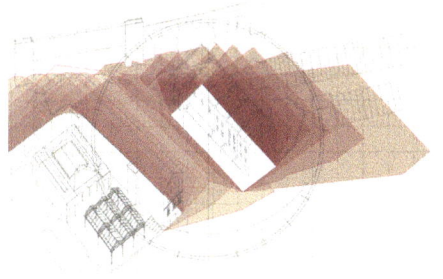

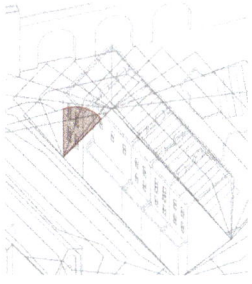

7.30am - 12pm   7.30am - 3pm

The Drawing Chamber is located on the darkest area of the site, as determined by light and shadow studies taken from morning to late afternoon. The form of the Chamber is generated by the intersections of the shadows from the railway viaduct and the buildings on Chalk Farm road.

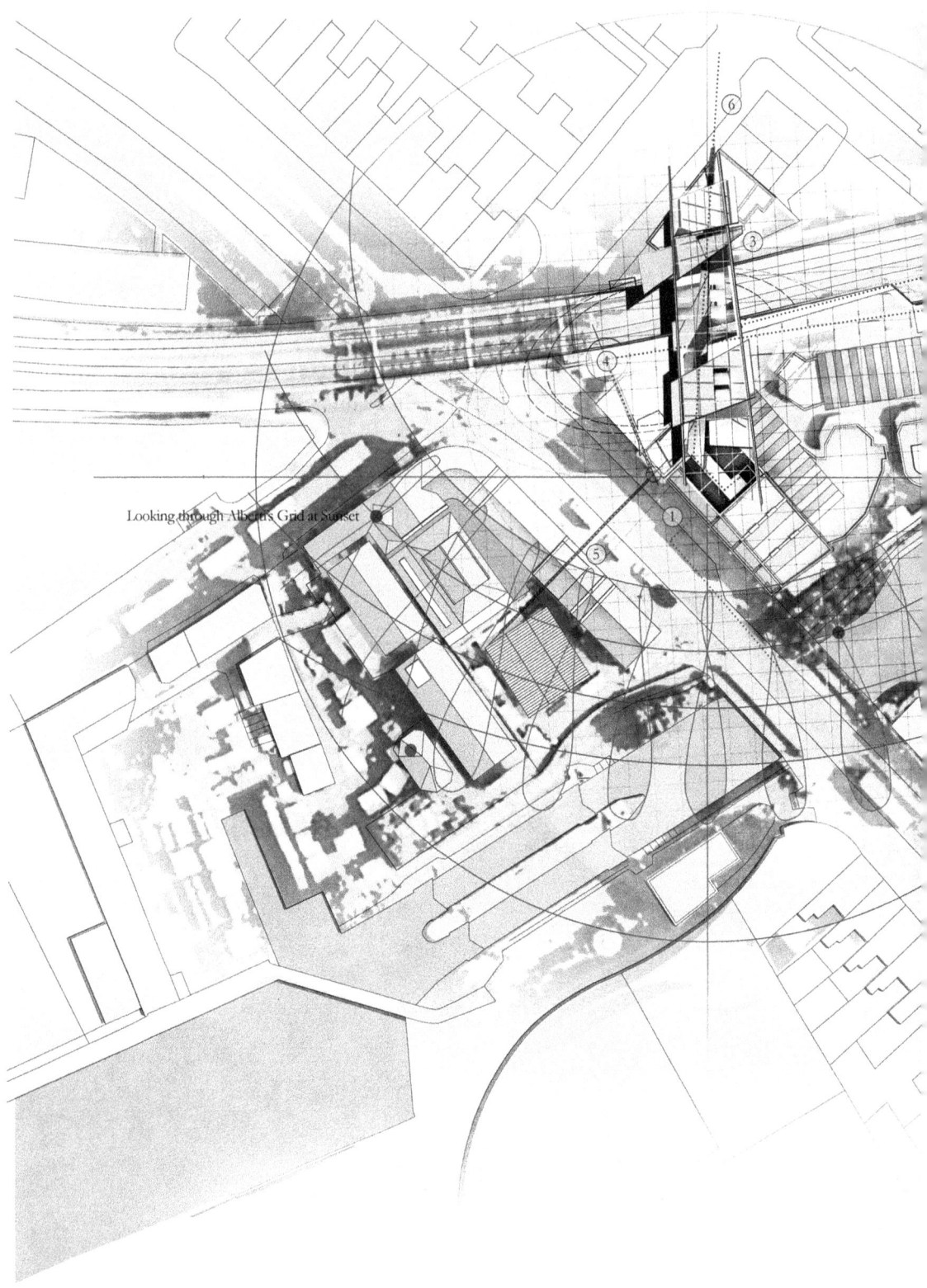

Key:
1: Main entrance for both students and visitors
2: Access to outdoor space
3: Private vertical access
4: New opening providing access to the courtyard and the Market
5: Access to the Wood Workshop
6: Alternative route to Castlehaven Park

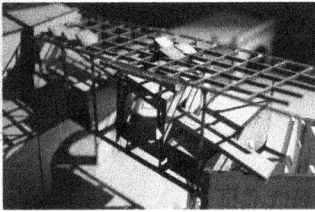

16:00
Drawing objects by means of Alberti's Window

8:00
Walking through the Bridge Gallery into the Lecture Room

...... Underground tunnel linking the School to the Wood Worskhop

...... Opening in the wall of the Wood Worskhop

...... Gallery Courtyard at sunrise

6:00
Entering the Powder Room

The School's programme is designed to suit the specific light conditions at different times during the day.

147

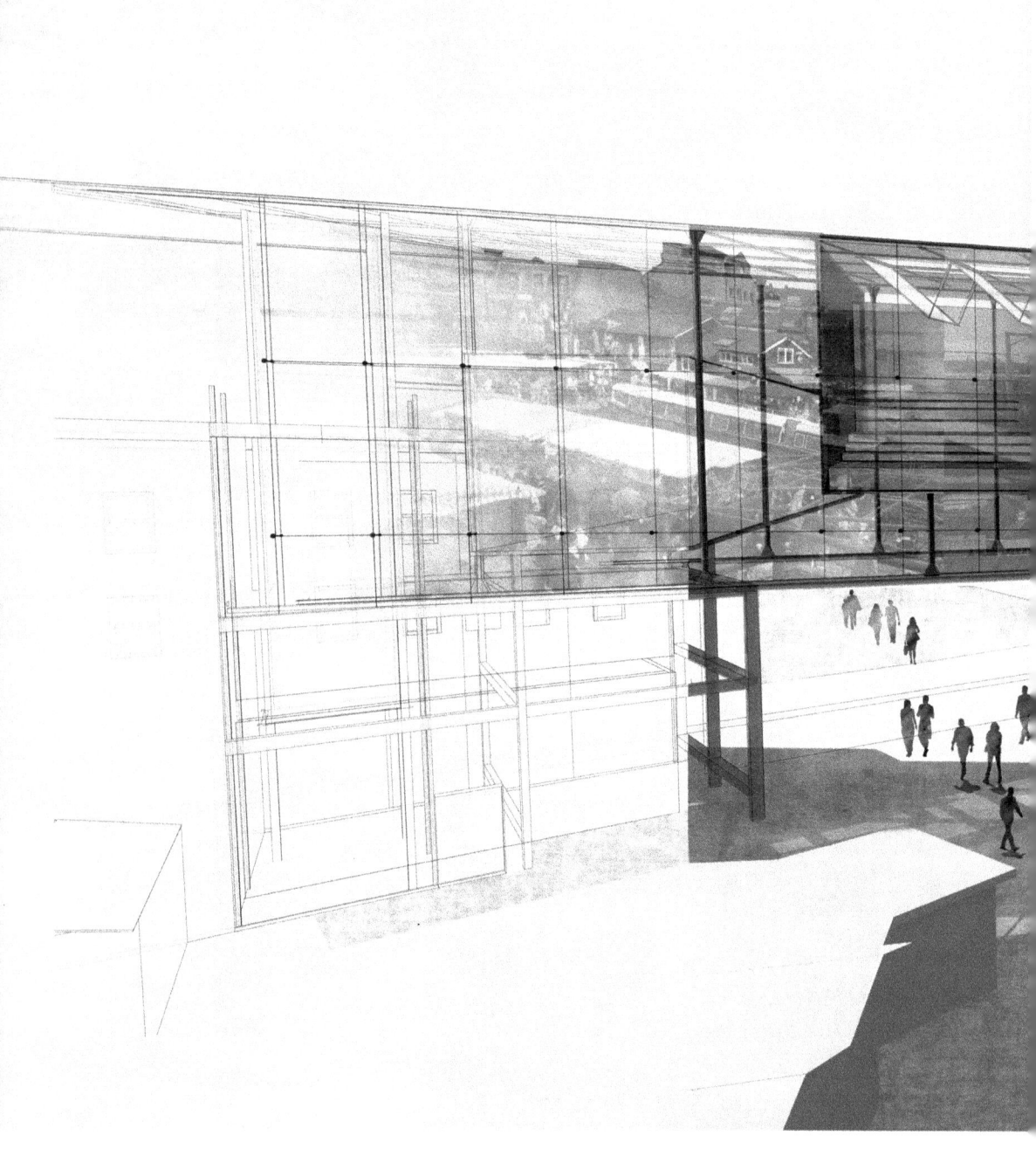
View of the School from the viaduct terrace.

Holy Trinity Church, Camden

II.
Bridge Gallery
Drawing the urban landscape

Lecture Room

III.
Alberti's Room
Drawing the object

IV.
Drawing Chamber

Viewing corridor directed towards the Holy Trinity Church

The Drawing Chamber

The Powder Room

BIBLIOGRAPHY

Ando, Tadao and Richard Pare, *The Colours Of Light* (London: Phaidon, 1996).

Arnar, Anna Sigrídur, *The Book as Instrument* (Chicago: The University of Chicago Press, 2011).

Berger, John, *Ways of Seeing* (London: Penguin, 1972).

Cook, Peter, *Morphosis, Buildings and Projects* (New York: Rizzoli International Publications Inc., 1989).

Diller, Elizabeth and Ricardo Scofidio, *Scanning, The Aberrant Architectures of Diller and Scofidio* (New York: Harry N. Abrams Inc., in association with the Whitney Museum, 1993).

Forty, Adrian, *Words and Buildings, A Vocabulary of Modern Architecture* (London: Thames and Hudson, 2000).

Hagen, Margaret A., *The Perception of Pictures: Alberti's Window* (New York: Academic Press, 1980).

Hill, Jonathan, *Actions of Architecture, Architects and Creative Users* (London and New York: Routledge, 2003).

La Charité, Virginia A., *The Dynamics Of Space* (Lexington, Ky.: French Forum, 1987).

Stéphane Mallarmé, *Un Coup de Dés Jamais N'Abolira Le Hasard* (Paris: La Table Ronde, 2007). The book was first published on 10 July, 1914 by the Imprimerie Sainte Catherine at Bruges.

Putnam, James, *Art and Artefact: The Museum as Medium* (London: Thames and Hudson, 2009).

Ranciere, Jacques, *Mallarmé: The Politics of the Siren* (London: Continuum, 2011).

Ruskin, John, *"Unto This Last": Four Essays on the First Principles of Political Economy*, ed. by Lloyd J. Hubenka (Lincoln: University of Nebraska Press, 1967).

Ruskin, John, *The Stones of Venice* (London: J.M. Dent, 1907).

Ruskin, John, *The Elements of Drawing* (New York: Dover Publications Inc., 2012). First published in 1857.

MORRIS' PLEASURE GARDEN: THE VIEWING FOLLY

SEAR NEE NG

The design proposal is woven around William Morris' London residence which flanked Red Lion Square and the idea that traces of his presence and journeys around the Square have all been erased, removed and/or altered. On this premise, what remains is the visual relationship between the seventeenth-century Square and the building. Therefore the design of a Viewing Folly, as part of a Pleasure Garden, is used to recreate to some extent, this relationship.

The architecture of the Folly is a mathematically calculated space which frames views in an attempt to provide the 'perfect' experience of Morris' house. The visual qualities can be experienced at different positions and levels. The architectural journey requires many explorative shifts in capturing different viewpoints before the revelation and sublime experience of the final view is revealed.

The project is further designed to engage with seasonal and environment changes. During summer, the dense leaves and branches of the surrounding trees merge with the architectural framework and alters the admission of light through the opening for optimum viewing conditions. As a result, the space and the view becomes distinctively defined at this exchange.

Alternatively, the 'bare' structure of the Folly is able to blend with the trees during winter, visually disappearing and forming a continuous landscape with the other elements like the open-air Cinema in the Garden.

While the proposal explores the different visual experiences in the space, the design simultaneously aims to re-enact and explore the different ideologies apparent while researching the Arts and Crafts Movement. The Folly attempts to challenge relationships between architecture and users by means of integrating and redefining the roles of the artefice and artefact.

(right) Arts and Crafts Architecture: In a letter to Andrea Scheu in September 1883, William Morris wrote 'I got a friend (Philip Webb) to build me a house very medieval in spirit which I lived for 5 years'.[1]

This statement could imply that the spacious entrance hall and tall staircase tower, which were medieval in planning to begin with, was the 'sacred' moment Morris had wanted to create in his house.

Hence the sublime moment is calculated to occur when the low winter light filters into the staircase tower. The dramatic effect of this moment can be experienced upon entering the foyer.

[1] Jan Marsh, *William Morris & Red House: A Collaboration between Architect and Owner* (Great Britain: National Trust Books, 2005), p. 19.

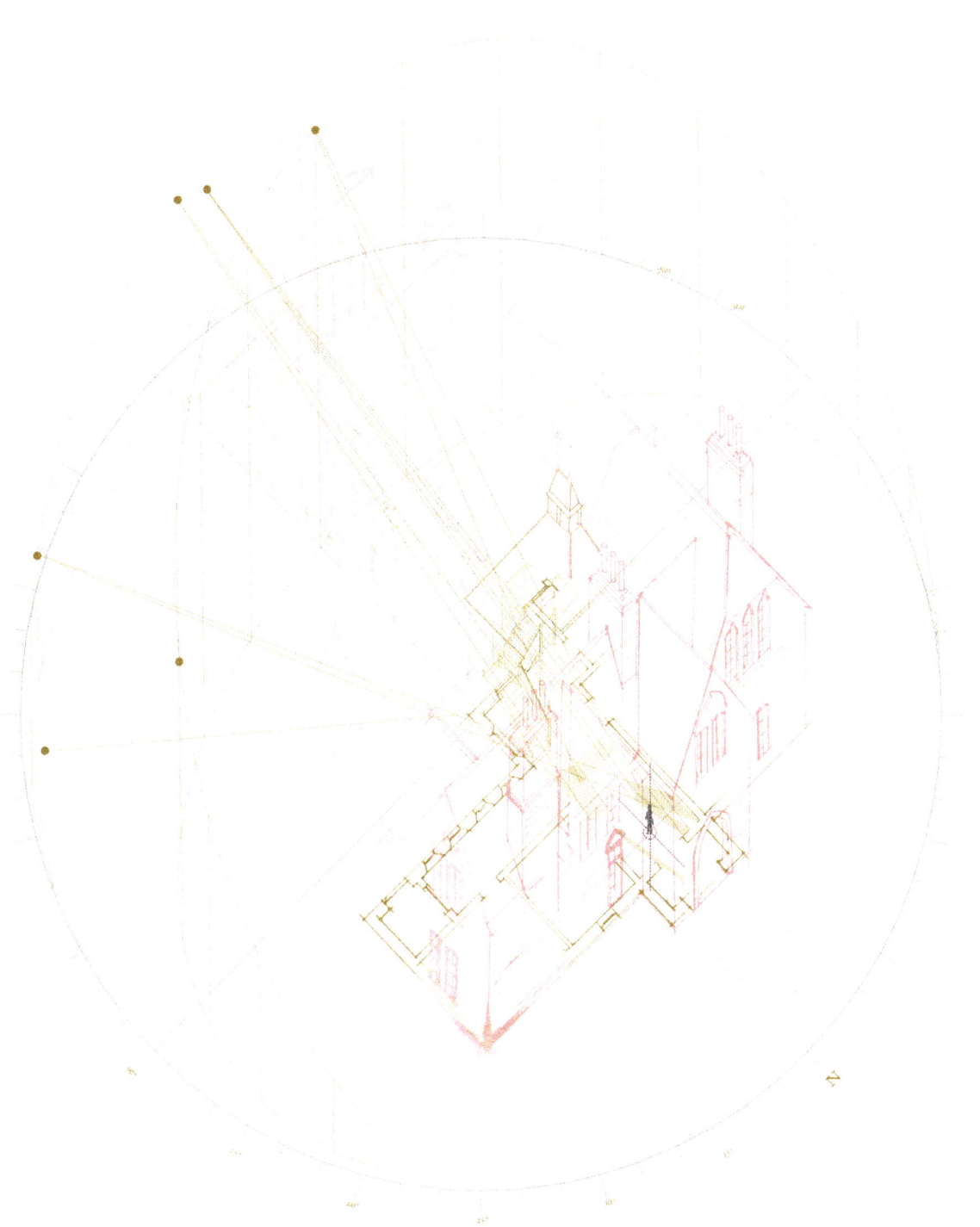

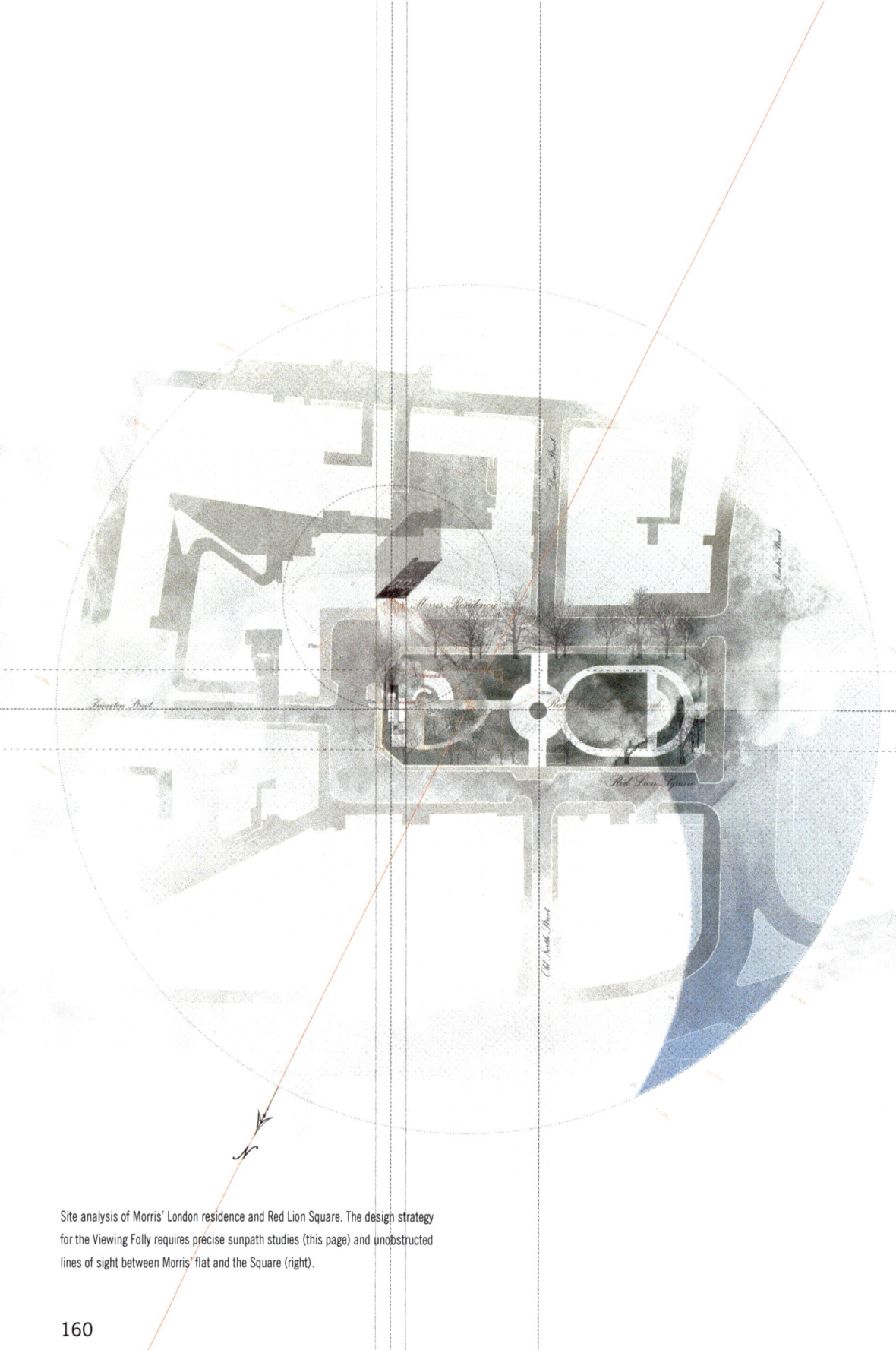

Site analysis of Morris' London residence and Red Lion Square. The design strategy for the Viewing Folly requires precise sunpath studies (this page) and unobstructed lines of sight between Morris' flat and the Square (right).

(this page) The Viewing Folly.

(right) The Viewing Folly and the Landscape Cinema, both set within Morris' Pleasure Garden in Holborn.

THE ARTS AND CRAFTS SCHOOL OF CABINET CONSTRUCTION

SEAR NEE NG

Camden Lock Market used to be known for its artist community, craft workshops and studios. This was the site of a home-grown art scene which flourished during the 1970s. Currently, there are no visible examples of this form of craftsmanship and the products on sale at the Market are merely commercial commodities. Noticeably, this shift in focus from local handmade goods to mass produced souvenirs has brought about a sense of detachment between the Market and the surrounding local community.

The key notion of 'Made in Camden' attempts to rediscover some of the ideas concerning the Arts and Crafts which used to characterised Camden. This is mainly explored through the ethics of the word 'craft', and challenges the dominating reality of mass-production. Hence, it is important that the context of Camden Lock Market where commercial objects are currently mass-produced forms part of the design proposal. Proposed as a School, the premises primarily facilitates craftsmanship.

In this instance, the idea of mass customisation is encouraged as a form of Arts and Crafts. This allows for new inventions and creations in crafting to become adaptable to future technologies.

The School is designed to be accessible from adjacent shops, existing site openings and routes. This design strategy creates access for the local community, vendors, merchants, artists and student-craftsmen, and enables them to become part of the School's programme. The integration of School and site, private and public features enables the act of 'making' and the skills of craftsmen to be exhibited and shared.

These activities are extended to the market to enhance the public experience. More importantly, the architecture is no longer a mere enclosure for the craftsmen but is part of and acknowledges the quality of the crafts by enabling the ongoing act of 'making' and skills of the craftsmen to be celebrated.

This project was nominated for the 2014 RIBA President's Bronze Medal.

(right) The settle is a very important piece of furniture for Morris as it symbolised the moment when his theories and the results of 'making' came together. Hence in this instance, it is referred to as the 'monument' in relation to Morris' Arts and Crafts pursuits.

The settle was moved from Morris' flat in Red Lion Square to the Red House. This piece of furniture is adorned by the artist Dante Rossetti - the nineteenth-century English poet, illustrator, painter and translator - who also painted the sides and the panels of the cupboard doors.

Technically much of the early furniture was of uneven quality as ignorance of the basic principles of construction led to mistakes being made by the craftsmen. These were corrected laboriously through trial and error. Surviving versions of the 1859 furniture in the Red House frequently bore traces of the modifications and alterations needed to strengthen the structure for stability. To Morris, those were the mark of life.

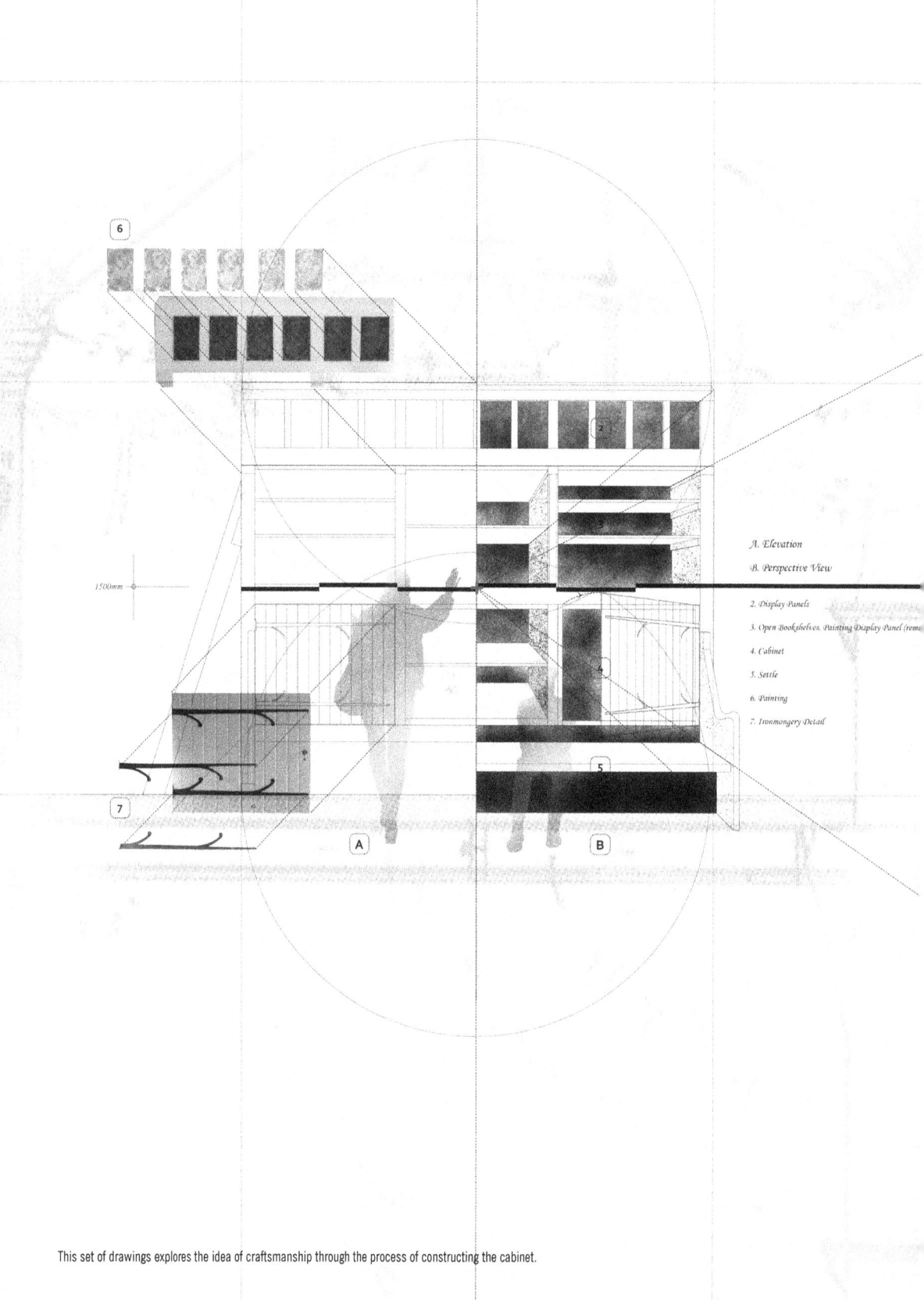

This set of drawings explores the idea of craftsmanship through the process of constructing the cabinet.

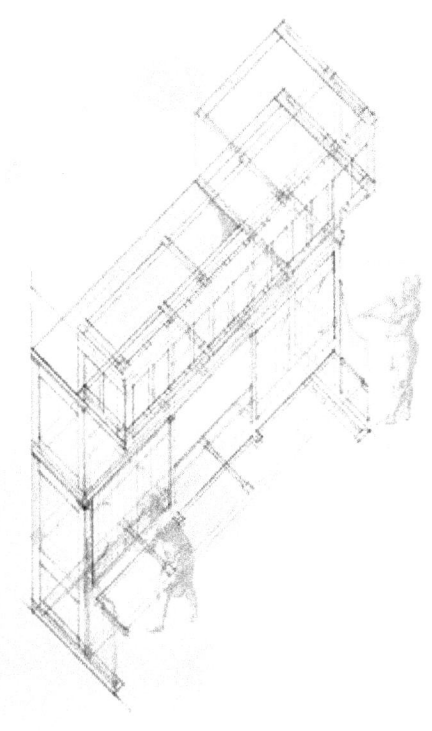

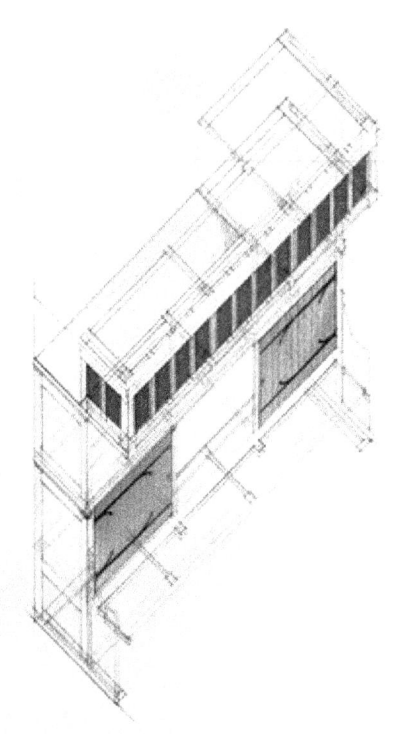

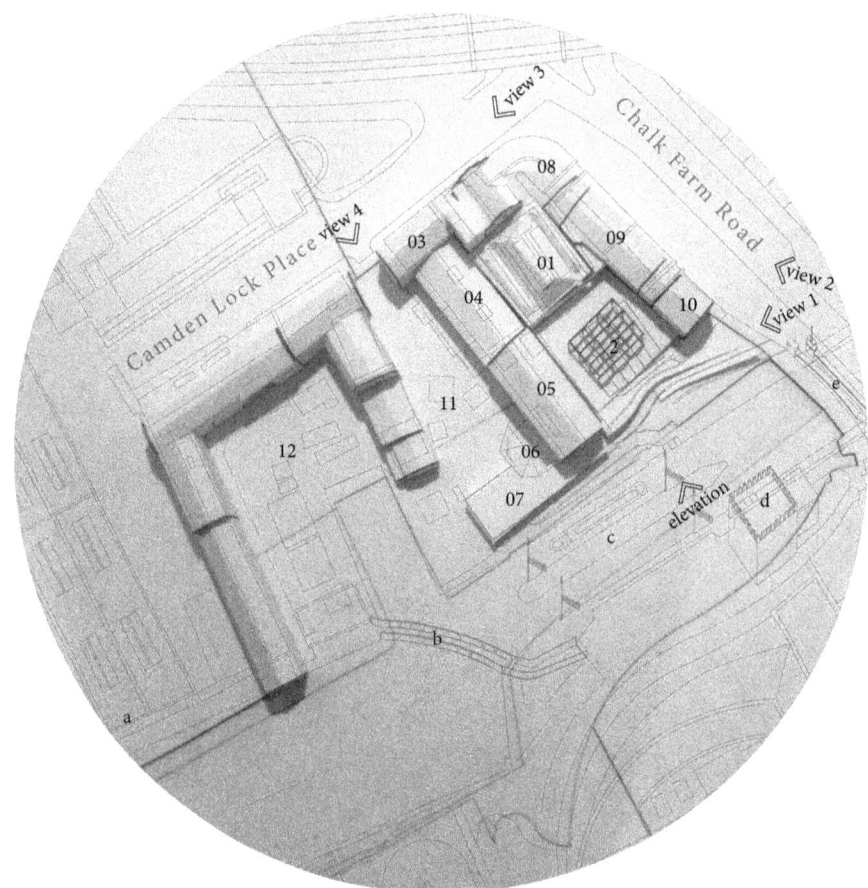

Site model of Camden Lock Market
The Market is made up of two former industrial buildings consisting of a timber warehouse and a bottling plant, two former timber yards and a newly built Market Hall.

Key:
1. Camden Lock Market Hall
The Market Hall was designed after a classic Victorian trading hall and built in 1991.
2. Dingwalls Club (Basement) and East Yard Open Market (above ground)
Some of these old buildings were sub-let on short leases as craft workshops in 1972.
3-4. Retail
5. Lockside Lounge consisting of bars and pubs
Dingwalls Club celebrated its fortieth year in the music business in 2013. This venue in the heart of Camden has a capacity for five hundred, and has sustained a legacy of bands, musicians and DJs whose music has defined each decade.
6-7. Lockside Lounge of bars and pubs
8-10. Retail
11. Middle Yard
The cobblestone courtyard has been restored to its original state.
12. West Yard
The yard is surrounded by industrial buildings from the Victorian period.

Listed Buildings and/or Places:
a. The Interchange Building
Built in 1896, this building was originally used to transfer goods between the canal and railway.
b. Roving Bridge
The cast iron profile of the grade II listed Bridge, built in 1845, makes it one of the best known structures in Camden.
c. Lock Keeper's Cottage
This early nineteenth-century Cottage is now the Regent's Canal Information Centre. The additions and alterations to this building are dated c.1975.
d. Hampstead Road Lock
This pair of canal locks are dated c.1818-20, but have since been altered in c.2000.
e. Hampstead Road Bridge
This 1876 bridge over the Grand Union Canal and towpaths is a public road. It replaces an earlier inadequate brick bridge dated c.1815.

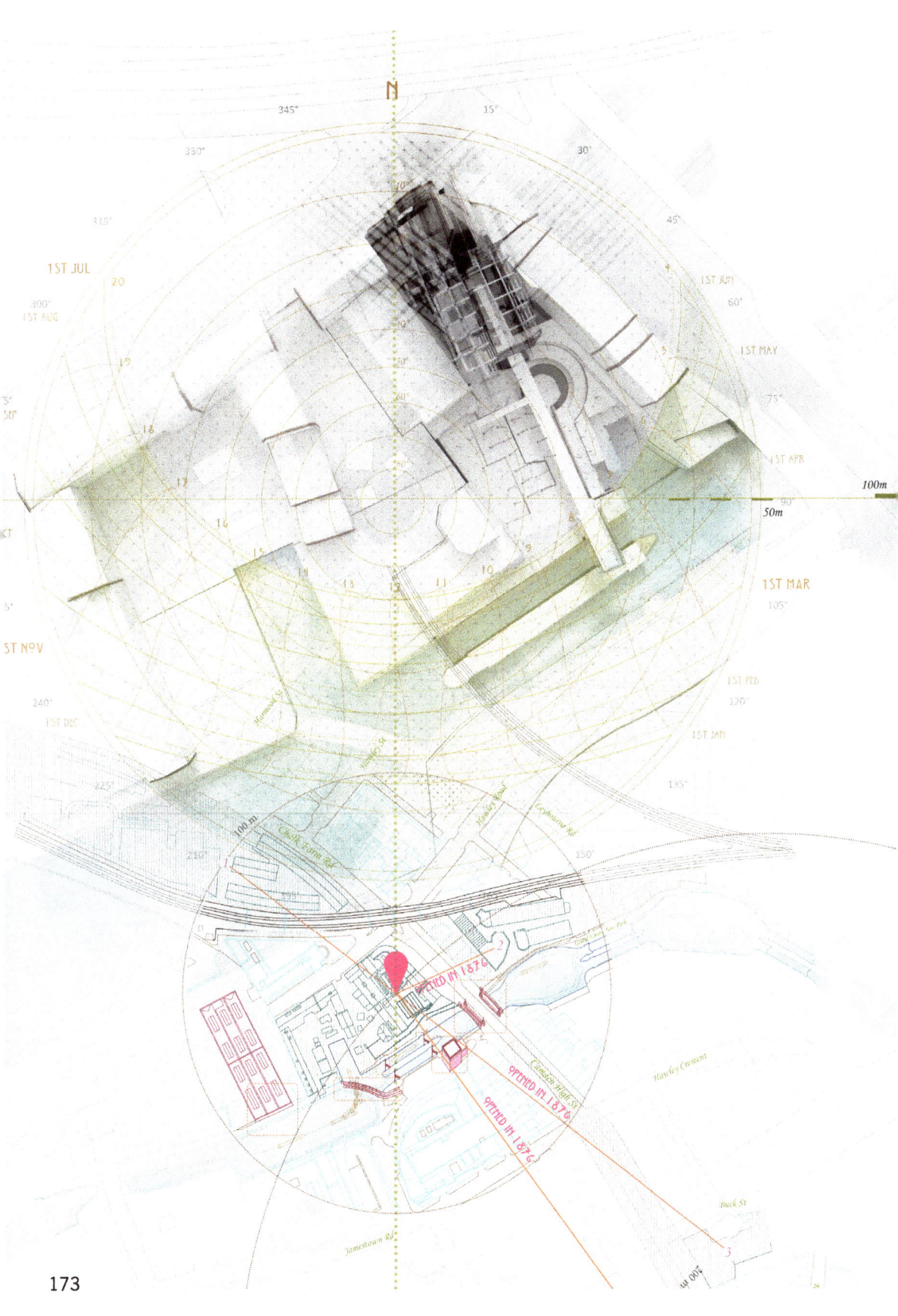

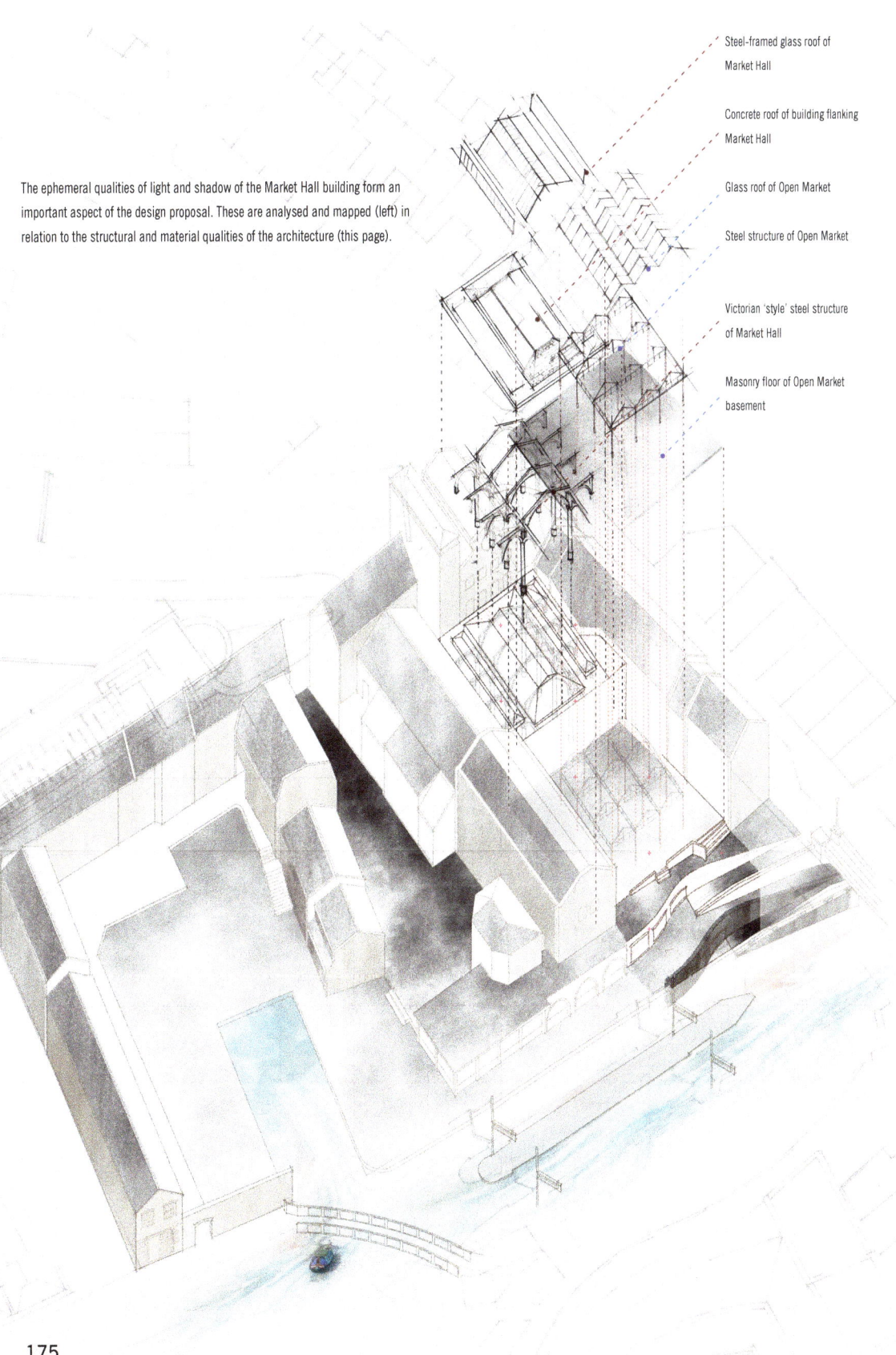

The ephemeral qualities of light and shadow of the Market Hall building form an important aspect of the design proposal. These are analysed and mapped (left) in relation to the structural and material qualities of the architecture (this page).

Steel-framed glass roof of Market Hall

Concrete roof of building flanking Market Hall

Glass roof of Open Market

Steel structure of Open Market

Victorian 'style' steel structure of Market Hall

Masonry floor of Open Market basement

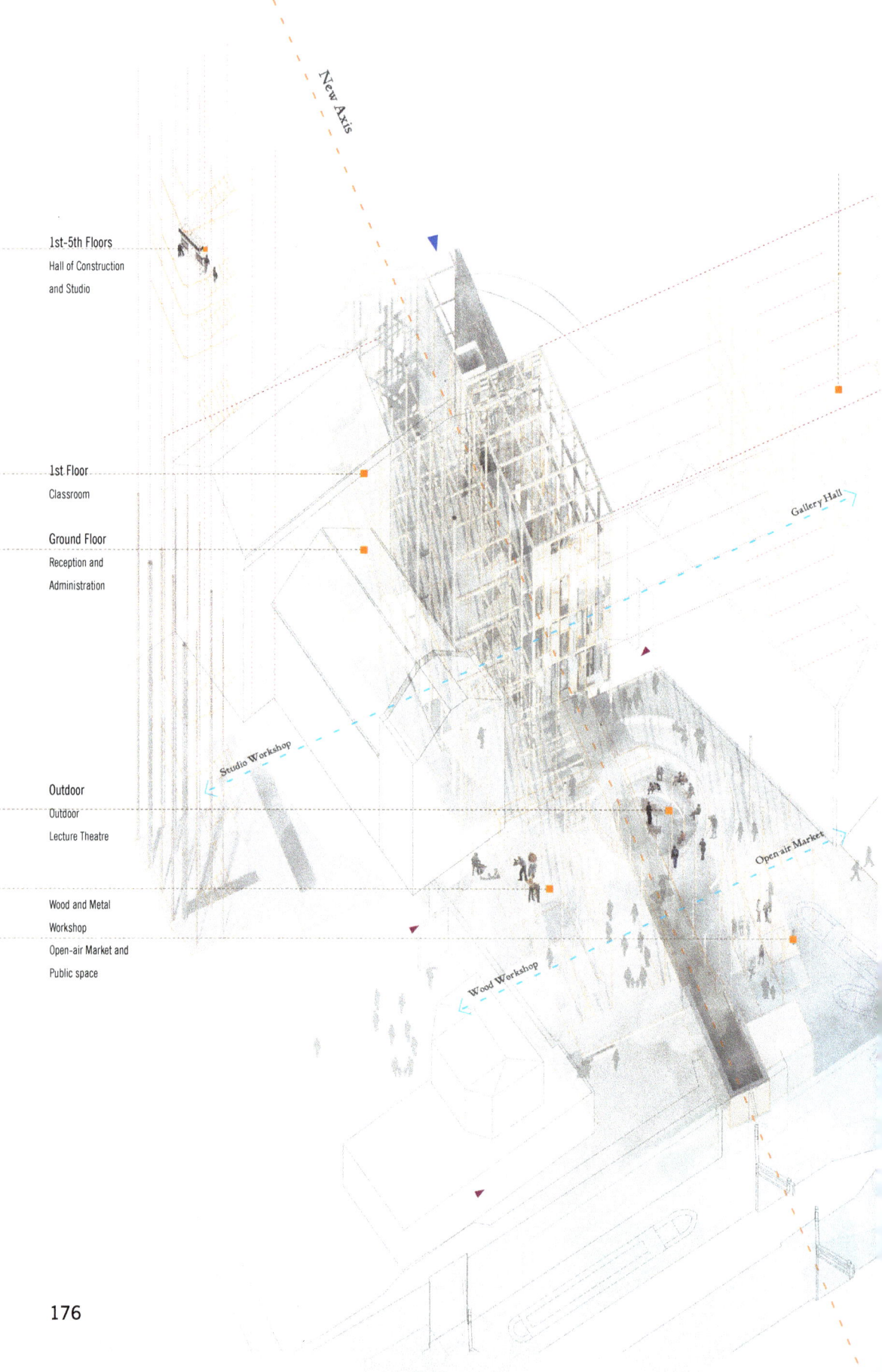

1st-5th Floors
Hall of Construction and Studio

1st Floor
Classroom

Ground Floor
Reception and Administration

Outdoor
Outdoor Lecture Theatre

Wood and Metal Workshop
Open-air Market and Public space

(left) Axonometric drawing showing the modular construction system of the School.
(this page) Axonometric drawing showing in detail the modular system, and the installation of the light enhancing mirrors and reflective panels of the Gallery within the School.

The Hall of Construction is designed to celebrate craftsmanship though the making of the architecture.

The Market Workshop

(this page and right) The Construction Studios and Workshop

The Gallery Hall

BIBLIOGRAPHY

Borg, Alan, and David E. Coke, *Vauxhall Gardens: A History* (New Haven: Yale University Press, 2011).

Downing, Sarah-Jane, *The English Pleasure Garden: 1660–1860* (Buckinghamshire: Shire Publications Ltd, 2009).

Geddes, Robert, FAIA, Dean Emeritus, *'Kahn and the Civic Realm'*. This lecture was delivered at the Museum of Modern Art (MOMA), New York on 28 July 1992, and published in *Progressive Architecure*, November 1992, as 'Perspectives: "Kahn's FDR Memorial Design"', <http://archweb.cooper.edu/exhibitions/kahn/index.html> [accessed 10 January 2014].

Graham, Dan and Alexander Alberro, *Two-Way Mirror Power* (Cambridge, Mass.: MIT Press, 1999).

Harris, Jennifer and William Morris, *William Morris Revisited* (London: Crafts Council, 1996).

Hollamby, Edward, *Red House, Bexleyheath, 1859, Philip Webb* (London: Phaidon Press Ltd, 1991).

Krauss, Rosalind E., *'Grids'*, *October,* vol. 9, summer 1979, pp. 50–64.

Ledoux, Claude-Nicholas and Michel Gallet, 1736–1806, *Claude-Nicolas Ledoux: unpublished projects,* ed. by Michel Gallet (Berlin: Ernst & Sohn, 1992).

Marsh, Jan, *William Morris & Red House: A Collaboration between Architect and Owner* (Great Britain: National Trust, 2005).

Pérouse de Montclos, Jean-Marie, *Etienne-Louis Boullée, 1728–1799: Theoretician of Revolutionary Architecture* (London: Thames and Hudson, 1974).

Morris, William, *William Morris and Company [Ruskin House] Ltd.: metal casements, stained glass, decorative ironwork* (London: The Firm, 1910).

Schumacher, Thomas L., *The Danteum: Architecture, Poetics, and Politics under Italian Fascism* (London: Triangle Architectural Publishing, 1993).

ADAPTABLE ARCHITECTURE

SEAR NEE NG

Abstract

The concept of movement in architecture has always remained a challenge especially given the assumed permanence of the built environment. On this premise, issues of adaptability, which we have yet to satisfactorily address, still resonates as an important consideration with regards to architecture at present. Cedric Price theorised that the consideration of movement in architecture can provide individuals with opportunities to decide, use and access spaces freely. However, such notions of freedom were generally perceived as ephemeral. Therefore, in the course of exploring the notion of adaptability in architecture, the issue of time will be included for specific readings and discussions. This paper investigates different types of adaptable architecture and especially the user-specific approach in relation to new possibilities concerning use, and the construction of architectural space. The discussion draws from Cedric Price's 1961 proposal Fun Palace, London, for its theoretical contributions and Atelier Bow-Wow's BMW Guggenheim Lab, 2011, New York and 2012, Berlin, as realised projects.[1] Drawing from the design principles of Fun Palace, the paper will explore the definition of adaptable architecture on the urban and tectonic scales. The urban scale includes complex associations with context, culture and social events while issues of accessibility, programme and physical adaptability are analysed at a tectonic scale. The paper will then examine the Lab in New York and Berlin which currently serve as examples of adaptable architecture today. The common trait of both architectural practices is their continuous usercentric research and experiments. In this instance, the term 'adaptable architecture' further speculates on the extended role of adaptability in relation to the built environments of the future.

Introduction

The proposal Fun Palace was a collaborative effort between Price and theatre director Joan Littlewood, and was conceived primarily as 'a people's workshop or university of the streets'.[2] Movement was an integral element of the architecture and hence the 'self-participatory element of the activities' was designed to include 'a degree of control by the users of their physical environment'.[3] This argument extended to the idea that over time, concepts of movement can provide individuals with 'greater utility and usefulness'.[4] Although Price's manifesto was not realised in his lifetime, Japanese architects, Atelier Bow-Wow demonstrated a similar vision five decades later when they designed the Lab as a mixed-use public space, conceived as a 'mobile laboratory about urban life'.[5] The intended life span for Fun Palace was ten years while the Lab lasted a year. The paper will first examine the idea of movement in relation to Fun Palace. Price's theory concerning movement took into account issues of accessibility and physical adaptability, which responded to the users, the physical context and organised events. This analysis will be compared to specific readings of the Lab in New York, which was dismantled and subsequently reconstructed in Berlin. Regardless of its impermanence, the approach to accommodating movement in architecture encompasses the complexity of both design and time considerations, and crucially, is user oriented. The paper will provide examples where ideas of adaptable architecture are becoming more prominent and have been integrated into the realm of architecture with long term prospects. The hypothesis argues that adaptability in design practice is quintessential and not addressing the issue undervalues and limits our engagement with the urban environment.

In Fun Palace, the architectural components like the radial, base-fixed escalators and portable walkways were designed to provide users with greater control, where the routes to various destinations can be controlled and/or altered by the individual user. This enabling of choices 'convert what is considered a healthy uncertainty, that is, one which not cowed by doubt, into delight in the unknown'.[6]

Although greatly reduced in size as compared to Fun Palace, the Lab adopted similar principles regarding adaptability and movement that were expressed through spatial configuration and programming. Atelier Bow-Wow recognised the important relationship between movement in architecture and the behaviour of users, and explored this through research concerning behaviorology and void metabolism. Behaviorology is 'an independently organised discipline featuring the natural science of behaviour'.[7] In this instance, it is approached as 'a means to organically integrate the built environment across different scales', with 'architecture as its site and medium'.[8] The word 'metabolism' first appeared in architectural discourses at the 1960 *World Design Conference* in Tokyo.[9] The vertical core, representing the idea of 'lifelines', and used to generate the other detachable aspects of the design proposal were of special significance to the Metabolists.[10] This notion of core metabolism from the 1960s is different to void metabolism. The latter is an urban formula which references the landscape of Tokyo, and especially the void spaces that occur when buildings are rebuilt. This process of regeneration revolves around, and is influenced by the character of these void spaces.[11]

The idea of adaptability in the Lab embraced a wide range of issues which included site selection and construction methods. These were further reflected in the design proposal where public participation was encouraged through the induction of movement. Although the building was temporary, the theoretical readings and design methodologies concerning movement in architecture, and the resulting effects on the user were apparent in the ambition of the project.

Adaptable Architecture

Accordingly to Price, 'architects should constantly recall the uses of buildings – namely, use, misuse, reuse, disuse and refuse'.[12] From the 1960s to the early 70s, Price's visionary thinking contributed to the development of new architectural philosophies regarding time and space within the city. Another influential British establishment called Archigram, which Price was known to have worked closely with, took a particular interest in non-static built forms. Instead, spaces were designed to inform and be informed by the dynamic and complex economical, social and cultural changes apparent in society. To Price, the term 'adaptable architecture' was closely linked to the notion of movement, and this includes the different ways in which architecture is accessed. Hence the provision of flexibility in terms of form and use is important.[13] A work of architecture was no longer conceived as a cohesive structure but instead, approached as a series of unstable systems, continually transforming, reorganising and rearranging itself through the processes of expansion and retraction.[14]

Price's lifelong vision for a city of the future contested the controlled manner in which the users could use and access works of architecture. In his proposals, the movements of the users were integral to the design process and this experimental approach allowed the work to adapt to changes and variations. These improvisations were capable of adjustments to allow for and accommodate unplanned events.[15] It was also during this time that Fun Palace was conceived.

The visionary aspects of adaptability and provision of flexible spatial configurations were key architectural issues during the 1960s. However, the range of suggestions and solutions in this particular field also varied considerably as the understanding of value and usefulness changes from user to user.[16] One typology that called for such attention during that period was the office building. The introduction of the open plan to provide supposedly 'adaptable' and 'flexible' spaces was in response to a rise in demand.[17] While this form of 'planning' appeared to offer infinite flexibility, it did not offer greater utility nor improve the relationship between the users and their built environment.[18] This was mainly because all activities were confined within the impermeable enclosure, with means of access limited to designated openings. Hence the need for a theoretical argument could have started through the asking of key questions concerning how cities and buildings are used and occupied by people. The questions extended to the implications of including a time frame to take into account changes in the environment.

Fun Palace and Programmatic Adaptability

The suitability and feasibility of Fun Palace cannot be fully determined as Camden Town in the 1960s was still recovering from post-war damages, and was just beginning to regain its popularity. The proposal was conceived as a place of endless spatial and programmatic possibilities where a radically rotatable escalator, full-span travelling gantry crane and movable roof as well as screens, come to play with theatrical effects. Hence while even the only limitation was 'one's imagination', the project remained unrealised.[19]

Price derived the presupposed program through research and meticulously documented his surveys. His devotion to understanding the needs of the users was evident in his collection of articles and notes, which formed and informed, to a large extent his working methodology. He acknowledged that architecture was too slow in solving immediate problems and hence, for this reason, he opposed the development of permanent buildings that were limited to particular functions.[20] Instead, he stressed the need to construct for adaptability because the future requirements for current spaces remain unpredictable. Therefore, the idea of adaptable architecture in this instance is one that fosters the relationship between the people and the architecture. This is achieved through design that enables architecture to be consciously programmed as adaptable. After which, this architecture is also one which can be demolished as part of its adaptable 'features' in order to cater for the next change. Hence works of architecture will not risk becoming a liability to the city once it has outlived its use.

Three Types of Movement

The three types of movements examined here involve that of the user, in architecture and during the processes of constructing and dismantling.

To encourage individuals to enter freely without the interference of a prescribed pathway, the planning of Fun Palace deliberately excluded a main entrance.[21] This design was to allow the architecture to adapt to the unpredictable movement of people. The ambition of Fun Palace was to break away from known conventions but, putting such theory into practice also required extensive technical research. In order for the main programs to be distributed across the compound to create generous areas for movement with minimal visual and physical obstructions, the structural columns, floor, wall, and roof, need to be eliminated. This would allow the auditorium, exhibition spaces and platforms to float within the main space. These juxtapositions would encourage activity and further allow for the creation of new activities and experiences.

The movements of the users are enhanced with the provision of different methods to access the space. Adaptability in this instance is largely linked to the physical aspects of the architecture, in particular to issues of constructability. This provides operational immediacy through the movement of the architecture, working in tandem with the constant movement of people that this induces. Hence in this shifting labyrinth of programs and spaces, the idea of adaptable architecture is partially realised.

Price also extended the ideology of adaptability to issues of materiality. A steel frame structure was employed for ease of construction, while the walkways, walls and floors were hung off the travelling gantry crane. The environmental system included 'vapour barriers, warm air curtains, fog dispersal plants and horizontal and vertical lightweight blinds'.[22]

Although the planned life span for Fun Palace was a mere decade, this schedule did not imply an immediate end for the architecture. As previously mentioned, a new approach to issues of adaptability ensured that the building would be designed to adapt and alter to suit future requirements. This further implies that the theory concerning continuous evolution in architecture is an ongoing argument and requires to be constantly challenged. The work must be subjected to being repeatedly designed and interrogated over time.

While Fun Palace may have remained a speculative project, it holds many valuable lessons with regards to its design considerations and methodologies. More importantly, the research and design processes raise many important questions and especially, the need to integrate usercentric material into long term planning schemes.

Adaptable Architecture Revisited

Price's ideas for Fun Palace are revisited, more than five decades later, by Atelier Bow-Wow in their proposal for the Lab. The project was located in the East Village, New York City, as an experimental urban intervention comprising of part urban think tank, part community centre and part gathering space where public exhibitions, lectures and social events were hosted. The architecture, like Fun Palace, was temporary and designed to adapt to the changing events.[23] Through the movement of the people and the 'moving' building, the architecture of the Lab aimed to increase interactions between the public and the proposed spaces. When confronted with a complex contextual situation, the challenges are not restricted to just the spatial constraints but include the broader social and technical aspects of the design and construction processes.[24] Hence, the architectural and design intentions of the Lab can be argued to bear similarities to the theory of movement in Fun Palace.

BMW Guggenheim Lab, New York

Atelier Bow-Wow was greatly influenced by the ideas of the Metabolists group formed in Japan during the 1960s and 70s. In the work of the latter, the urban environment was approached as a 'changing and dynamic city'.[25] Even today, the contest between private and public spaces remains one of the biggest architectural challenges in Tokyo. Hence like many other Japanese architects, the interest in leftover and/or in-between spaces is a prominent aspect of Atelier Bow-Wow's design practice. Their focus on adaptability aims to create additional moments for the public and the architecture to interact, which subsequently present opportunities for new discussions within the urban context. The two theories that are important to this argument, behaviorology and void metabolism, are applied throughout their practice.

In order to illustrate the effects of sequential events on one's behaviour, Yoshiharu Tsukamoto from Atelier Bow-Wow used the example of seasonal changes in Japan. During the annual blossoming of flowers, especially during the plum and cherry blossom festivals, people are 'coaxed outside for the event, individually and of their own violation'.[26] This unexpected gathering of people from which an 'animated' and uniquely Japanese public space emerges, allows for different behaviours to 'synchronise and overlap'.[27] According to Tsukamoto, the resulting 'synergy' from the synchronisation of the 'different rhythms of lives, activities and cycles' can be identified even if there are no buildings.[28] This knowledge, and the corresponding relation to a 'suitable material or location' can be used to inform and form buildings and urban spaces.[29] Hence the design of good public spaces in addition to responsive architecture remains the fundamental inspiration for their practice.[30] The paper explores this design methodology and Atelier Bow-Wow's experiments with concepts of movement in relation to Price's ideas.

A sliver of land between First Park and Houston street at Second avenue was identified as a potential location for the Lab. This site was in a half ruined state and had remained unoccupied since a fire during the 1980s. The architecture inserted into this cavity offered various settings to accommodate and control the different types of movement. Largely inspired by the idea of a theatrical stage, the architecture was designed to adapt and perform.[31] Although the building was not a theatre in the conventional sense given that it had no distinct stage or audience space, it was able to transform according to programmatic requirements by means of manipulating the spatial divisions. The moveable display screens moved vertically, the travelling roof screen provided shading as appropriate and, all other equipment could be controlled manually. The public's curiosity was triggered by these moving components, as well as the translucent mesh skin that offered glimpses of the interior. When the Lab was not in operation, the architecture was stowed away and the site returned to the pedestrians.

The Lab was composed of a system of modular structural components and designed to be assembled by the public. The notions of lightness to further encourage public participation and extend ideas of adaptability through construction were addressed by the use of carbon fiber.[32] The Lab demonstrated that the creation and use of architecture can be altered through public participation. From their design experiences in Tokyo and the Lab in New York, Atelier Bow-Wow's work which argues for an adaptable architecture to serve as a catalyst between public and private spaces, has been markedly reinforced. While the programme aimed to foster interactions between people and place, the architecture acted as a bind for the fragmented site.

The design of programmes where a visitor could be 'stimulated or informed', 'react or interact' within the built environment is a key similarity regarding the proposals for the Lab and Fun Palace. Hence even though the Lab was temporary, the architecture demonstrated the application and feasibility of theories concerning movement and provided material to inform current practice.

BMW Guggenheim Lab, Berlin: Portable, Adaptable Architecture

Post New York, the Lab was dismantled and transported to Berlin to continue with research concerning movement and architecture. This act of displacement was to test solely, the issue of portability. This aspect was to be demonstrated through the efficiency of construction, and the ability of the building to adapt to new events on a new site. This also meant that the extensive site and user studies conducted in New York were disregarded.

In spite of the new and different site conditions, the Lab was reconstructed within a short time and without apparent alterations. The architecture, as before, provided flexible use that responded to the changing events. This reconstruction has seemingly demonstrated the successful delivery of such spaces and may perhaps even fulfill the criteria of an adaptable architecture. However, the new site of an open courtyard space with a single entrance made the Lab a standalone entity, with minimal site engagement. In addition, the isolated location meant the architecture was unable to inform and/or be informed by any user patterns. This situation references the concept of the open plan office discussed previously, with regards to a space that has flexible aspects, but yet was still restricted to fixed designated openings and an impermeable enclosure.

Hence physical and material adaptability without proper considerations for context, people and movement limits discussions of this reconstruction to issues of portability. In this instance, the term 'adaptable architecture' refers only to the physical aspects of the architecture. This example further highlights the ambiguity surrounding discussions of adaptability, and the misconceptions regarding ideas of infinite flexibility that are associated with ideas of adaptable architecture. From this discussion, it is clear that every site is unique and that architectural theory and methodology cannot be simply duplicated without site-specific research. Otherwise, the resulting contradictions will devalue the role of architecture in relation to people and context.

Fun Palace Recap

In retrospect, it is important to remember that Fun Palace was designed with different levels of programmatic adaptability that prioritised the user. In his vision for a user-led architecture of the future, Price also factored in the inevitability of a changing society and built environment. He believed that architecture should not outlive its usefulness. Therefore, the fundamental quality of adaptable architecture lies in its ability to be changed, if not adapted, to suit new situations. Price believed that architecture could contribute to society and the city through renewal, and the ability to be differently useful.

The Lab challenged conventional architectural planning and construction methods, and further demonstrated how adaptability was achieved through site studies and understanding different types of human behaviour. In contrast, the stint in Berlin showed that negligent duplication which is neither site nor user-specific renders the notion of adaptability redundant. More importantly, the key design intention of fostering relationships between the architecture, people and context are lost in the latter. Nonetheless, the discussions involving adaptable architecture, and ideas of an extended lifespan for buildings, hints to an optimistic future with innovations to designing for specific locations and user needs.

In many ways the Lab takes on board some of Fun Palace's theoretical and design approaches, and answered some of the earlier questions raised. Crucially, the idea of adaptability in architecture continues to influence architectural discourse today. The idea of designing for users in this manner, and for a work of architecture to be able to adapt to programmatic and environmental changes requires continuous research as well as the constant reworking of architectural design processes.

Future Projects

The notion of usercentric and adaptable works of architecture is reflected in the 2013 winning proposal for the Jean-Jacque Bosc bridge by the architecture firm Office for Metropolitan Architecture (OMA). The design spans over the river Garonne in Bordeaux, France, and was described as a 'generous platform for pedestrians and public programs, as well as flexibility in accommodating the future needs of various types of traffic'.[33] The platform stretches into the land to create seamless connections at either ends that are the municipalities of Bègles and Floirac. Separate lanes with specific widths are designed across the surface of the platform for each different vehicle. This allows the architecture to adapt to the different vehicular needs and rates of change in the future. More importantly, the largest section of the bridge is dedicated to pedestrians.

The proposal is approached as an urban intervention with the aim of creating generous amounts of new public spaces. These spaces can be adapted for different events, facilitated by the closing of the vehicular lanes. Hence 'the bridge itself is not the "event" in the city, but a platform that can accommodate events of the city'.[34]

In this paper, the definitions of movement, accessibility and adaptability in architecture have been addressed and explored. While the examples of adaptable architecture discussed are mainly associated with public spaces and/or projects, the application of the ideas discussed could be expanded to different architectural typologies.

This reworking of concepts will enable innovative outcomes that can inform and reshape the future of adaptable architecture.

[1] BMW is the commonly used abbreviation for Bayerische Motoren Werke AG, a German luxury vehicles, motorcycle, and engine manufacturing company founded in 1916. Unless otherwise stated, all references and mentions of the Lab in this paper refer to the BMW Guggenheim Lab in New York.

[2] Cedric Price, *Cedric Price Works II* (London: Architectural Association Publications, 1984), p. 56.

[3] Price, p. 56.

[4] Price, p. 11. The argument is furthered by this extract: 'This bears a strong resemblance to the British philosophical concerns of Jeremy Bentham and John Stuart Mill's deep passion for personal freedom, while closer examination of Price also shows marked affinities to Benthamite Utilitarianism'.

[5] This project began as a co-initiative of the Solomon R. Guggenheim Foundation and the BMW Group. The Lab was set up in New York, dismantled and reassembled in Berlin and Mumbai in 2012 and 2014 respectively. <http://www.bmwguggenheimlab.org> [accessed 15 Jan 2014].

[6] Price, p. 54.

[7] Yoshiharu Tsukamoto and Momoyo Kaijima, 'Architectural Behaviorology' in *The Architectures of Atelier Bow-Wow: Behaviorology*, trans. by Steven Chodoriwsky (New York: Rizzoli International Publications, 2010), pp. 8–15. The quote is unpaginated.

[8] Tsukamoto, *The Architectures of Atelier Bow-Wow: Behaviorology*, pp. 15 and 11.

[9] Yoshiharu Tsukamoto, 'Void Metabolism', in *City Catalyst: Architecture in the Age of Extreme Urbanisation, Architectural Design*, 219, ed. by Alexander Eisenschmidt (London: John Wiley and Sons, 2012), pp. 88–93 (p. 90). This was part of a manifesto by the architects Kiyonori Kikutake, Kisho Kurokawa, Fumihiko Maki and Sachio Otaka, and the architectural critic Noboru Kawazoe.

[10] Tsukamoto, *The Architectures of Atelier Bow-Wow: Behaviorology*, p. 13.

[11] Tsukamoto, *The Architectures of Atelier Bow-Wow: Behaviorology*, p. 13.

[12] Price, p. 36.

[13] 'Flexibility in the construction and destruction of enclosures is alone insufficient to achieve the degree of immediacy of change… means of movement and access throughout the complex also needed to be capable of adjustment'. Price, p. 56.

[14] The architectural proposals Plug-in-City, 1964 and Instant City, 1968 by Peter Cook, The Walking City, 1964 by Ron Herron, all members of Archigram, were similarly programmed with these qualities.

[15] Price, p. 56.

16. For clarification, it is essential to present a contrasting example of what flexibility could have meant as the concept of the open plan office was known to have incited such misunderstandings in the 1960s.
17. William Kremer, 'The Pleasures and Perils of the Open-Plan Office - BBC News', *BBC News, 2013* <http://www.bbc.com/news/magazine-21878739> [accessed 04 Jan 2014].
18. 'The concept of the office as a "communications matrix and information node is too generalised to be useful, while the perceptive definition of a "mind-oriented living space" if taken in isolation is too ambiguous'. Price, pp. 54–55.
19. Price, p. 56.
20. Price, p. 56.
21. Price, pp. 59–62.
22. Price, p. 11.
23. BMW Guggenheim Lab, *Lab Design: Architectural Animation, 2011* <https://www.youtube.com/watch?v=KLge3maZPHI> [accessed 18 December 2013].
24. Christopher D. Brazee, *East Village/Lower East Side Historic District – Designation Report*, pp. 7–8. The area has changed drastically since the 1830s as a result of immigration.
25. Tsukamoto, 'Void Metabolism', p. 90.
26. Tsukamoto, *The Architectures of Atelier Bow-Wow: Behaviorology*, p. 12.
27. Tsukamoto, *The Architectures of Atelier Bow-Wow: Behaviorology*, p. 12.
28. Tsukamoto, *The Architectures of Atelier Bow-Wow: Behaviorology*, p. 12.
29. Tsukamoto, *The Architectures of Atelier Bow-Wow: Behaviorology*, p. 12.
30. Tsukamoto, *The Architectures of Atelier Bow-Wow: Behaviorology*, p. 12.
31. In an open lecture, Atelier Bow-Wow described the design process of the pavilion, which included studies of theatrical stages. BMW Guggenheim Lab, *Lab Programs: Yoshiharu Tsukamoto of Atelier Bow-Wow, 2011* <https://www.youtube.com/watch?v=fe3_IgtU2el> [accessed 28 December 2013].
32. The largest building component could be handled single handedly.
33. The proposal measures (44 x 545)m. 'OMA Wins Competition to Design Jean-Jacques Bosc Bridge in Bordeaux', dated 19 December 2013 <http://oma.eu/news/oma/leads-the-final-round-fo-pont-jean-jacques-bosc-bridge-international-competition-in-bordeaux> [accessed 5 January 2014].
34. Clément Blanchet, director of OMA France. <http://www.archdaily.com/460821/oma-wins-its-first-bridge-pont-jean-jacques-bosc> [accessed 5 January 2014].

THE INVISIBLE ICON
AND
THE URBAN OBSERVATORY

2014/2015

CONSTANCE LAU

Essentially the Pavilion was an 'exhibit about exhibition, which 'exhibited a new way of looking'.[1]

The notion of multiple interpretations starts with *Looking for Mies*' Barcelona Pavilion.[2] The trajectory of the original Barcelona Pavilion from a temporary exhibition space to its status as an icon representing twentieth-century architecture is especially significant given that the building existed for a mere six months. Until its reconstruction in 1986, the Barcelona Pavilion was essentially a series of photographs, drawings, sketches and correspondence associated with its commission, design and construction. Hence given its history, one can argue that there exist several versions of this building.

Referencing its history from the original 1929 building to the 1986 reconstruction, the narratives concerning the Barcelona Pavilion engage with issues of temporality, site-specificity, context, identity and programme. The site of Kensington Gardens is acknowledged for the Serpentine Pavilions during the months of June to October. Similar to Mies' original building, the designs for these Pavilions are required to respond to a range of concerns.

More importantly, the design proposal for another translation of the Barcelona Pavilion places itself within the argument that supports the notion that there are different readings of this building. Hence the narrative for the architectural proposal, a pavilion set in Kensington Gardens, will encapsulate one of these interpretations.

This proposal for an Urban Observatory and Auditorium translates the earlier ideas and explorations into the different views, viewpoints and manners of interpreting and presenting a work of architecture. The design narrative is henceforth constructed around a new definition of an Observatory. The body of work is seen as a continuation of the design arguments and research presented earlier, particularly with regards to contextual issues. This is especially relevant given the surrounding diversity, which includes the Royal Parks, grade I listed monuments and buildings, museums and residences. Significantly, the site-specific and permanent qualities of this design proposal can be read as a counter-balance to earlier arguments.

The projects by Iga Martynow analyse the use of the grid as an architectural concept and its direct associations with Mies' Pavilion. These readings are used to generate site-specific responses which are integrated into the design from the scale of the masterplan of Kensington Gardens, down to the detailing of the eventual architectural construct. In the design proposal for the Theatre of Transparencies, the conceptual and spatial application of the grid extends to both the horizontal and vertical planes. The narratives of performance and therapy are woven into the gaps between these two planes, and the qualities of time and movement are used to alternate the function and occupation of the spaces.

The projects by Kyriakos Eleftheriadis explore Mies' relationship with the art movement Dadaism, the works of the Russian Avant-Garde, and especially El Lissitzky's development of the *Proun*. Concepts concerning the *Proun* are extended and employed to generate an architectural language. More importantly, material attributes are introduced in a precise and systematic manner to the design narrative and architectural programme. Hence the presentation, arrangement and reading of these new pieces of work are able to meticulously reveal the development process of transforming a painting into a building.

---

[1] Beatriz Colomina, 'Double Exposure, Alteration to a Suburban House (1978)', in Birgit Pelzer, Mark Francis and Beatriz Colomina, *Dan Graham* (London, Phaidon Press Ltd., 2001), p. 88.

[2] This phrase references Daza Ricardo's book *Looking for Mies* (Barcelona: Actar Publishers, 2008).

GARDEN OF ECHOES

IGA MARTYNOW

Since 2000, the Serpentine Gallery commissions a temporary summer pavilion on an annual basis. The pavilions serve as means of raising funds for the Gallery through privately hosted events as well as a place to house exhibitions and educational programs which are open to the general public.

Mies van der Rohe's 1929 Barcelona Pavilion serves as the main architectural precedent which influenced the design of this project. The research concentrated on the figure of the grid apparent in Mies' works, and was further inspired by the writings and projects by Rosalind Krauss, Superstudio and Le Corbusier. The design proposal aims to translate readings from a two-dimensional grid, mostly used in painting, into a three-dimensional architectural proposal.

The analysis concluded with two distinct types of grids, namely one involving the use of hierarchy and the other, without. The first was used to determine the site boundaries within Kensington Gardens and historical, contextual and visual information were layered onto the site in a strict hierarchical order. The latter grid was used to indicate subsidiary grids within these established boundaries. The idea of a 'democratic' and rectilinear grid was the factor which influenced the design of the Garden Pavilion. The level changes within the project are carefully choreographed to illustrate the relationship between the rules of the grid pattern and the plans which become more fluid and inhabit the spaces inbetween as the structure descends towards the water.

Hence the research on the subject of the 'grid' concluded in a design proposal in which the boundaries between landscape and building were fluid and overlapped. This concept is further enhanced by the material selection, largely inspired by Le Corbusier's notion of *'transenna'*.[1] The result is the dematerialisation of the boundaries separating the existing site and the building imposed onto it.

---

[1] Sarkis, Hashim, *Le Corbusier's Venice Hospital and the Mat Building Revival* (Munich: Prestel, 2001). 'In Venice there is this special characteristic called *"transenna"*, that is, the way buildings, water, and light merge into a completely different condition where there are not single buildings anymore but a whole architectural compound'. p. 32.

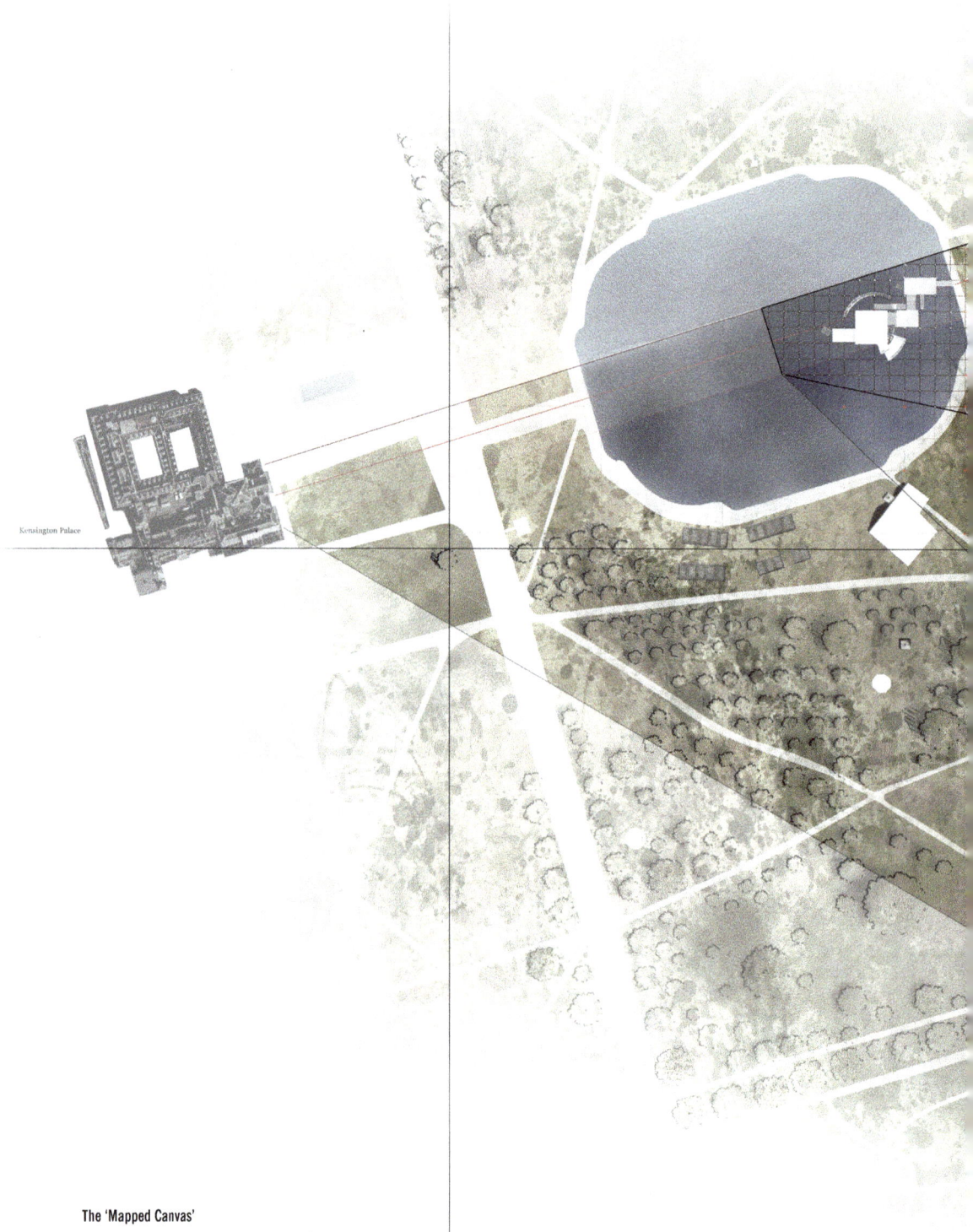

The 'Mapped Canvas'

A hierarchical order is applied to the use of different grids in this drawing. The layering of grids follows an ordering principle which highlights the different boundaries including historical, contextual and visual that are applied to the design proposal. The analysis reference Le Corbusier's Venice Hospital project, Mies' use of the grid in his design work, the planning principles of Kensington Gardens and the existing geometrical arrangements, patterns and grids surrounding the Serpentine Gallery.

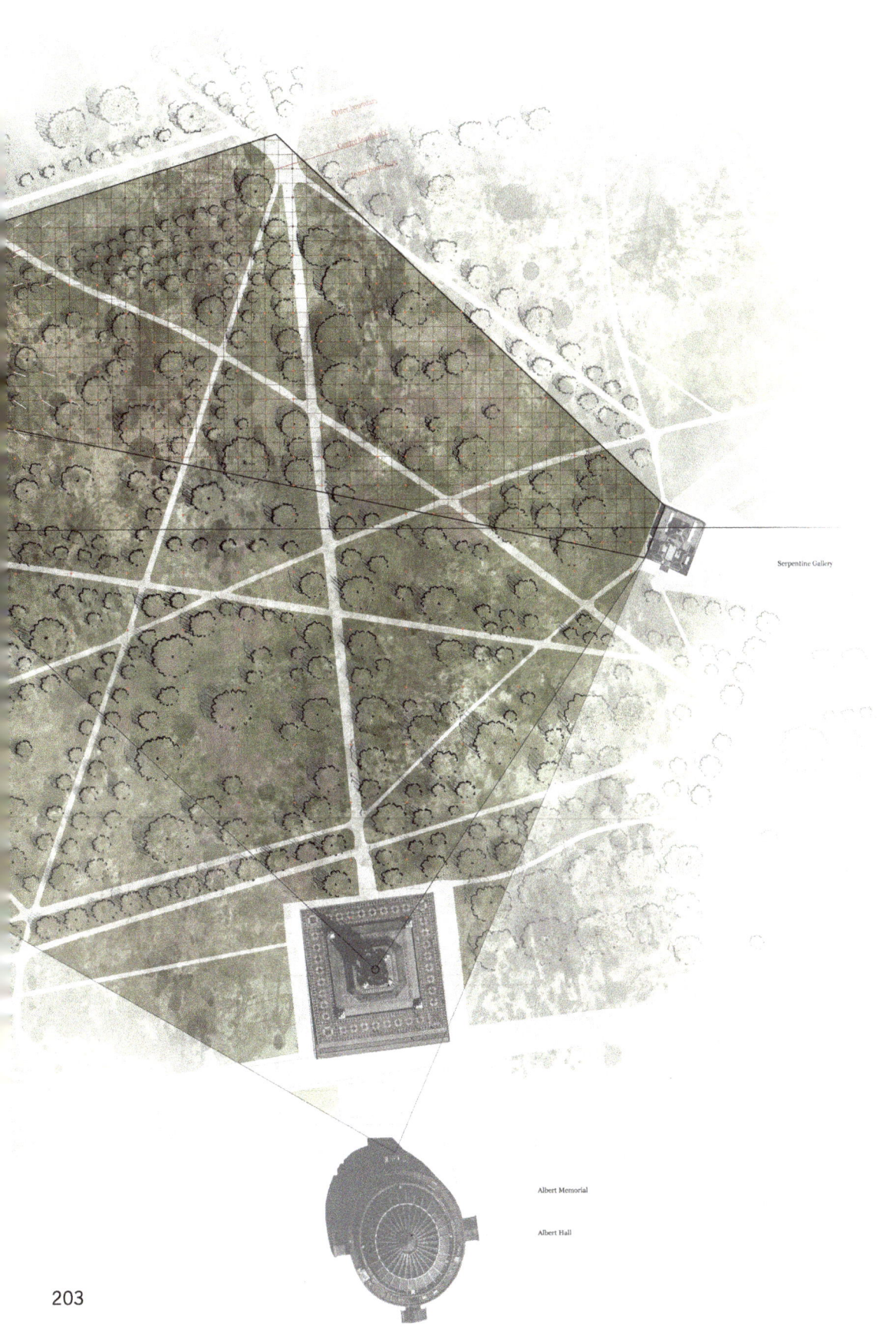

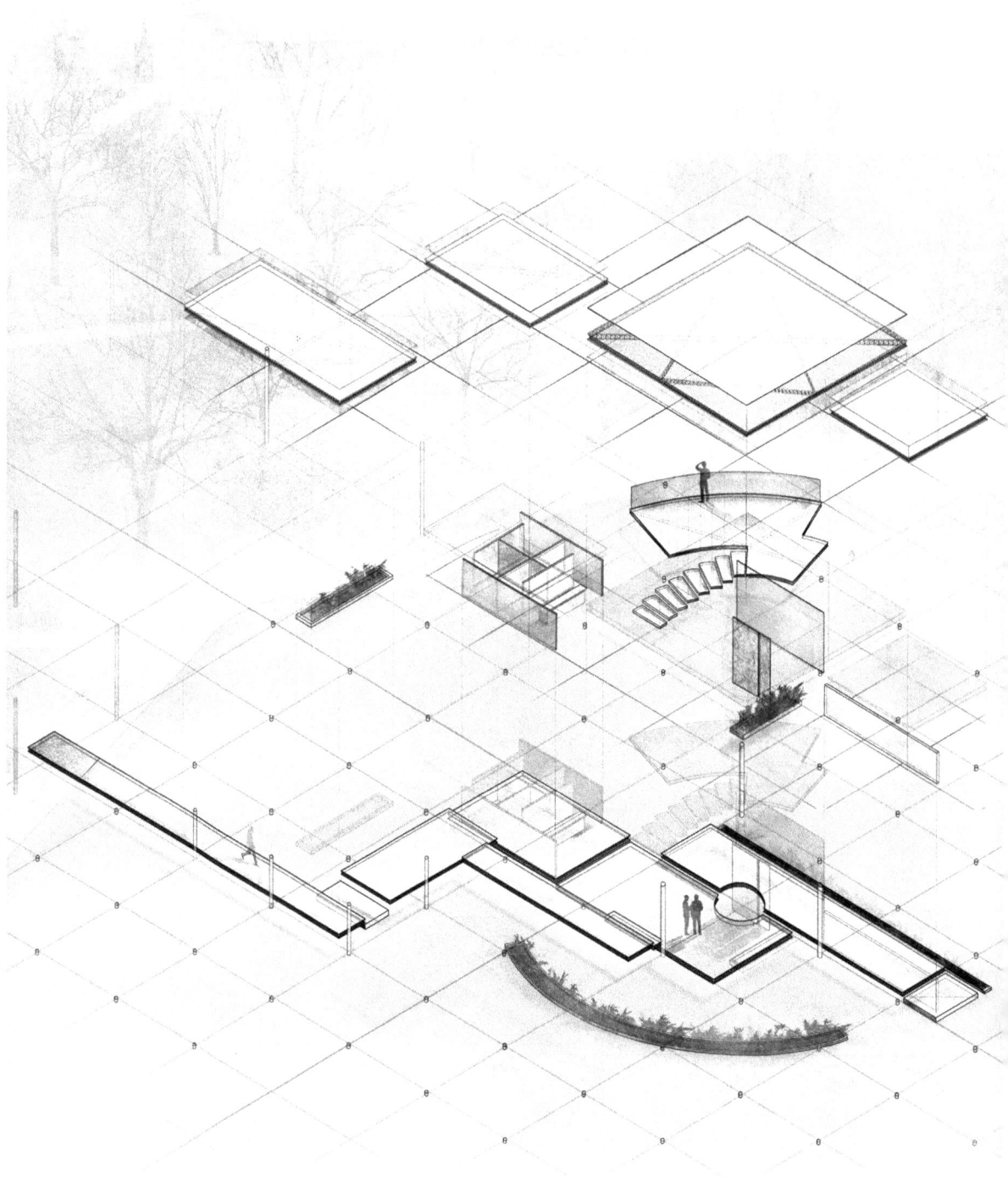

Echoing of the Grid
Exploded isometric drawing depicting the vertical echoing of the grid. As the grid descends, the Garden Pavilion breaks away from the rigid order imposed onto the site and begins to inhabit the in-between spaces.

TOP LEVEL - Roof
The design of the roof closely follows the
rectilinear grid imposed onto the site

MID LEVEL - Walls
The design of the walls is set off slightly from
the rectilinear grid

LOW LEVEL - Pathways
The design of the pathways flows freely between
the rectilinear grid

WATER LEVEL
The design breaks away from the grid through
the introduction of a circular form

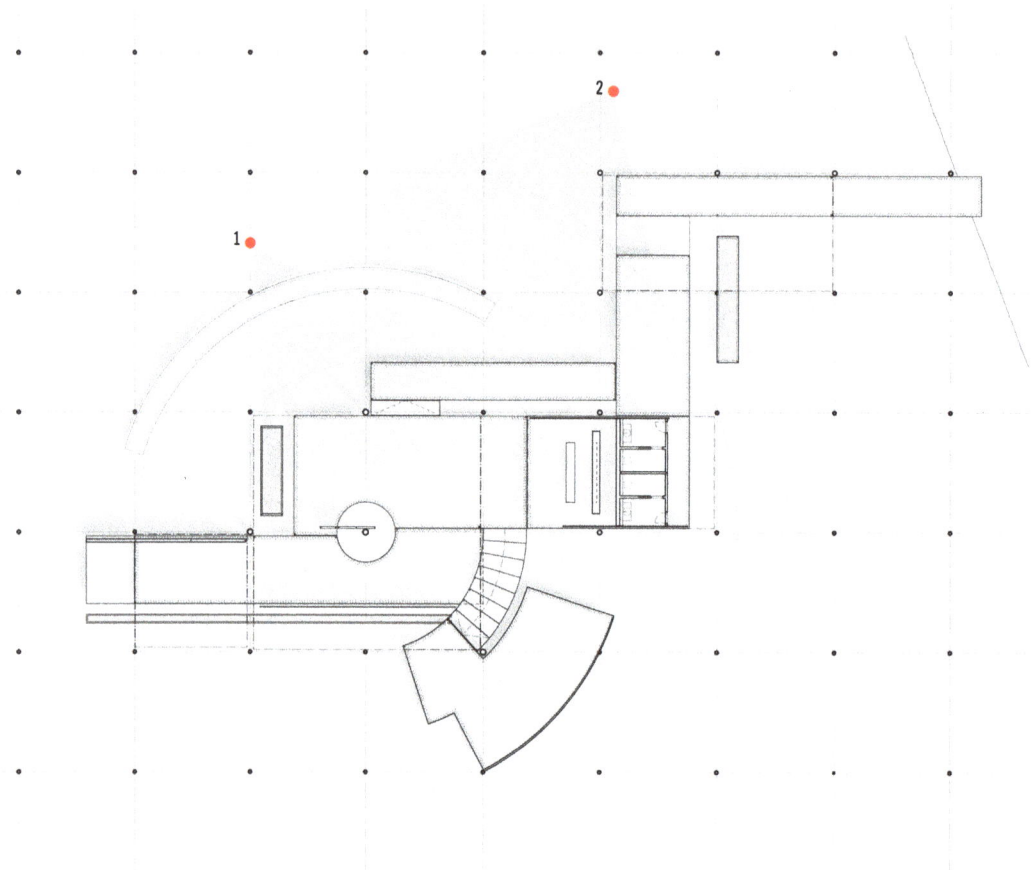

(this page)
Plan of the Garden Pavilion

(right, top)
Champagne reception (view 1)
Concept image describing the central space of the Pavilion, floating above the water. The image also depicts the idea of the structure echoing vertically as it descends down into the water.

(right, bottom)
Entrance (view 2)
Concept image describing the means of entering the Pavilion via the public entrance. The pathways inhabit the spaces between the grid, similar to the manner in which the footpaths occupy the ground between the trees in Kensington Gardens.

THEATRE OF TRANSPARENCIES

IGA MARTYNOW

In contrast to the Garden of Echoes project which was centered on issues concerning structural clarity, this project explored ideas of structural complexity. The previous body of research was extended to include the concepts of transparency, flexibility and modularity.

The program combines a self-help centre with a community theatre. This juxtaposition allows for the use of the creative arts as means of rehabilitation, and to help integrate people in recovery back into community life.

The site is located at the corner of two streets and is accessible and visible from both sides. There are no theatres or community centres within the immediate context. The building is raised to simultaneously encourage public access, and emphasise the idea of the site as a stage and the city as the audience.

The main architectural strategy played on the typology of the theatre which revolved around the traditional and linear relationship between the audience, stage and backstage. This relationship is extended to the surrounding site, where the city functions as the audience and the building assumes the role of a stage. The idea of flexibility is further manifested within the theatre space and designed to accommodate multiple arrangements in response to different stage configurations. The results reference modern theatre and exploit key features of the design concerning ideas of flexibility and modularity.

These ideas are integrated within the key concept of 'transparency'. Key readings include Colin Rowe and Robert Slutzky's *Transparency; Literal and Phenomenal* (1997)[1] and Anthony Vidler's discussions in *The Architectural Uncanny: Essays on the Modern Unhomely* (1992).[2] Hence the design explores ideas of structural, material, phenomenal and programmatic transparencies. These architectural qualities are used in the blurring of boundaries, and the resulting spaces are simultaneously layered, overwhelming and intimate. This theatre not only provides the community with a social facility but as a work of architecture is able to generate a spectacle of transparencies, and serves as an innovative addition into the local fabric.

---

[1] Colin Rowe and Robert Slutzky, *Transparency; Literal and Phenomenal* (Basel, Berlin and Boston: Birkhauser Verlag, 1997).

[2] Vidler, Anthony, *The Architectural Uncanny: Essays on the Modern Unhomely* (Cambridge, Mass.: MIT Press, 1992).

Spectacle of Transparencies

This exploded isometric drawing identifies and highlights the various qualities of transparencies throughout the building. The properties of literal transparency are expressed by means of the short façade of the building which is designed to expose the activities within to the pedestrians. Phenomenal transparency is interpreted through the spatial arrangement of the interior volumes which enables visitors to 'sense' the other spaces within the building without actually seeing them.

The structure of the building is exposed and clearly expressed. The choices of cladding materials range from transparent in the front façade, to translucent on the side façades, to opaque for the Therapy rooms.

This drawing also depicts ideas of modularity and flexibility which are expressed throughout the project. The stage and the therapy rooms are designed using modular components, and can be reconfigured and/or rearranged as appropriate.

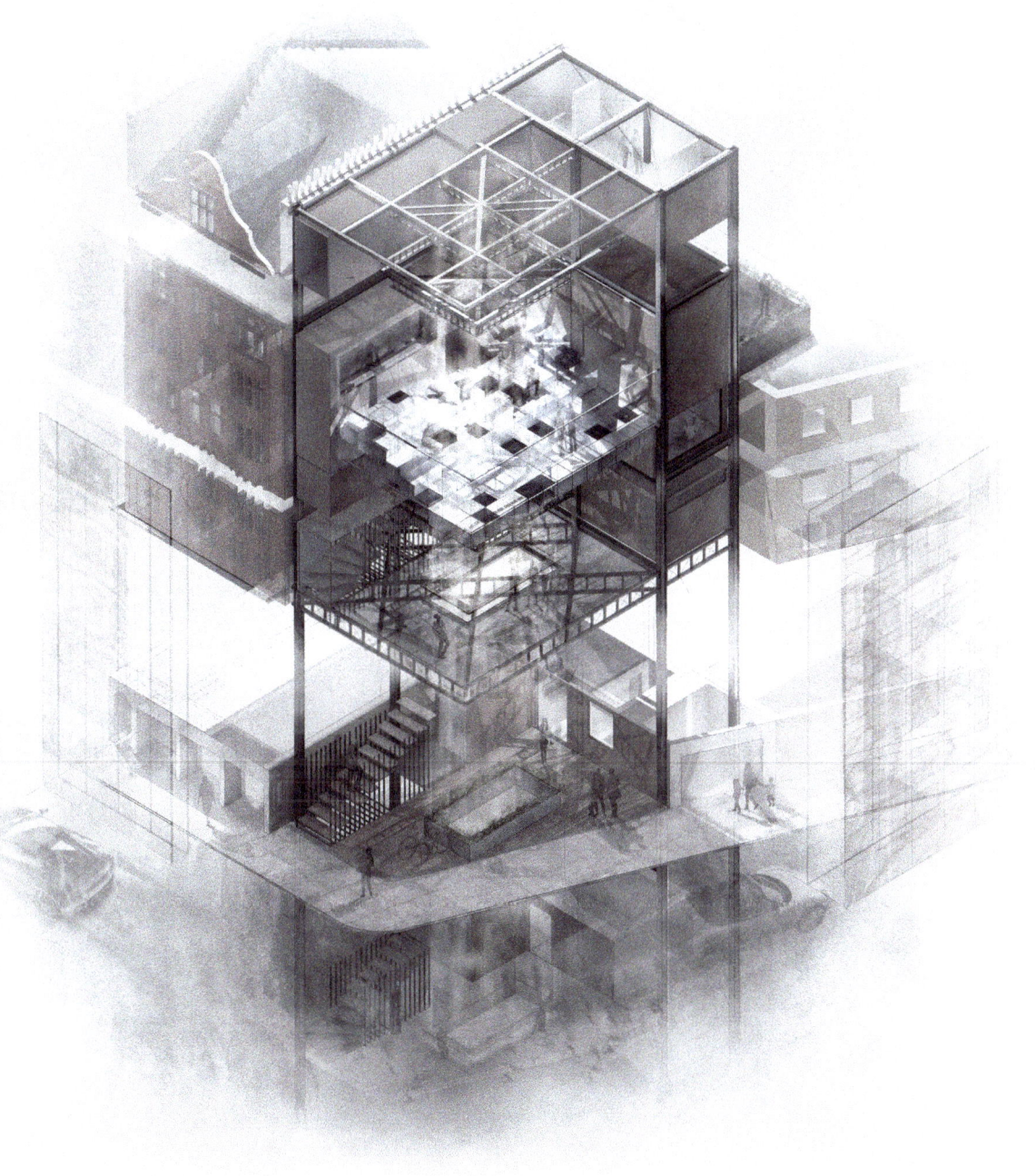

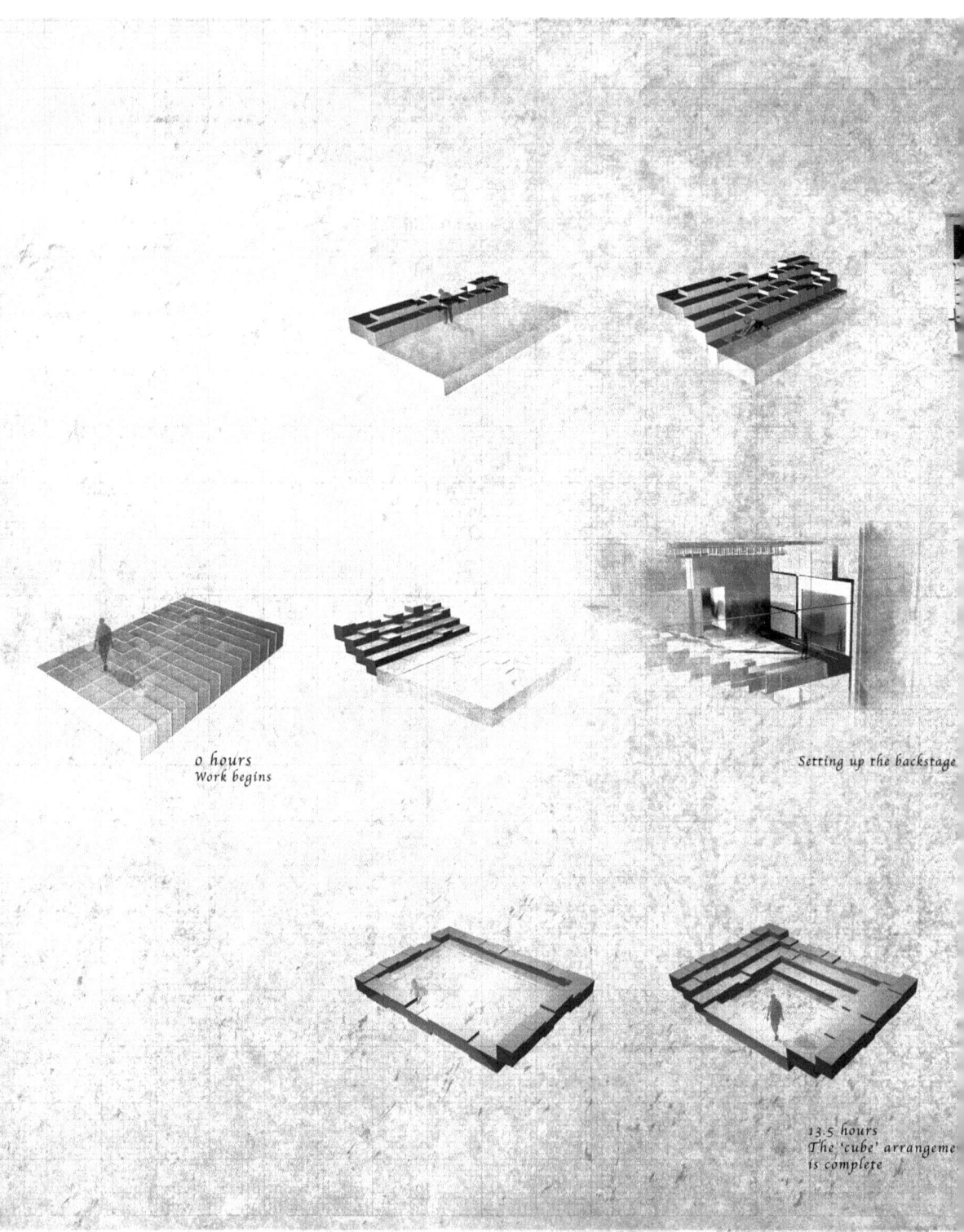

0 hours
Work begins

Setting up the backstage

13.5 hours
The 'cube' arrangement is complete

The 'deployable' stage is described by means of this timeline drawing which shows the setting-up process for the different stage configurations.

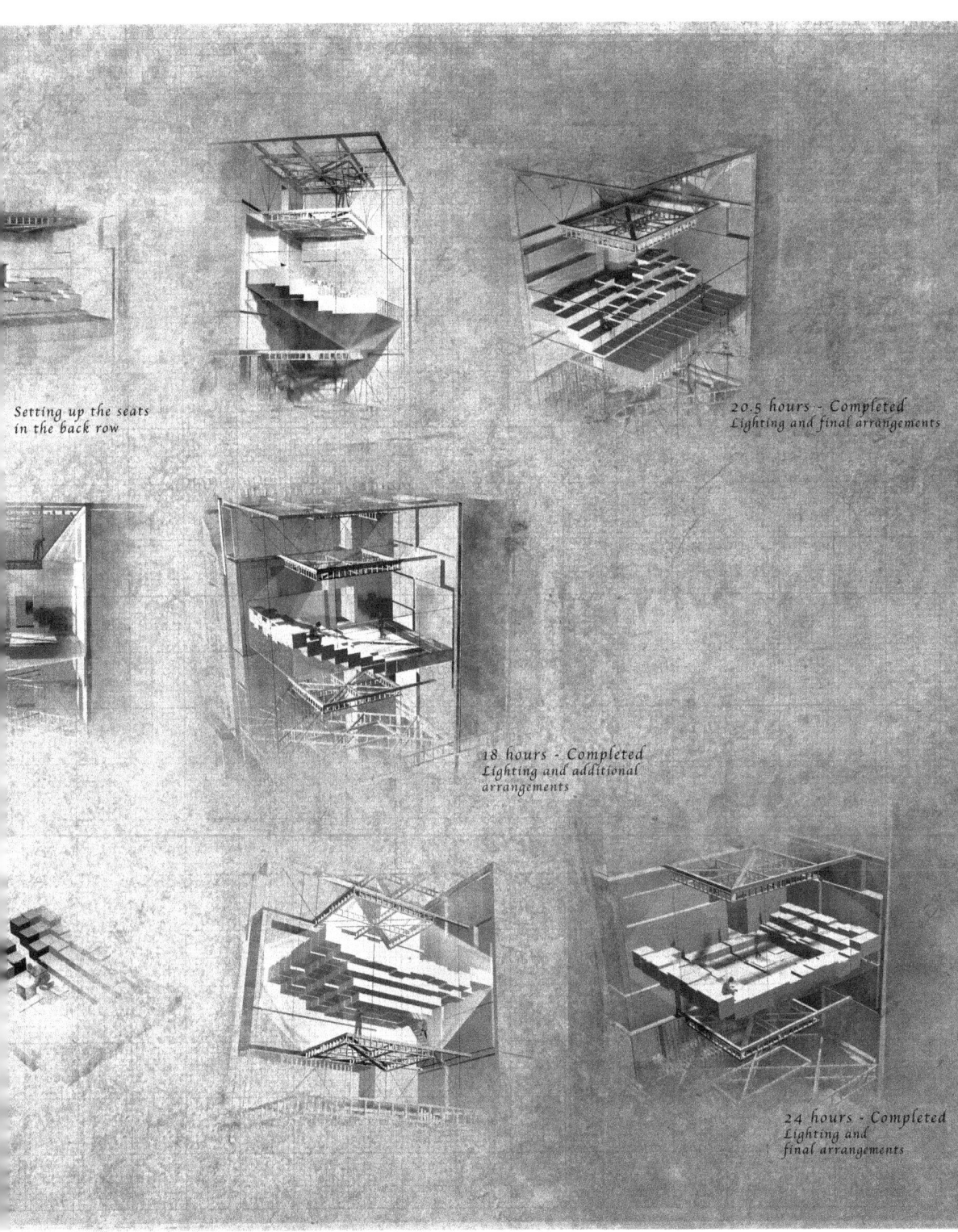

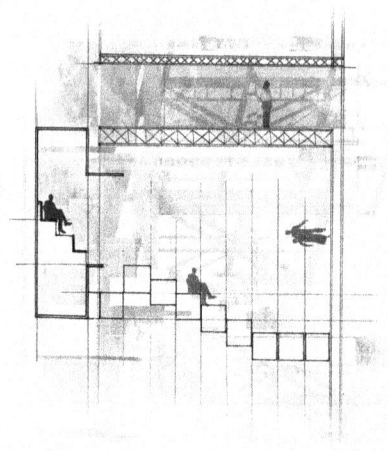

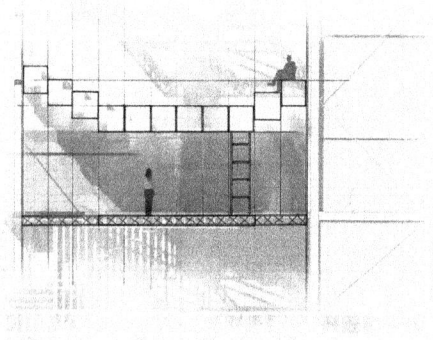

The spaces in the building adapt to accommodate the performances using three different stage configurations.
The relationship between the backstage which is highlighted in the drawing, stage and audience alter with each configuration.

The stage configurations are based on three key references. In the first (top), both the horizontal and vertical planes are utilised. In the next configuration (middle), the architecture of the stage becomes part of the performance. Finally (bottom), the performance takes place amongst the audience.

Section showing the Therapy rooms.

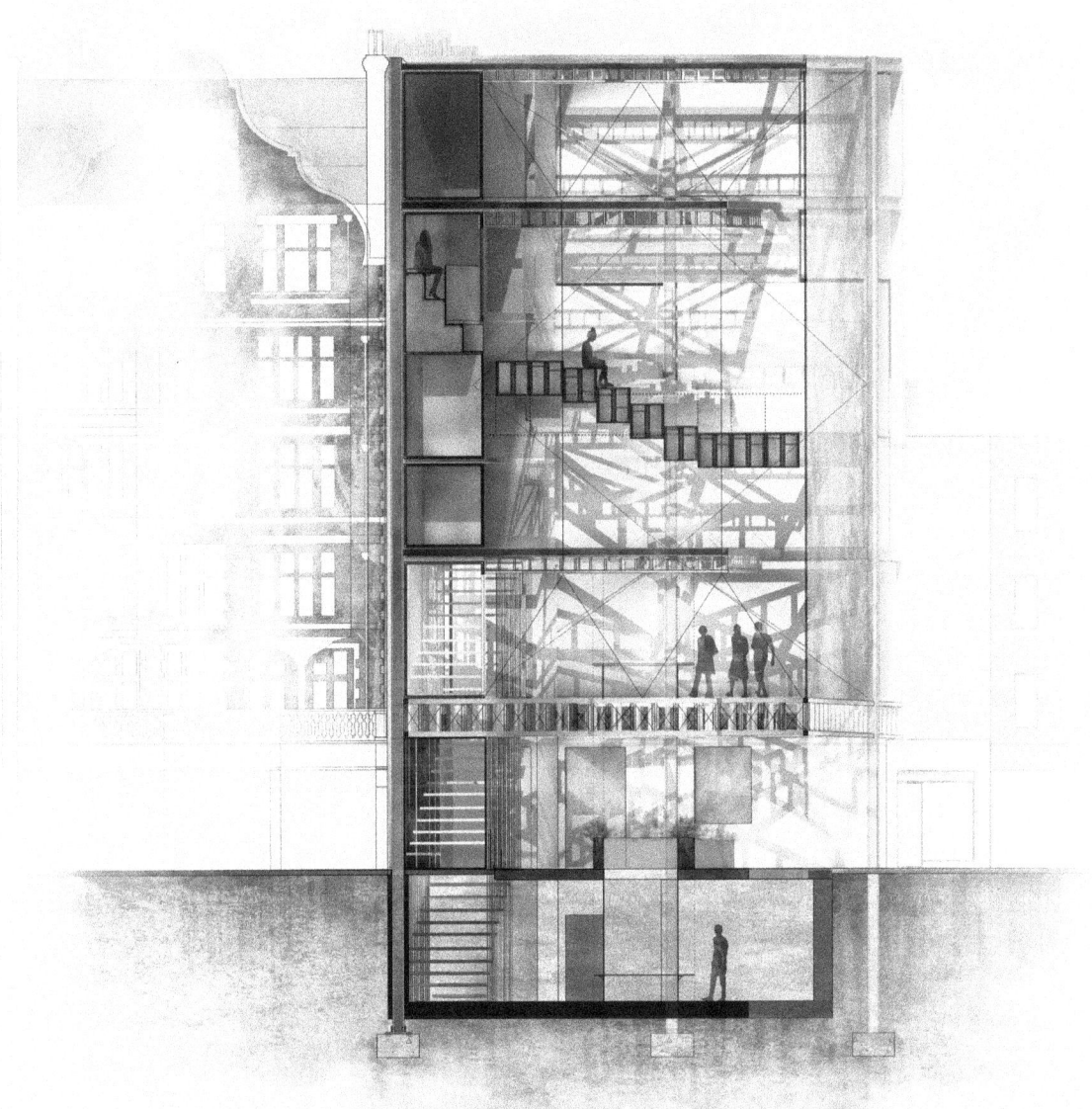

Section through the main Theatre.

City as Backdrop
This view from the audiences' perspective illustrates how the city is used as a backdrop for the ongoing performance. The boundary between the Theatre and the city becomes indistinguishable as the play of transparencies visually enables the interior to extend onto the site and vice versa.

Transition Point
View from the Therapy rooms, which dually functions as the backstage, onto the stage with the audience in sight. The location of these rooms is also read as a transition point to allude to the notion of reflecting on the journey that an individual experiences while going through recovery.

City as Audience
This view illustrates the idea of the city acting as an audience to the performances taking place within the building. The façade is shown as a membrane which wraps around the performance to create an intimate space within a space.

BIBLIOGRAPHY

'Bernard Tschumi Architects', Tschumi.com <http://www.tschumi.com/projects/3/> [accessed 25 January 2015].

Blank, Peter, 'Presidential Lectures: Peter Eisenman Home', Prelectur.stanford.edu, 1998 <http://prelectur.stanford.edu/lecturers/eisenman/> [accessed 25 January 2015].

Calvino, Italo, Invisible Cities (Italy: Giulio Einaudi Editore, 1972).

Krauss, Rosalind E., 'Grids', *October,* vol. 9, summer 1979, pp. 50–64.

Krauss, Rosalind E., *The Originality Of The Avant-Garde and Other Modernist Myths* (Cambridge, Mass.: MIT Press, 1986).

Lang, Peter and William Menking, *Superstudio* (Milano (Italy): Skira, 2003).

Mathews, J. Stanley, *From Agit-Prop To Free Space* (London: Black Dog Pub. Ltd., 2007).

Puente, Moisés, *Conversations with Mies Van Der Rohe* (New York: Princeton Architectural Press, 2008).

Rowe, Colin, *The Mathematics Of The Ideal Villa and Other Essays* (Cambridge, Mass.: MIT Press, 1982).

Rowe, Colin and Robert Slutzky, *Transparency; Literal and Phenomenal* (Basel: Berlin and Boston: Birkhauser Verlag, 1997).

Sarkis, Hashim, *Le Corbusier's Venice Hospital and the Mat Building Revival* (Munich: Prestel, 2001).

Schuiten, François and Benoît Peeters, *Les Cités Obscures: La fièvre d'Urbicande*, vol. 2 (France: Casterman, 1985).

Vidler, Anthony, *The Architectural Uncanny: Essays on the Modern Unhomely* (Cambridge, Mass.: MIT Press, 1992).

Wigley, Mark and Constant (Nieuweuhuys), *Constant's New Babylon, The Hyper-architecture of Desire* (Rotterdam: Witte de With, Centre for Contemporary Art and 010 Publishers, 1998).

Zimmerman, Claire, *Mies van der Rohe* (Germany: Taschen GmbH, 2006).

TATLIN'S WORKSHOP

KYRIAKOS ELEFTHERIADIS

Mies van der Rohe's 1929 Barcelona Pavilion was hailed as a turning point in his work. The design of this building accelerated the trajectory of his architectural language from the use of classical and neo-classical forms to 'a new architecture' which would come to be known as Modernism. The design of the Barcelona Pavilion further symbolised the new world and democratic ideals associated with the emerging Weimar Republic.

Kenneth Frampton characterised Mies' career as divergent, and a constant struggle between three factors. These were 'the technological capacity of the epoch, the aesthetics of avant-gardism, and the tectonic legacy of classical romanticism'.[1]

Vladimir Tatlin's iconic proposal for the headquarters of the Third Communist International, 1919-20, embodied similar architectural ambitions, but was attempted in a very different period.[2] The main intention of Tatlin's Tower was to flaunt the rising influence of socialism in the Soviet Union during the 1930s. The construction of the Tower struggled with design and construction issues which were also apparent in Mies' Pavilion, and especially his unrealised proposal for a glass skyscraper in Friedrichstrasse, Germany.[3]

Since 2000, the Serpentine Pavilion program in London commissions different renowned architects to contribute a work of architecture annually. These temporary structures are located in close proximity to the existing Serpentine Gallery in Kensington Gardens and serve as expressions of the architects' interests regarding specific issues in architecture. The built works further reflect the architects' aesthetic and technological concerns.

The design of Tatlin's Workshop adopts a similar approach and the proposed Pavilion is a workshop for material and construction testing. The form of this Pavilion is explored through the aesthetics of the Russian Avant-Garde and specifically El Lissitzky's *Prouns*.[4] The project encapsulates the essence of Mies' architecture through demonstrating the limitations of building technology at present, and the design's association with classical forms. More importantly, Tatlin's Workshop highlights questions of buildability in relation to technological advancements, and the functionality of the form in relation to programme. These issues were similarly raised in discussions concerning Tatlin's Tower and Mies' glass skyscraper, both of which were never constructed.

[1] Kenneth Frampton, *Studies in Tectonic Culture: The Poetics of Construction in Nineteenth and Twentieth Century Architecture* (Cambridge, Mass.: MIT Press, 1995), p. 283.

[2] The Communist International, also referred to as Comintern, was an international organisation of communist parties with a similar vision of world communism. It was founded after the dissolution of the Second Communist International in 1916. The Comintern was officially dissolved in 1943. The Tower is also known as the project for the Monument to the Third International.

[3] The design was conceived by Mies in 1921 as a competition entry for Berlin's first skyscraper. The proposal demonstrated Mies' idea of non-load bearing exterior walls.

[4] *Prouns* were a series of geometrical abstract paintings first created by El Lissitzky in 1919. The exact meaning of the word was never clarified but the work would lay the ground for further experiments in architecture and exhibition design.

(right) Tatlin's Workshop is presented as a manifesto in which the building poses as a beacon. This 'formal' manifesto simultaneously combines the ambitions of Vladimir Tatlin and Mies van der Rohe.

EL LISSITZKY'S *PROUN* AND THE BIRTH OF ARCHITECTURAL FORM

El Lissitzky (1890-1941) was an artist, designer, photographer, typographer, polemicist and architect. He was an important member of the Russian Avant-Garde, and helped develop the art movement Suprematism with his mentor, Kazimir Malevich. He also designed numerous exhibition displays and propaganda works for the Soviet Union. Lissitzky communicated to the west his personal ideas and concepts of art, as well as those of his colleagues working in Russia after the 1917 October Revolution. These included Wassily Kandinsky, Alexej von Jawlensky, Mikhail Larionov, Kazimir Malevich and Vladimir Tatlin.

Lissitzky grew up in Vitebsk, a small Jewish town in Belorussia, where he took art lessons in 1903 from the Russian painter Iurii (Yehuda) Moiseevich Pen who was also Marc Chagall's teacher. In 1909, after being turned down by the St. Petersburg Academy of Art, Lissitzky left Russia for the first time to study architectural engineering at the Technische Hochschule in Darmstadt, Germany. In 1912, he travelled to Germany, France and Italy during his studies but was forced to return to Russia during the summer of 1914 after the outbreak of World War I. He enrolled as a student of engineering and architecture at the Riga Polytechnical Institute (Rizhskii Politekhnicheskii Institut) which was temporarily quartered in Moscow, and graduated on 3 June 1918 with the qualification of engineer-architect. He worked in various architectural offices in Moscow and St. Petersburg during the years 1915–16.[1]

In 1919 Lissitzky was invited by Marc Chagall to join the Vitebsk Art Labor Cooperative as a professor of architecture and graphics art. The arrival of Malevich and subsequent collaborations were to have a profound influence on Lissitzky. Later that year, he created his first *Proun*.

Prouns were described by Lissitzky as an 'interchange station between painting and architecture'.[2] There are suggestions that the word '*Proun*' was an acronym based on the Russian words '*proekt utverzhdeniaa novogo*' or 'project for the affirmation of the new'.[3] Executed as designs for spatial constructions, *Prouns* consist of geometrical forms which appear to exist and float in a cosmic space. The *Proun* is further defined as a moment between conceptualisation and physical realisation during the process of architectural representation. The key function is to introduce into the painterly space the role of the form generator. The construction of a *Proun* 'begins on the flat plane, passes through three-dimensionally constructed models and continues to the construction of all objects of our everyday life'.[4]

Hence Lissitzky went beyond his mentor's definition of a typographic space with the addition of a fourth dimension. This is the element of time which is characterised by movement. This new type of cosmic space created by *Prouns* symbolised the post-Russian Revolution utopia he had envisioned. The vulnerability of Suprematism was in part due to 'the absence of material and structural interests' inherent in its theoretical background. This was needed to address the immediate problems of the revolutionary society, most of which required practical solutions.[5] Lissitzky's new, and more materialistic view of the design process was represented by the newly founded revolutionary educational institutions which attempted to connect theory with serious scientific analysis. 'This materialist view of creativity merged with scientific and technological developments gave birth to the new concept of artist-constructor or artist-engineer'.[6] This was the new role for an artist in the new world, as envisioned by Lissitzky.

Lissitzky's explored his new spatial concepts through a series of architectural proposals. His Wolkenbügel Skyscraper, 1924, Moscow, is often discussed alongside the works of Tatlin, another key member of the Russian Avant-Garde. Many of the *Prouns* that Lissitzky produced can be read as relief constructions, which was a mode that Tatlin had developed.[7] However, most of the information regarding Tatlin's constructions are simply based on photographs and catalogues of the time.

Lissitzky was adamant that only 'universal' forms should be used in this new manner of spatial constructions. Hence geometrical forms were reduced to their essential elements and the sphere was characterised as 'the crystallisation of the Universe'.[8] These basic geometrical forms were significant for the Russian Avant-Garde artists and appeared as the square and triangle in Malevich and Tatlin's works respectively. The *Proun* was a new system of form exploration where spatial qualities were articulated through material and structure. These properties are also relevant to architecture. Hence by transforming the square into a cube, Lissitzky symbolically bridged Malevich's Suprematist concepts concerning immateriality and Tatlin's Constructivist theories.

[1] Nancy Lynn Perloff and Brian Reed, *Situating El Lissitzky: Vitebsk, Berlin, Moscow* (Los Angeles: Getty Publications, 2003), p. 6.
[2] Sophie Lissitzky-Kuppers, *El Lissitzky: Life, Letters, Texts* (London: Thames and Hudson, 1992), p. 325. First published in 1968.
[3] Lynn Gumpert, 'El Lissitzky's Proun I. Kestnermappe' <http://monoskop.org/images/c/cf/Gumpert_Lynn_1979_El_Lissitzkys_Proun_I_Kestnermappe.pdf> [accessed 09 May 2016].
[4] Puts Henk, ed., *El Lissitzky, 1890 – 1941: architect, painter, photographer, typographer* (London and Eindhoven: Municipal Van Abbemuseum, 1990), p. 17.
[5] Christina Lodder, *Russian Constructivism* (London and New Haven: Yale University Press, 1983), p. 20.
[6] Lodder, pp. 106–10.
[7] El Lissitzky, 'New Russian Art; A Lecture' in *El Lissitzky: Life, Letters, Texts*, pp. 333. Tatlin's corner constructions are generally acknowledged as an important innovation which challenged the notion of painting and its depicted content. Lissitzky in his lecture on 'New Russian Art' specifically commented on these counter-reliefs.
[8] Lissitzky-Kuppers, p. 345.

The architectural and landscape elements in Kensington Gardens are explored in relation to Lissitzky's *Proun* concept. This drawing represents an abstract reading of the site and further references the manner in which Mies' collages are presented.

This drawing shows the careful selection of specific elements in Kensington Gardens
in relation to the site for the proposed Tatlin's Workshop. The formal relationships
between these elements are expressed through readings of Lissitzky's *Proun* concept,
and Mies' collages.

(this page) This drawing, titled 'The Technological Capacity of the Epoch' is an expression of specific materials and technical details which were used in the design and construction of the Barcelona Pavilion.

(right) Similar to the site drawing, the final form of the design proposal is explored through ideas and processes of form generation that Lissitzky introduced with his *Proun* studies, and Mies explored in his projects through his collages. The investigation starts in a typographic space where the Sackler Gallery and Carriage Drive are first translated into pure geometrical forms. The dimension of time and the associated concept of movement is introduced through the linearity of the road. The triangular boundary of the site is also an important site consideration.

The triangle is a significant form in Tatlin's theories and the circle further references the spherical forms associated with Lissitzky. The glass box pays homage to Mies. Similar to readings of Tatlin's Tower from which key concepts are derived, this design proposal explores the notion of form as an independent entity. Textures and the qualities of transparency are employed to bring an aspect of materiality to this form in the final step. This design process explores the hypothesis that Tatlin's Workshop exists in a space between painting, sculpture and architecture.

The project is composed of three basic elements which are designed to make two architectural spaces consisting of the workshop and design studio. The underground workshop houses machinery for the testing of new materials and creation of new forms, and the design process takes place within the suspended volume.

The three basic elements reference key projects and design precedents. These include the glass crane which supports the whole structure and contains a lift like Tatlin's Tower. The suspended travertine block with the stairwell references the innovative qualities of the free hanging onyx wall in Mies' Pavilion. Finally, the Miesian glass box which serves as the design studio encapsulates Mies' ambitions as apparent in the Barcelona Pavilion. The composition of these elements and the final form of Tatlin's Workshop raises questions of technical possibilities, form and function in architecture. Consequently, the project highlights the reoccurring question in design practice concerning the hierarchy of 'form before function or function before form'.

THE VYGOTSKY CENTRE OF EVOLUTIONARY ANTHROPOLOGY

KYRIAKOS ELEFTHERIADIS

Lev Semenovich Vygotsky was educated as a lawyer and philologist, and had contributed to literary criticism before he began his career as a psychologist following the Russian Revolution in 1917.[1]

Moscow during the 1910s was a place of experimentation and innovation where unorthodox trends in the arts, science and humanities emerged. Between 1913-17, Vygotsky was simultaneously enrolled at Moscow University to study law and Shaniavsky University for history and philosophy. He pursued all these 'ideas from seemingly disparate fields' and was especially interested in theatre. He admired Stanislavsky's Art Theatre, and later used Stanislavsky's notes for actors in his 1934 book *Thought and Language* (*Myshlenie i rech*).[2]

Vygotsky's multi-faceted interests were evident in his ability to integrate commentary on Shakespearean plays, philosophical readings, and clinical studies of the mentally retarded. He was also 'a man of practice who founded and directed a number of research laboratories, including the first Russian Institute for the Study of Handicapped Children'.[3]

The proposal for the Vygotsky Centre can be read as a continuation of the design language adopted for Tatlin's Workshop. The form of the Centre is explored through the location of the *Proun* as a middle point between painting and architecture. Similarly, the *Proun* is used to explore the relationship between the architectural forms in a typographic space. These forms which are derived from precise site studies are informed by the programme of the building, and the function of each space at each stage of the design process.

This project further references Ivan Leonidov's Lenin Institute, 1927, which was to be located in Moscow, Russia. The choice of Moscow which epitomised the 'new world' was important to Leonidov as this proposal symbolised the 'center of knowledge'.[4] The two projects share formal architectural readings like the exaggeration of scale, the use of glass volumes and the role of the sphere as the dominant form. The utopian aspects of the project highlight once again, the struggle with the technological capacity of its time.[5] Similarly, the geometrical language and exploitation of building materials beyond their structural capabilities are key issues which the Vygotsky Centre adopts, and attempts to answer architecturally in the twenty-first century.

---

[1] Lev Semenovich Vygotsky, *Mind in Society, The Development of Higher Psychological Processes*, ed. by Michael Cole, Vera John-Steiner, Sylvia Scribner and Ellen Souberman (Cambridge Mass. and London: Harvard University Press, 1979), p. 1. The spelling of 'Semyonovich' appears in some sources.

[2] Lev Semenovich Vygotsky, *Thought and Language*, trans. and ed. by Alex Kozulin (Cambridge Mass. and London: The MIT Press, 1986). First published in English in 1962. p. xiii. Shaniavsky University was for a short while, the center of academic liberalism and innovation.

[3] Vygotsky, *Thought and Language*, p. xi.

[4] This was Leonidov's 1927 diploma project. The aim was to address the needs of contemporary life through maximising the possibilities of technology. The Lenin Hills area where the city of Moscow was expanding towards, and was new at the time, was chosen as the project site. The project consists of a library, five reading rooms and an auditorium with a varying capacity.

[5] The approach regarding the application of formal references are also apparent in the proposals of early utopian architects in post-revolution France like Claude-Nicolas Ledoux and Étienne Louis Boullée.

The four subjects of the anthropology

In his first piece of writing, *The Psychology of Art* (1925) Vygotsky argued that 'psychology cannot limit itself to direct evidence, be it observable behaviour or accounts of introspection'. The process of psychological inquiry is an investigative process, and hence the psychologist, like the criminal investigator, must take into account 'indirect evidence and circumstantial clues – which in practice means that works of art, philosophical arguments, and anthropological data are no less important for psychology than direct evidence'. Hence issues of culture and consciousness 'constituted the actual subject of inquiry', while psychology 'remained a conceptual tool' as opposed to the process of psychological inquiry being 'a goal in itself'.[1] These concepts are reflected in the study of constructivism which argues that knowledge is an artefact of social interactions between individuals, their environment and tools such as language.

Basically, social constructivism follows ideas from cultural psychology where groups construct knowledge with one another. The approach was also raised in 1934 by George Herbert Mead who approached the study of human experience from the view that communication is essential to social order as opposed to just the individual.[2] The work of Vygotsky places emphasis on social interaction to enable learning. He strongly believed that community plays a central role during the process of teaching an individual person how to learn, and favoured the concept of learning as a construct which is mediated by language via social discourse. He further emphasised that culture plays an important role in the cognitive development of a person.

The study of human in addition to just natural and/or biological functions was important to Vygotsky and hence 'psychology was a method of uncovering the origins of higher forms of human consciousness and emotional life rather than of elementary behavioural acts'. This remains a 'trademark of Vygotsky's lifework'.[3]

Vygotsky's knowledge and varied interest across the humanities and sciences was used to expand upon his experiments and studies concerning the zone of proximal development. This started with his revelation that the work produced by the different schools of psychology in the 1920s which included behaviorism, reflexology and psychoanalysis to name a few, not only differed in theoretical and/or methodological grounds, but even their facts were incompatible. Hence he concluded that 'the divisions among the systems of psychology were so serious and their basic theoretical premises so liable to various interpretations' that they should be considered as 'different sciences' as opposed to 'a number of schools within one science'.[4] More importantly, 'some of these systems of psychology were so closely connected with philosophy and the humanities' that Vygotsky found no reason to limit the study of psychology to within the 'conceptual framework of science'.[5]

Vygotsky's key interests in the development of language in relation to thought are reflected in his work *Thought and Language*. This book is put forth in the form of a 'critical dialogue in which the survey of conflicting approaches is interspersed with experimental data and theoretical constructions'.[6] This further complicates the reading of Vygotsky's work as in addition to a large collection of writing, there are gaps in the original manuscripts. Much of his work was never properly edited and due to illness, he often dictated his papers, 'a practice which resulted in repetitions and dense or elliptical prose'.[7] Given the exceedingly numerous and varied implications of his theory and limited time due to failing health, Vygotsky's focus was on 'opening up new lines of investigation rather than pursuing any particular line to the fullest'. Hence most of his studies were pilot investigations conducted by his students and not prepared for publication.[8]

To Vygotsky, 'anthropological and sociological studies were partners with observation and experiment in the grand enterprise of accounting for the progress of human consciousness and intellect'. Significantly, his theoretical approach and method of experimentation served to break down some of the barriers that were traditionally erected between 'laboratory' and 'field'.[9] It is with this view of Vygotsky's experimental spirit that the term 'evolutionary anthropology' seems highly appropriate for the design proposal.

Many thanks to A/P Tan Aik Ling, associate professor of science education and the assistant dean for Professional Development at the National Institute of Education, Nanyang Technological University in Singapore. Her research interests focuses on science teaching and learning in science classrooms, with a particular focus on science as inquiry.

[1] Vygotsky, *Thought and Language*, trans. and ed. by Alex Kozulin (Cambridge Mass. and London: The MIT Press, 1986), p. xv–xvi. First published in English in 1962.
[2] George Cronk, 'George Herbert Mead (1863 – 1931)' <http://www.iep.utm.edu/mead/> [accessed 31 May 2016]. Mead died in 1931, his book *Mind, Self, and Society*, ed. by Charles W. Morris (Chicago: University of Chicago Press, 1934) was published after his death.
[3] Vygotsky, *Thought and Language*, p. xv.
[4] Vygotsky, *Thought and Language*, p. xviii.
[5] Vygotsky, *Thought and Language*, p. xix.
[6] Vygotsky, *Thought and Language*, p. xxx. The participants in this imaginary dialogue have been noted as William Stern, Karl Bühler, Wolfgang Köhler, Robert Yerkes and Jean Piaget.
[7] Vygotsky, *Mind in Society, The Development of Higher Psychological Processes*, ed. by Michael Cole, Vera John-Steiner, Sylvia Scribner and Ellen Souberman (Cambridge Mass. and London: Harvard University Press, 1979), p. x.
[8] Vygotsky, *Mind in Society*, p. 11.
[9] Vygotsky, *Mind in Society*, p. 14.

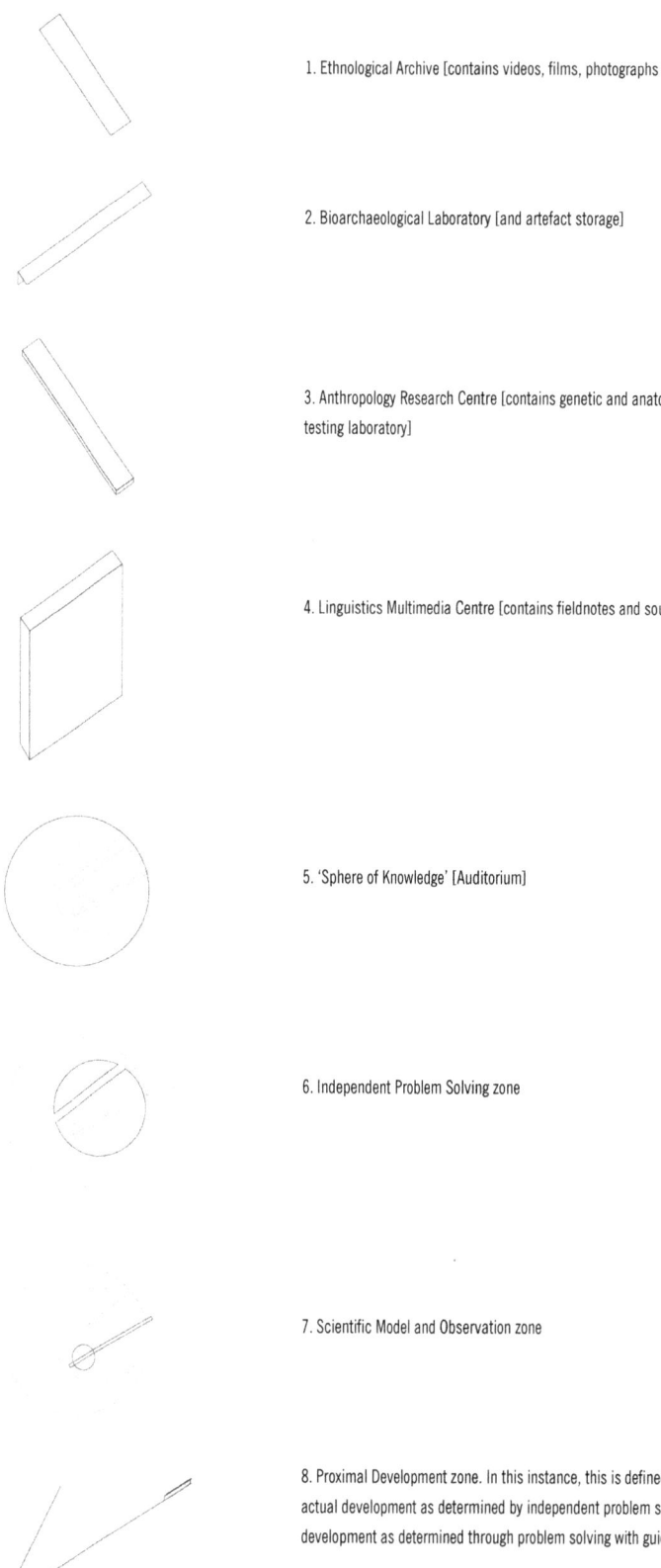

1. Ethnological Archive [contains videos, films, photographs and fieldnotes]

2. Bioarchaeological Laboratory [and artefact storage]

3. Anthropology Research Centre [contains genetic and anatomical material as well as a testing laboratory]

4. Linguistics Multimedia Centre [contains fieldnotes and sound recording manuscripts]

5. 'Sphere of Knowledge' [Auditorium]

6. Independent Problem Solving zone

7. Scientific Model and Observation zone

8. Proximal Development zone. In this instance, this is defined as the distance between actual development as determined by independent problem solving, and the level of potential development as determined through problem solving with guidance.

The ambition for the design proposal revolves around ideas for 'a centre of knowledge in the new world'. The project site for the Vygotsky Centre is located in an existing carpark between the Dana Centre and Science Museum in South Kensington, London. The chosen site is directly connected to five existing buildings, all of which inform the development of the design concept. The Science Museum and Natural History Museum located to the east of the site will assume the role of the 'knowledge archive'. The Darwin Centre will be the 'sample archive'. The material from both these archives are required to support the research activities in the Vygotsky Centre. The Dana Centre was created as a public venue for contemporary science debate and this facility is a crucial aspect of the programme, given that the subject of evolutionary anthropology still evokes arguments. Hence this activity will take place in the central auditorium of the building. Finally, Imperial College embodies the notion of ground breaking research and the discovery of new knowledge. These are traits that this new Centre will attempt to emulate. All these roles will be defined and the facilities connected by means of the new Vygotsky Centre.

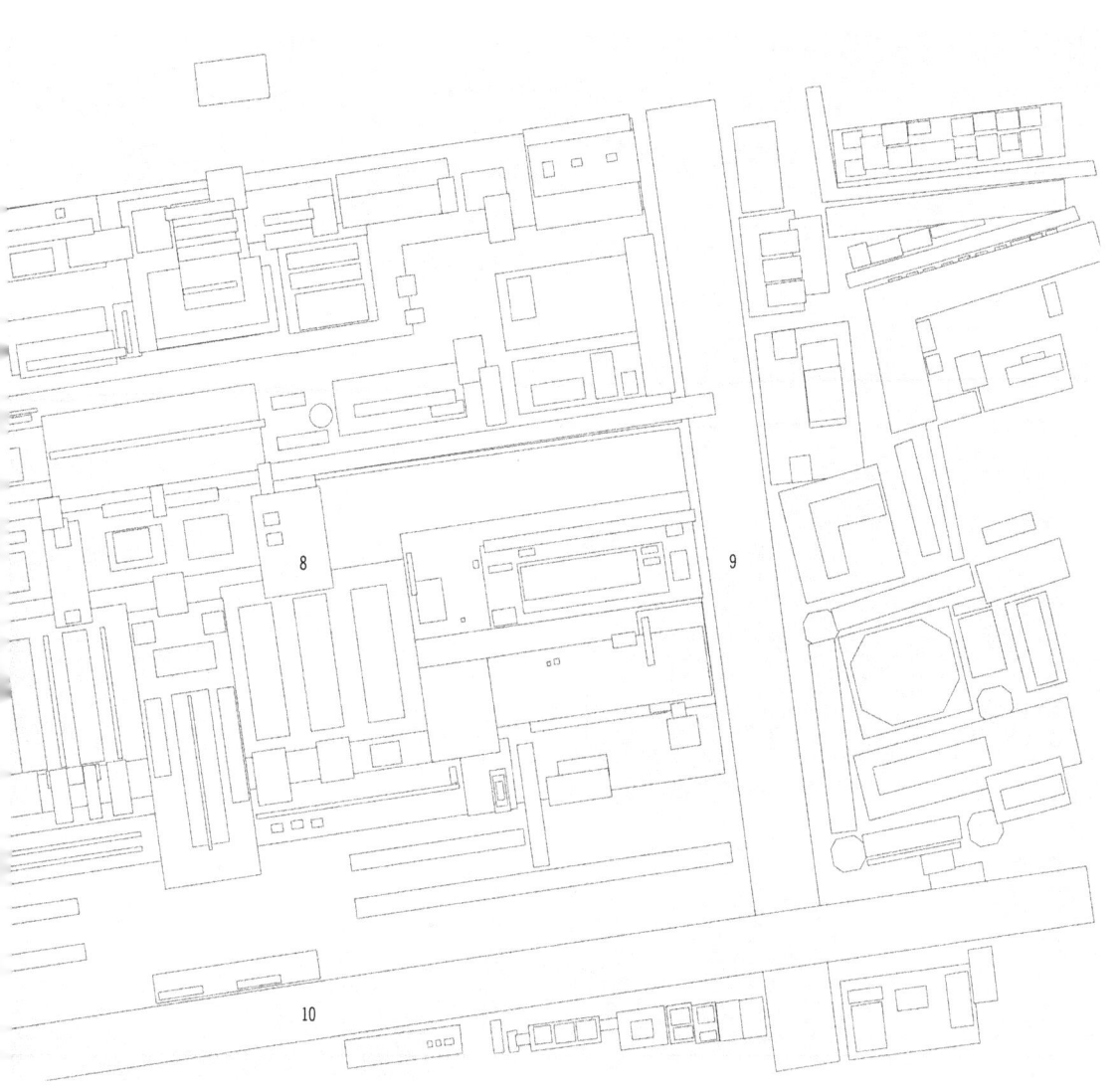

1. The Dana Center is now known as the Dana Library and Research Centre. This new facility contains the Science Museum's Library and Archive Services, and the Research and Public History Department.
2. The Darwin Center is part of the Natural History Museum and contains the Cocoon building, Attenborough Studio and Zoology Spirit building.
3. Queen's gate
4. Imperial College road
5. Imperial College
6. Science Museum
7. Museum lane
8. Natural History Museum
9. Exhibition road
10. Cromwell road

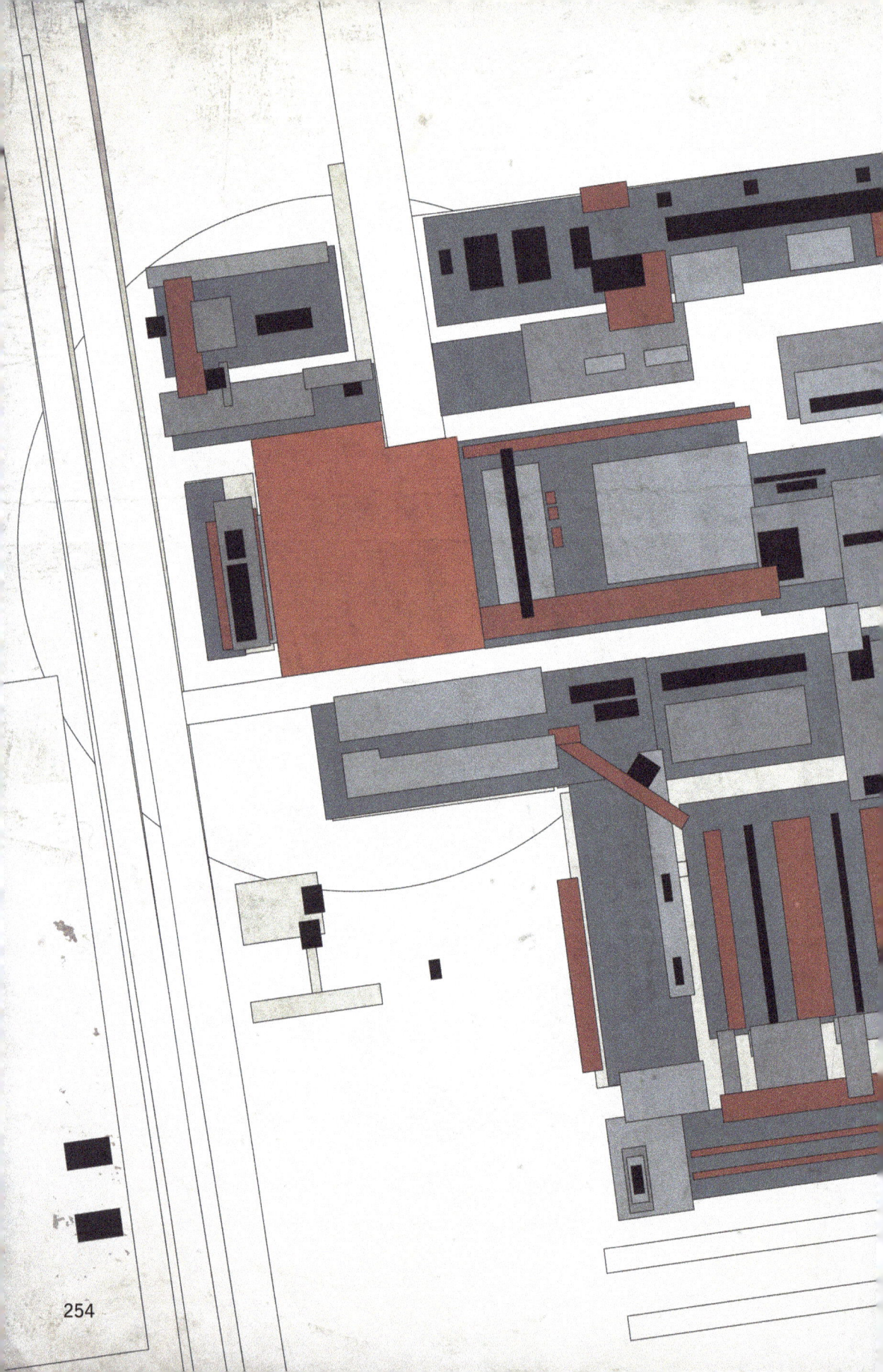

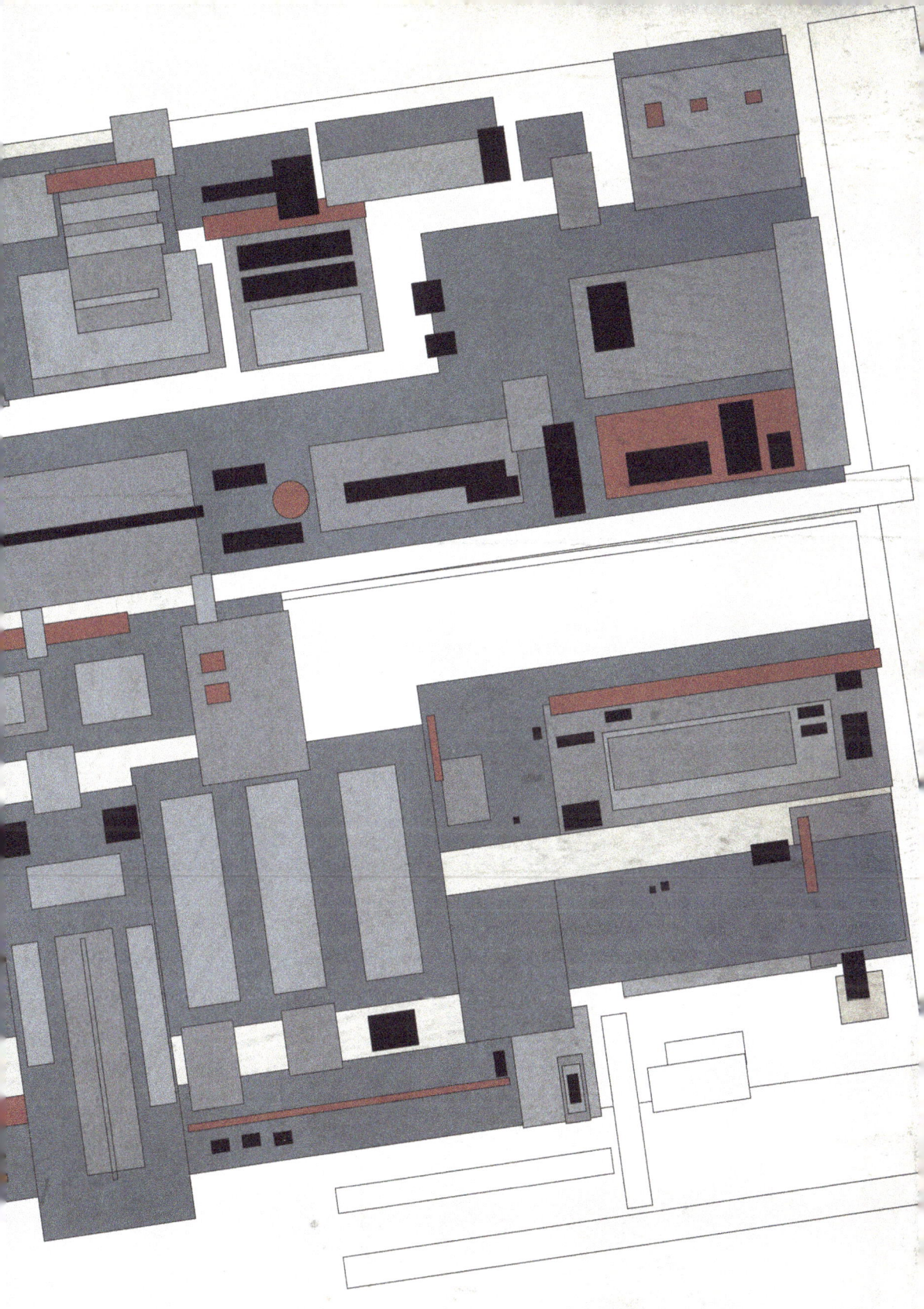

The forms of specific site elements are 'isolated' in order for their spatial relationships to be explored typographically.

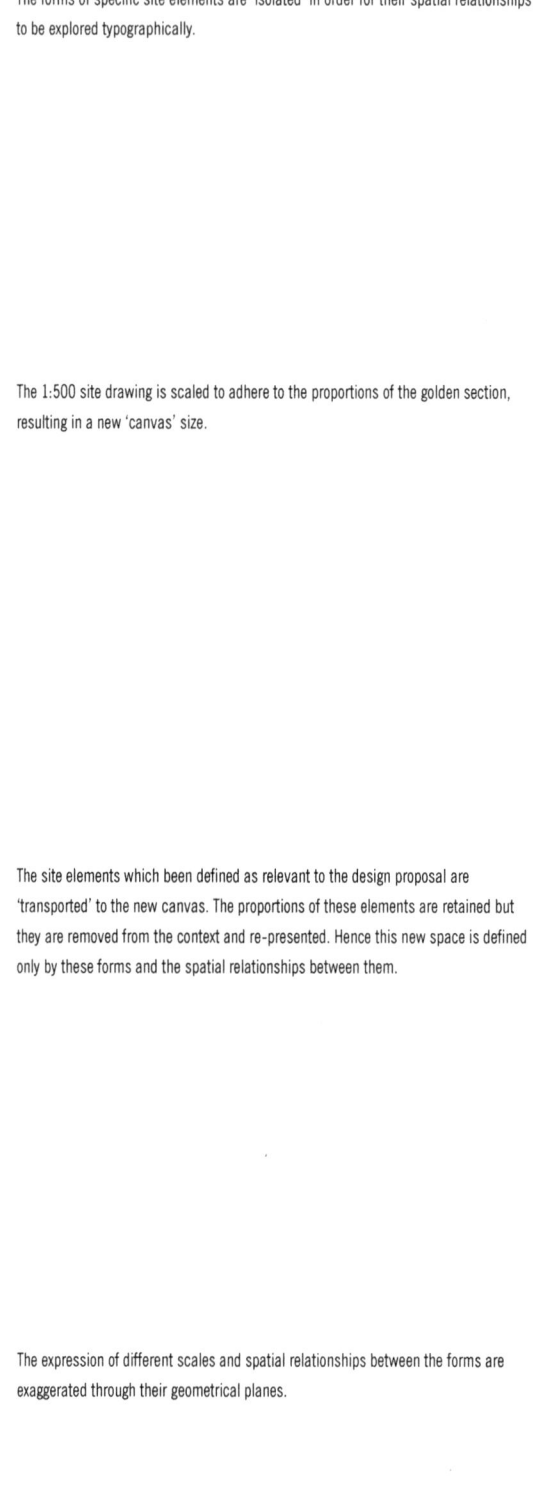

The 1:500 site drawing is scaled to adhere to the proportions of the golden section, resulting in a new 'canvas' size.

The site elements which been defined as relevant to the design proposal are 'transported' to the new canvas. The proportions of these elements are retained but they are removed from the context and re-presented. Hence this new space is defined only by these forms and the spatial relationships between them.

The expression of different scales and spatial relationships between the forms are exaggerated through their geometrical planes.

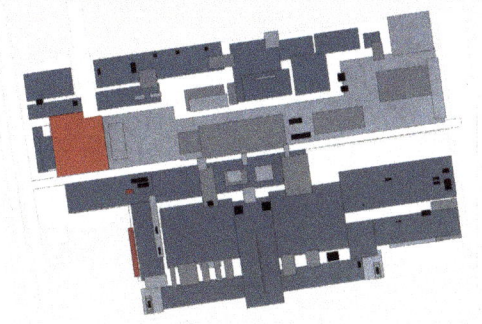
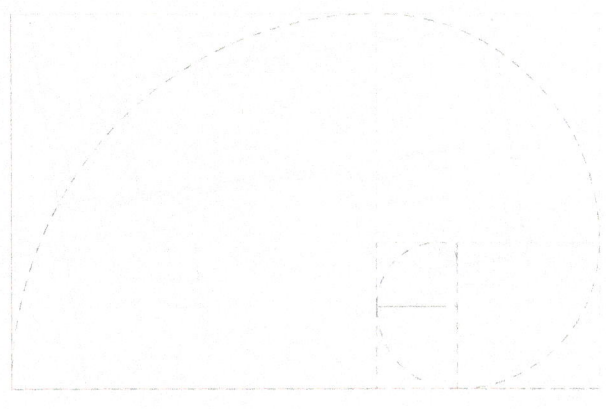
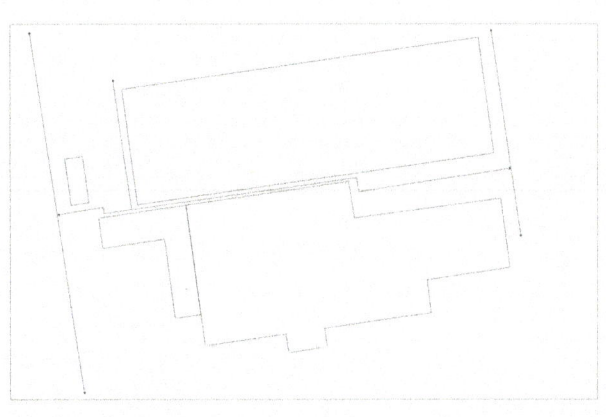
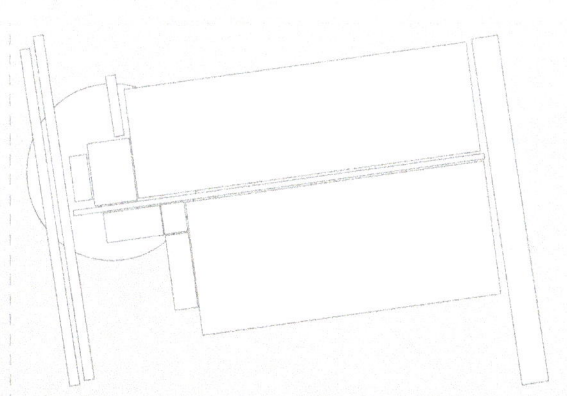

The exploration process extends to the site in the form of this (left) 'site *Proun*' drawing. This development drawing starts with the reading of the project and site as two-dimensional geometrical shapes.

This is the first moment the *Proun* concept becomes apparent in the design process and hence this drawing (above) is termed 'initial *Proun*'. The process of form generation follows the steps detailed previously, and further references a process similar to the design of Tatlin's Workshop. The generated forms are systematically transformed into habitable spaces.

In this instance, the dynamic relationships between the spaces are expressed through the surrounding buildings, the circulation routes in and out of the site, and the main spaces in the Centre. The location where all these spaces connect and cumulate becomes the core of the project and houses the auditorium. At this point, discussions of materiality and function are still non-existent.

The 'initial *Proun'* drawing is layered with programmatic values and explored through a third dimension in addition to the introduction of perspective. This process creates a new drawing, 'initial project *Proun* 1'.

The auditorium occupies a cylindrical form that is suspended at the heart of the sphere. This exceedingly intimate space is designed to bring about a unique connection between the lecturer and the audience. The timber structure of the auditorium is chosen to contrast with the industrial materials of the outer skin. The space between the two skins is inhabited by structure and circulation. The transparent quality of the spherical skin changes under different light conditions which enables the space to visually dematerialise. This effect visually alters the appearance of the spaces in the building.

The formal relations are retained in the transformation from a two-dimensional painting exploration to a spatial architectural proposal with material qualities, a distinct program and functions.

The architecture is experienced as a materialised *Proun*. The encounter with the building upon approach is dominated by the volumes overhead. These forms have been designed to 'float' in space and are defined by their proximity to each other.

As night falls, the transformation of the architecture is an event onto itself. The structure is gradually revealed as the dimming light visually dissolves the 'skin' of the building. The eventual dematerialisation of the volumes turns the auditorium into a beacon.

BIBLIOGRAPHY

Benjamin, Walter, *The Work of Art in the Age of Mechanical Reproduction*, trans. by J. A. Underwood (London: Penguin Books, 2008). First English edition of the essay was published in 1968.

Boyd, Robert and Peter Richerson, *The Origin and Evolution of Cultures* (Oxford: Oxford University Press, 2005).

Colomina, Beatriz, *Privacy and Publicity: Modern Architecture as Mass Media* (Cambridge Mass.: MIT Press, 1996).

Frampton, Kenneth, *Modern Architecture: A Critical History* (London: Thames and Hudson, 1980).

Frampton, Kenneth, *Studies in Tectonic Culture: The Poetics of Construction in Nineteenth and Twentieth Century Architecture* (Cambridge Mass.: MIT Press, 1995).

Gombrich, Ernst Hans, *The Story of Art* (London, Phaidon, 1995).

Henk, Puts, ed., *El Lissitzky. 1890-1941: Architect, Painter, Photographer, Typographer* (London and Eindhoven: Municipal Van Abbemuseum, 1990).

Lissitzky-Kuppers, Sophie, *El Lissitzky: Life, Letters, Texts* (London: Thames and Hudson, 1968).

Lodder, Christina, *Russian Constructivism* (London and New Haven: Yale University Press, 1983).

Margolin, Victor, *The Struggle for Utopia: Rodchenko, Lissitzky, Moholy-Nagy, 1917-1946* (Chicago Illinois: Chicago University Press, 1997).

Perlof, Nancy-Lynn and Brian Reed, *Situating El Lissitzky: Vitebsk, Berlin, Moscow* (Los Angeles: California, Getty Publications, 2003).

Quetglas, Josep, *Fear of Glass: Mies Van Der Rohe's Pavilion in Barcelona* (Basel: Birkhauser, 2001).

Vygotsky, Lev Semenovich, *Mind in Society, The Development of Higher Psychological Processes*, ed. by Michael Cole, Vera John-Steiner, Sylvia Scribner and Ellen Souberman (Cambridge Mass. and London: Harvard University Press, 1979).

Vygotsky, Lev Semenovich, *Thought and Language*, trans. and ed. by Alex Kozulin (Cambridge Mass. and London: The MIT Press, 1986). First published in English in 1962.

SPATIAL WRITING AND NON-LINEAR ARCHITECTURAL NARRATIVES

SOTIRIOS VARSAMIS

SOCRATES

I call 'geometric' those figures which are records of the movements we can express in few words.
[...]
This, dear Phaedrus, is the most important point: **No geometry without the word. Without it figures are accidents, and neither make manifest nor serve the power of the mind.** By it, the movements which beget figures being reduced to acts, and these acts clearly designated by words, each figure is a proposition that can be combined with others; and we are able in this way, without paying any more heed to sight or movement, to recognize the properties of the combinations we have made; and as it were, **to construct or enrich space, by means of well linked sentences.**
[...]
For a time he [the geometer][1] gets away from images, and yields blindly to the destiny imposed on words by the **machinery of the mind.** [emphasis added][2]

Paul Valéry, Eupalinos or the Architect

Introduction and Research Question

In the passage above, Paul Valéry, in a Platonic style, in his imaginary dialogue between Socrates and Phaedrus about architect Eupalinos, defines which figures can be considered to be geometrical and how they relate to architecture and the experience of space. I find it an interesting starting point for exploring the geometry of language and/or the language of geometry because it was written at the heart of modernism (1921) and, looking back in history and theory of architecture, suggests an approach to design or a methodology for how to 'construct space by means of well linked sentences'. This is a fundamental question for studying the relations between narrative and architecture: how words could be organised in relation to their own geometry or to a geometrical concept, and/or how geometry could transcend its abstract nature and transform into a language itself able to transfer meaning and experiences relating to the world of the senses but also to memory and imagination, like any other language. This is also the main question of my own research and design work, which aims to locate the area where the disciplines of text and architecture meet, and explore how an understanding of this relationship could contribute to the creative process of design: in other words, how is it possible to bring text and architecture together and examine cases where buildings can be read and texts drawn?

Because it seems like a very wide area to explore, my own research started by looking at palindromes, since they are expressed both in literature and architecture. As the quote above suggests, in literature, palindromes can be considered 'geometric figures', in the sense that they are 'records of movement' that can be expressed in 'few words'; in particular, the fewest words possible. In architecture palindromes are traditionally associated with thresholds, passages, domes, arches and fountains – often written or inscribed on them.

As literary structures, palindromes have a specific geometry, that of mirrored symmetry, which generates or 'records' a movement of motional and temporal reversibility. Either easily recognisable or very well hidden within poetic structures, and moving in one, two or three dimensions, they have the ability to open up to a spatial experience. This procedure of violating language through formal manipulation makes an opening to the experience of a poetic space,[3] the space and time veiled in the non-linear relation between sign and signifier inside the anagram.[4] Words do not mean only what they suggest with their materiality. According to Jean Baudrillard (1929–2007): 'The poetic anagram cuts across the two laws of the human word, as proclaimed by Saussure, that of the codified bond between the signified and its signifier and that of the linearity of signifiers'.[5] This way the palindrome is released to the invisible space of meaning. **[figure 1]**

In architecture domes, arches and fountains are some of the spaces traditionally associated with the palindrome, mainly because of their structural similarities. A palindromic arrangement of letters mirrors the reflective structure of the elements that constitute a vaulted form or a dome: a poetic form for the memory and the construction site. But the space domes and arches generate could be experienced similarly to that of the poetic anagram, a poetic space, according to philosopher Giordano Bruno (1548–1600), of infinite associations based on bi-partite divisions of pairs of extreme differences.[6] **[figure 2]**

Other architectural spaces related to palindromes are thresholds, passages and stairs as the spaces of combination that potentially contain all possible connections that mirror symmetry allows them to have – those expected and those not. Their structure is, like text, a sequence of elements that can contribute an infinite multiplicity of combinations to the creation of the spatial experience. Thresholds and passages have the ability to link spaces as well as link the links between spaces, in all different directions. Stairs and corridors are made from distinct elements that reflect themselves and always have a centre of balance, a mirrored surface where there are reflected moments in their temporal and motional repetition. To put it simply, thresholds, passages and corridors look simultaneously in two, or more, different directions, exactly like the palindrome. **[figure 3]**

Spatial Writing and Architecture

Such devices as the palindrome – although overlooked for centuries and, as Georges Perec (1936–1982) very vividly describes, 'treated ... as aberrations, as pathological monstrosities of language and of writing'[7] – are at the heart of a growing interest both in literature and architecture that looks at writing either as 'writing as practice, as work, as play', as Perec claims, or as an interdisciplinary 'critical-spatial practice'[8], according to architect, historian and theoretician Jane Rendell.

For Perec the practice of writing under constraints like palindromes[9] determined almost his whole creative outcome and was used as a methodology to generate literature but also space and spatial experience. For example, in his most famous book *Life A User's Manual* (1978), Perec used a series of superimposed mathematical constraints to generate a book/building in the form of a Parisian block of flats, as well as the lives and stories of its inhabitants.

The main constraints Perec used are Bi-Latin squares (Sudoku), the Knights' move on a 10x10 chessboard, and lists of elements and actions to distribute within the books' chapters. Apart from the main constraints, he used numerous smaller ones like lipograms, acrostics and also palindromes, some obvious and others very well hidden within this extremely complex literary structure. In this way Perec designed the mechanism for a book/space that in the end wrote itself and where the author was just the moderator of these devices. For the reader, who is totally unaware of the constraints used, the book is experienced like an actual building through processes of memory, imagination and recollection. Perec in this example uses literature and text as his tool not only to design the building down to its smallest details, decorations and relation of spaces, but also to determine its time and the interactions of events and humans within the building. Such a methodology is not much different from any architectural design process where certain abstract geometrical and mathematical constraints are used to generate space, spatial experience and at the end a life's user manual. But, more importantly, Perec with his constraints turns writing into a 'critical-spatial practice' with the highly self-referential nature of his design and the ingenious incorporation within the structure of the book/space of the idea of the clinamen, otherwise the error or mistake that leaves the work unfinished and creates the fracture between the abstract world of language and mathematics and the world of the senses. As a book/space *Life A User's Manual* raises questions about the nature of language, authorship, narrative, space and life itself.[10]

But looking back in history, the palindrome and Perec's constraints manifest that methodologies of writing as a spatial critical practice are a form of tradition. For example, I believe that palindromes were considered very literally as a sort of architectural writing, in that letters shared similar values to the buildings blocks on which they were inscribed: the threshold, the dome, the arch or the fountain itself. This kind of writing that could be expressed spatially in text and textually in architecture, I call spatial writing and it includes examples from both text and buildings. This text-space is organised more like a building-space; it is multi-layered, three-dimensional, temporal, based on movement, and the geometric characteristics of its elements can transfer forces, create bodies and as a result be experienced retrospectively over time, like a building.

Tracing the tradition of *spatial writing*, there are plenty examples where words were called bodies, poems were called objects and books were organised like a body or a temple. For example, according to architect and author Indra McEwen (1945), Vitruvius believed, from his studies of the ancient Greek temple, that the ideal proportion derives from the human body, which makes the temple a translation or interpretation of the body in space. He attempted to transfer these ideas into the structure of his *Ten Books on Architecture*, organising or 'building' his book as a translation of the 'human body of architecture'.[11] Publilius Optatianus Porphyrius (fourth century AD) a poet of Constantine the Great, very carefully calculated and designed his poems like a fence, jewels or a ship travelling in a sea of letters – an image that we also meet later in Mallarmé's *Un Coup de Dés*.[12] Bruno, in one of his emblematic images, draws the image and writes the poem of a palindromic mnemonic tree that through a process of geometric manipulations starts to grow and its shadow escapes to the third dimension to create the known universe.[13] In another of his emblematic images, Bruno provides an interpretation of the ancient Latin palindrome *in girum imus nocte et consumimur igni* [trans. we enter the circle at night and we are consumed by fire] where words become moths or the body of the 'enthusiast' flying around the flame ready to be consumed by her/his inclination.[14] But also very commonly known is the ancient Greek palindrome νίψον ανομήματα μη μόναν όψιν [trans. wash your sins not only your face] that was used to be written on fountains, often in a circular way, with the most celebrated example being the fountain outside the temple of Agia Sophia in Konstantinopolis. [figure 4]

Narrative

To understand *spatial writing* and how it becomes a practice, narrative plays an important role because it stands between the textual and the architectural. It is the key concept to recognise the operations of *spatial writing*, to understand its methodology and use it to design space. In general, narrative could be viewed as the mechanism that predetermines the way we move within textual and architectural space, or how we experience these spaces through 'reading' them.

In writing, narrative is the underlying structure upon which a story is built; it is like the genetic code of the linguistic material that determines its arrangement on the page. It is not identical to the story itself – although story and narrative very often coincide – but rather narratives are more about how this story is recounted. Thus, narrative can be examined as an autonomous system. In general, a written narrative could be either linear or non-linear, expressed either as a hierarchical sequence of events in a temporal progression from one event to another, or as a non-hierarchical one where the unfolding of events and their time are organised in a more complex and multi-faceted way (as mentioned before for the palindrome, expressed following the law of mirror symmetry, or using Perec's various mathematical constraints). Non-linear narratives in general create more possibilities of reading or, to put it another way, more ways of moving within their structure and the possibilities of experience they create.

In architecture the narrative frequently coincides either with the decoration of a building, the draft that describes the building or with the story the building wants to tell.[15] Typically, architectural narrative is equated with the stories recounted by architectural features, for instance, sculptures, friezes, or paintings applied to the building, or as the stories the building's form itself is meant to communicate, as is the case with monuments or memorials. It is very rare that the narrative in architecture is seen as a more abstract and autonomous structure that underlines the whole building, describes its parts and is even able to build it. For example George Hersey, reading Vitruvius, studied the Greek temple as an algorithmic narrative that provides all the necessary information for the building's scale, distribution of spaces and spatial features, and the relation between architectural elements all inscribed on a three-dimensional grid.[16]

On a greater architectural scale, such as that of the city, it is even more rare to find narrative treated as something distinct and independent of the stories recounted by its elements. But there are some important exceptions. One such example comes from Latin semiotic theory or the rhetorical strategies of Cicero, who perceived the city as a repository of signifiers, an argument in motion, that constructs an actively evolving narrative upon which stories are built and multiple possibilities of reading and experience are provided.[17] For Cicero cities provided the material upon which books could be transcribed in memory with the use of various mnemonic techniques based on grids, lists and other constraints not very different from the ones mentioned before for Perec's *Life A User's Manual*. In a reverse action, a process of recollection to retrieve information from a book was equal to a walk in the city, either real or created within the orator's imagination.[18] In general this process is called architectural mnemonics and was used by researchers until the popularisation of printing when books became more easily accessible.[19]

In relation to *spatial writing* I see architectural narrative as being closer to what Vitruvius defines as *writing on architecture*, when for the first time in history he creates a language not only to talk about architecture, but also to use it as an essential descriptive and design tool. To write on architecture Vitruvius borrows terminology from the disciplines that traditionally deal with writing, such as history and poetry, distinguishing two types of writing: one tells a story (history), and another constructs the system upon which this story is told (poetry). Following Vitruvius' view, we can consider the building as a narrative rooted in both the geometric and descriptive qualities of writing, one that constructs the scaffold upon which the other is told. In this sense, drawing can be seen to be the equivalent of a text in literature, the medium that carries both the story and its structure. Similarly writing could be the equivalent of designing, an active practice that produces texts and drawings. Vitruvius for the first time crosses the boundary (or possibly defines the boundary) between the disciplines of architecture and literature and examines how texts are drawn in order to write *on architecture*.[20] Of course for Vitruvius such a type of writing had also a very practical significance as the book and the building with its various elements, styles and rhythms had to be remembered and easily recollected for the drawing table as well as for the site. Nowadays, with the vast amounts of information available, our different technology and drawing techniques there is not such a need anymore. But I believe that by looking backwards to such devices of *spatial writing*, we could develop methodologies so that content and structure are not seen as separate elements but are developed together from the very first stages of the design process. In that context the architect could be seen less as the *author* of a space, but more as the moderator of experiences, like Perec who designed a system, which is able to generate a space/book that is experienced openly and differently for every reader.

Experience of both textual and architectural space is largely dependent on reading, or the way the individual decides to move through narrative. Reading both a written and an architectural narrative becomes an active and critical process of constant movement between the story and its structure, or to put it another way, the external space of the senses, politics, nature and social interactions and the inner space of our imagination (beliefs and ideas). For example, a palindrome's reading as a kind of narrative that both constructs (poetry) and tells a story (history) generates a very precise movement (forward/backward) and experience (repetition/reversion/cancellation). The palindrome on the one hand reminds the reader of text's spatiality and, on the other, of space's textuality. When reading a text – in particular a linear text – one gets so immersed within the story that one forgets that reading is also a physical operation that involves the human body in relation to material objects like the book or the words themselves; it is a movement within space, like walking around a circular fountain, being under a dome or stepping over the threshold.

The reader can burrow into linear texts and forget she/he is reading, but this is not the case in non-linear texts like the palindrome in which the reader remains in an indeterminate state between meaning and its materiality, remembering and forgetting.

A similar process takes place for architecture, except that it occurs in reverse. Architectural palindromes constantly remind occupants of space's textuality. Occupants or dwellers of architecture often get so immersed within the materiality of buildings, cities and other architectural structures that they forget architecture's ability to generate narratives. The occupant of architecture can easily burrow into 'linear architecture' and forgets she/he is submerged in space, but this is not the case in non-linear spaces like the palindromic ones where palindromic spatial experience produces an indeterminate state between materiality and meaning, memory and forgetting. As in literature, linear architecture could very briefly be described as one that follows a linear narrative, otherwise a hierarchical unfolding of relations between material objects and their meaning. A non-linear architecture follows more complicated geometric relations between material objects and meanings or concepts; in the case of the palindrome, an architecture that follows the non-hierarchical laws – as any hierarchy in the palindrome has been reversed and thus cancelled – of mirror symmetry, motional and temporal reversibility and cancellation of meaning.[21]

Literature's spatiality or architecture's textuality generates spatial experience for any kind of reader or occupant, though it will not necessarily be the identical spatial experience, as the next example aims to demonstrate. The palindrome's double horizontal and vertical symmetry displays exactly the above relation between body and the mind, image and memory, its perception (horizontal palindromic movement) and recollection (vertical palindromic movement). Each reader or occupant stands in the middle, fragmented, scattered and then recollected within the book like the Vitruvian man.

Stéphane Mallarmé's *Un coup de Dés*, a poem, a space, a design

But how could such a tradition of *spatial writing* and concepts like non-linear literary and architectural narratives relate to the architectural practice and to student work within a studio like Westminster's DS 03 that primarily works with narrative? I am going to use the example of Mallarmé's *Un Coup de Dés* (A Throw of the Dice) as a case of *spatial writing*, which will be analysed as an architectural structure, as a room of thoughts, and look at ways that this poem could form the base for design work.

Un Coup de Dés was written in 1897 and is considered to be Mallarmé's most famous work. It is a unique poem, unbound and composed by words that seem to be floating randomly within the white pages. At first glance it seems to be very disorientating, and a reader can easily feel lost as you he/she does not know how to read this poem, where to start from, and how to move from word to word, from phrase to phrase or from page to page. But we can only be certain of one thing: that Mallarmé definitely had a very important reason for meticulously placing his words within the space of the poem, and for using different font sizes – in times when there was no editing and publishing software available – to create a unique poem that even now looks very contemporary, unique and definitely very enigmatic. I believe that within the tradition of *spatial writing*, where other similar examples of poetry belong, Mallarmé designed his book as a space, a room of thoughts, where the poem/space is the dice itself; it is a very carefully constructed literary cube and the way to read the poem is to move or orientate ourselves within its physical structure…

Un Coup de Dés is a spatial object by itself, but also a product; the poem is made in space and is to be experienced in space, and this is the only way it reveals its meaning. According to Mallarmé's critic Virginia A. La Charité: 'Poetic gamesmanship is an important part of Mallarmé's esthetic of space, for it is in space that he moves the words/pieces and it is in space that meaning occurs'.[22] The readers are the producer of this space because they have to mobilise all of their existence to 'read' the poem, their mind, memory, knowledge as well as their moment and place in our culture. *Un Coup de Dés* is made as a scaffold of ideas within which the mind is free to travel. The space of the text is self-produced, produced by itself and by the self, and like a building cannot be seen in only one instant but can be experienced only retrospectively. [figure 5]

Mallarmé had an established interest in formal writing; there are many examples of his writing poetry on cylinders (mirlitons), on Easter eggs, or on fans where he folds the words in order to create others.[23] Mallarmé also had an interest in 'language manipulation', and there are various examples of anagrams, charades and palindromes in his work, as for example in his *Vers de circonstance*[24] where, similarly to other examples from *spatial writing*, words were treated like objects.

Mallarmé's approach was detached, to a degree, from content: that is, the meaning as it is conceived in a more conventional way in poetry. The form, apart from its content, becomes the carrier of meaning. It seems that, for Mallarmé, thought and its poetic expression requires form. The experience of this poetic space, based on poetic form, is visual, perceptional and mnemonic in the sense that it creates a mental topography connected to the topology of the book. Language, apart from meaning, becomes a design tool for creating a formal landscape, a space of poetics or a poetics of space. Graphic manipulation is applied consciously to language in order to create space.

In the preface to *Un Coup de Dés*, Mallarmé uses the expression 'spaced reading' and states: 'the paper intervenes each time that an image, of itself, ceases to be or returns, accepting the succession of other'.[25] In his description, the paper itself becomes space, the space of images or of the intervention of images, and 'spaced reading' is the experience of nothingness. 'Spaced reading', according to Mallarmé, is the experience of this space, not the typical procedure of reading but a 'transparent'[26] reading through the pages or beyond the pages, which follows the hidden geometries layered by the poet: for example, poems within poems that follow different fonts, font sizes, numerous careful calculations and hidden geometries. The poem is read in multiple ways in multiple times and in multiple layers. When Mallarmé claims that you need 'transparency' to read the book, he means it literally. The reading of the poem demands transparency from line to line, from page to page and from poem to poems within.

Symmetry in general, and more particularly palindromic symmetry exactly in the middle of the book, ties this 'mental space' together.[27] Without symmetry Mallarmé's spatial structure would be dispersed and lost. When you read the poem, in a form of déjà vu, symmetry is what holds the two poles together. You read and re-read, experience and recollect the book, the architectural book and the space Mallarmé creates. Symmetry is less visual than experiential through mental processes of memory and recollection, related to the image of the words as well as to their meaning. In a similar way, in architecture, such symmetries make it easier to read a space as you know what to expect at the other side of a building or a structure.

Mallarmé treats the book as superimposed pages and images, but what keeps them together is not the binding of the book – which doesn't exist in the edition closer to his specifications – but the symmetry of a mental space. Mallarmé, knowing that the physical space of the book, the page, is two-dimensional, opens up the third dimension of space in memory.

The page becomes a mnemonic device and the scaffold upon which are built the images to be perceived and experienced by the mind. According to Mallarmé, the 'narrative is avoided' but narrative's geometry plays a significant role. We could go even further to claim that the poem itself becomes the room, a space that we are invited to inhabit: a room designed and first inhabited by Mallarmé out of his thoughts, a room that works as a scaffold for the reader to build onto it his own thoughts and generate an individual spatial experience. Even with his title, Mallarmé suggests the form of the cube for this space with the image of the dice; a room whose randomness of experience (of living) depends on the individual's actions, or a throw of the dice.

Mallarmé was fully aware of the importance of time to achieve his goal, and this is the reason why he decided to fracture time by breaking the narrative's linearity. The title, which is a direct reference to Heraclitus and his very well-known metaphor of time as a child playing dice by the river, suggests also that time is not linear, or maybe the experience of time within this room is not linear.[28] Apart from the game of dice introduced in the title, one of the most important elements of the poem is water, in the image of the sea or of whirlpools, and maybe those whirlpools are the passage, the 'corridor', that leads to this room, and maybe the wreck Mallarmé describes is that of language itself, suggesting that we have to destroy language, the way we know it and the way we use it, in order to inhabit that room.

But if *Un Coup de Dés* is a topological structure – a room of thoughts – how does someone orientate or locate herself or himself within the poem with reference to time, place or people? The time of reading is not linear because of where the words are placed and how. The reader does not know how to read the lines – from the left page to the right or within each page? – and sometimes has to move to other pages. The placement of lines, words and fonts creates uncertainty about what to read first, how to navigate the poem, and how to move within the pages. The time of experience of the text demands a similarly complicated imaginary reconstruction of the text, a forward/backward movement between the material object, the poem, and the room/space that this object creates in the reader's mind. A constant critical movement between image/perception/memory within the space of the poem that builds this room of thoughts. The image of the whirlpool[29] within the poem is possibly the one that describes this constant motional and temporal re-placement or re-orientation for both the body and the arts,[30] a movement towards a 'transcendental reality'.[31] But this is a whirlpool that cuts through the pages of the book; the whole book rotates or the pages of the book rotate around a hidden or invisible structure based on numbers, geometry and symmetry. It is like the frame of the fans on which Mallarmé wrote poems: these had the ability to fold/unfold the words upon themselves or upon other words. Similarly, the cylinder poems (mirliton) had to be rotated (like a whirlpool) in order to read the poem.

For Mallarmé 'A throw of the dice will annul chance'; by this, he claims that randomness will determine meaning, as meaning is as random as our re-placement, re-orientation within a spatial structure, a room or a room of our thoughts. Mallarmé seems to be aware of the danger that his poem will disperse meaning within the 'galaxy of signifiers'[32] it creates – moving infinitely outwards or collapsing to a centre – and palindromic symmetry is used to keep together the elements of this space, this 'universe', a galaxy of *constellations*.[33]

The act of reading becomes a bodily experience and the book transforms into a performative space that can be experienced by the body. Mallarmé considered himself not as an author but as an operator, similarly to Perec's self-generated book *Life A User's Manual*.

Looking backwards within the tradition of *spatial writing*, there are other similar examples of poetry organised in the shape of a dice. The most important one comes from Vitruvius who claims that the ancient Greek tragic poets, following a Pythagorean tradition, used to write in the form of a cube. According to Vitruvius, 'The Pythagoreans seem to have taken the image of the [literary] cube from dice', and it was used by the Greek poets because as text that follows the law of cubic poetry, it has a double function in the theatrical play: on the one hand to create 'immovable stability of memory', or to remember the words; and on the other to 'relieve the actors' speeches with these intervals', break up the linearity of the play with intervals of memorable poetry, contributing to the action's space.[34] There is also a very beautiful illustration by Renaissance scholar Cesare Cesariano (1475–1543)[35] in his interpretation of the above Vitruvius passage that this literary cube is presented among images of dice. It is difficult to determine how exactly Pythagoreans and Ancient Greek poets wrote cubic poetry or how Vitruvius incorporated similar techniques in his architectural writing, and later how Cesariano thought these examples worked within the text. This is mostly because there is not much research into this kind of formal poetry, but also because there is no original text surviving from the Pythagoreans and Vitruvius to explore such geometries and how they create space. Mallarmé's *Un Coup de Dés* – although it is difficult to determine if Mallarmé knew about the above examples – could easily fit (as enigmatic as it is) within such a tradition of cubic poetry referenced throughout the centuries to the throw of the *poetic* dice. Most importantly, Mallarmé's literary dice is published the way he wanted and we have the ability to move within the poem and experience its space the way he intended. We can throw the dice he carefully designed for us and generate meaning and produce various interpretations,[36] both in text as well as in design projects.

One such interpretation is the *Dream Machine*, designed in collaboration with architect Petros Ioannou. The *Dream Machine* is a device that, having as its starting point the above analysis of cubic poetry, proposes a space, a room of thoughts, where experience and time is fragmented and meaning is based in retrospect reading like the throw of the dice. Other references for the *Dream Machine* come from the work of artist Brion Gysin (1916–1986), who fully developed cut-ups – a literary technique in which text is cut up and rearranged to create a new text. Cut-ups could be traced back to Dadaists and as a technique was popularised by William Burroughs (1914–1997). Gysin was also the inventor of the original Dreamachine, a stroboscopic flicker device that produces visual stimuli.[37] **[figure 6]**

Our *Dream Machine* was initially designed for London to be placed on top of the Queen Elizabeth Hall, but due to its nomadic nature could be easily assembled, disassembled and transferred to other places and other dreams. The *Dream Machine* is a device that generates dreams for the city of London or London's dreams. Images from the surrounding cityscape and sky fuel the *Dream Machine*, which cuts them up, fragments and overlays them, creating the fabric of its interior and its user's dreams. The *Dream Machine* is an architectural study of cubic poetry and, by reversing Vitruvius' relationship between poetry and spatial form in text, it examines the poetic operations of form in architectural space. The immovable stability of the cube, which can be rolled like a dice and always be the same, provides the surface upon which the movable instability of London's images can be projected and, like a dice, always read differently. The images are drawn into the machine by a combination of analogue optic devices like scioptic balls, kaleidoscopes and teleidoscopes, which are enhanced by up-to-date lenses and projected on layers of surfaces made of wood, glass or Barrisol fabric. None of the images produced is manipulated digitally. When a user enters, the *Dream Machine* is completely shielded from the city's visual and acoustic overload. She or he can allow the machine to produce and manipulate images by itself or experiment with its parts, direct them towards specific parts of London, the river or a dramatic sunset. The 'dweller' has the ability to start or stop the machine and its parts at will and experiment with different configurations to find her or his favourable combinations of images, spots within the room, and meaning. The 'dweller', by moving the various parts of the machine or by moving within the machine, is exposed to the infinite combinations of images perceived and the meaning created by them, exactly as in dreams. The *Dream Machine* provides as many views – points of observation and opinions – as the images of London at every moment.

Another project that is based on Mallarmé's spatial qualities of *Un Coup de Dés* comes from studio DS03 and Ioana Vierita's Arts and Crafts Wood Workshop in Camden. I believe it is a fascinating example that shows how closely narrative and architectural form could work together to provide the fabric of space, and uses a methodology that explores what are the *invisible* and experiential elements of architecture. It also demonstrates clearly the importance of narrative-driven architecture within an educational environment, like in Constance Lau's studio where drawing becomes a 'critical spatial practice' and architectural constraints are able to create a language not much different, or in reverse, to Perec's example mentioned above – where literary geometrical constraints were used to create a space.

Conclusion

To return back to where we started, in a palindromic fashion, I would like to conclude by quoting again Valéry[38] who, in his book *Eupalinos*, gives an example of a small Greek temple where the architect has geometrically translated into space the 'mathematical image' of love as the proportions of a beautiful girl from Corinth. The visitor entering the temple, although unaware of the intention and action of the architect, experiences similar feelings to those the architect felt. The individual 'reader' of architecture translates the invisible geometry of space implanted by the architect into a similar erotic experience. In this example, according to Valéry, space 'vaguely awakens a memory which cannot reach its goal; and this beginning of an image of which you possess the perfection does not fail to incite and confound the soul'.[39] In this case the temple stands as an image of love. Image, its geometry and spatial distribution, becomes the agent of experience – not of the same experience, of the specific girl, but of a similar one that 'vaguely awakens a memory'. Valéry seems to believe that mathematics and geometry expressed in forms and images anchor experience in space. But for me this passage also concludes the difference between the story architecture wants to tell and the narrative we decide to choose in order to transfer the experience of this story. In this example the architect with her or his building wants to tell a story of love, but the narrative she/he is using is the temple itself, the structure upon which she/he decided

to construct the story, the language she/he used to tell this story, and its geometry. I believe that non-linear narratives in architecture have exactly this ability to draw our attention not only to the stories we want to tell but also to how to tell them, and consequently to explore how it is possible to use geometry as a language – especially in the era of Computer Aided Design (CAD) design and Virtual Reality – or an agent of forms that produce images able to incite imperfect memories based on random operations within a finite object like Mallarmé's literary dice, *Un Coup de Dés*.

[1] For Valéry the geometer could be both the poet and the architect.
[2] Paul Ambroise Toussaint Jules Valéry, *Eupalinos or the Architect*, trans. William Mc Causland Stewart (London: Oxford University Press, 1932), p. 45.
[3] 'To name it more precisely, using a word that has come to have great currency in recent literary studies, the formal approach constitutes a "poetics".' Anthony Matthew Mellors, 'Poetic Space and the Late Modernist Text: The Theory and Context of J.H. Prynne's Writings from 1960–1974' (PhD thesis, University of Oxford, 1992).
[4] In the 'dislocation' of the sign from its object, the Russian formalists located the 'poetic' because, according to them, the form of the poetic text 'allows the sign a certain independence as an object of value in itself'. According to Roman Jakobson, Russian linguist and literary critic (1896–1982), 'the poetic function projects the principle of equivalence from the axis of selection to the axis of combination' because we string words not only according to their meaning but also rhythmically or phonetically. Yuri Lotman (1922–1993) viewed the 'poetic text as a stratified system in which meaning only exists contextually, governed by sets of similarities and oppositions'. It is 'a system of systems' and is the 'most complex form of discourse imaginable', 'where even absence of certain devices may produce meaning'. According to Lotman, the 'poetic text' is so complex that 'a poem, in fact, can only be re-read, not read, since some of its structures can only be perceived retrospectively'. Eagleton, *Literary Theory*, pp. 85, 86, 89.
[5] Saussure quoted in Jean Baudrillard, 'The Extermination of the Name of God', in *Symbolic Exchange and Death* (London: Sage, 2002), p. 197.
[6] Giordano Bruno uses the emblematic image of the palindromic mnemonic tree to explain a rhetoric process that is able to construct the universe. Bruno notes that this tree, having all the qualities of the physical world, casts a shadow that takes the form of a circle. This shadow/circle is divided into two parts, and from there again to two more, and this goes on in a continuous process of 'two-member bipartite divisions'. This process of divisions of the palindrome's shadow creates a 'growth' of pairs, which enlarges constantly, pushing the multiplicity of these pairs to their 'extreme differences', until infinity. From that point and onwards, and by squaring or growing the circle, together with its divisions, Bruno slowly starts to create the universe, the sun, the moon,

the stars, the planets and the explanations of things. For details: Giordano Bruno, *On the Composition of Images, Signs & Ideas*, ed. Dick Higgins, trans. Charles Doria (New York: Wills, Locker & Owens, 1991), pp. 126, 248, 250.

[7] Georges Perec, 'History of the Lipogram', in *OuLiPo a Primer of Potential Literature*, ed. Warren F. Motte Jr. (Lincoln, NE and London: University of Nebraska Press, 1986), p. 98.

[8] Jane Rendell, having as a starting point 'the possibilities opened up for criticism by art- and site-writing', defines 'architecture-writing' as an interdisciplinary 'critical-spatial practice'. According to Rendell: 'Architecture-writing also demands that we consider the modes in which we write, as well as the medium in which we practice criticism, to be more than a description of content, but to define critical positions'. Jane Rendell, 'Architecture-Writing', *Journal of Architecture* 10, no. 3 (2005), p. 263.

[9] Perec, for example, wrote one of the largest palindromes, The Grande Palindrome (1969), comprising 5,566 letters or 6,372 characters, and a novel, *La disparition* (1969), without using the vowel e – the most common letter in the French language.

[10] Similar methodologies to generate space more or less successfully have also been used in architecture; for example in Bernard Tschumi's *Parc de la Villette* where the architect superimposed three different systems to distribute actions, movements and planes in order to generate – according to their website – 'a discontinuous building but a single structure nevertheless, overlapping the site's existing features and articulating new activities'. In particular in movements like deconstruction architecture is explored as a language able to generate and communicate meaning and its representatives have experimented largely with methodologies from linguistics and writing. Possibly the most well-known example is the collaboration between Jacques Derrida with Peter Eisenman for *Parc de la Villette* (Chora L Works), but relevant references are also found in the early works and drawings of Daniel Libeskind and Zaha Hadid.

[11] Indra Kagis McEwen, *Vitruvius: Writing the Body of Architecture* (Cambridge, MA: MIT Press, 2003).

[12] Publilius Optatianus Porphyrius and Giovanni Polara, *Publilii Optatiani Porfyrii Carmina* (Torino: In aedibus Paraviae, 1973).

[13] The operations of the mnemonic tree have been analysed in detail above.

[14] Bruno uses his own palindrome-emblem *Hostis non Hostis* and continues with the description of his emblem: 'The meaning of the butterfly is not difficult, which, seduced by the fascinations of splendour, goes innocently and amicably to meet its death in the devouring flames. Thus, "hostis" stands written for the effect of the fire; "non hostis" for the inclination of the fly. "Hostis", the flame passively; "non hostis", actively. "Hostis", the flame, through its ardour; "non Hostis", through its splendour …" His description provides a remarkable analysis for the meaning and the mechanism (actively/passively) of the ancient Latin palindrome. Fifth dialogue part IV, from Giordano Bruno, *The Heroic Enthusiasts (Gli Eroici Furori): an Ethical Poem, Part the First*, trans. L. Williams (London: George Redway, 1887), pp. 128–30.

[15] To use Daniel Libeskind's words to describe the Jewish Museum in Berlin, the building is meant to 'tell a story' and be experienced as one. Daniel Libeskind, *Jewish Museum Berlin* (Munich, London and New York: Prestel Verlag, 1999), p. 60.

[16] As Hersey claims: 'Vitruvius has constructed his Greek temple signified in the form of hierarchy. He had first arranged points, that is column bases, into a grid. He then bounds these points with a linear structure – the stereobates and its steps. Then comes the order. This constructs the four planes of the façades, which automatically produce the final result, a solid.' George L. Hersey, *Pythagorean Palaces: Magic and Architecture in the Italian Renaissance* (Ithaca and London: Cornell University Press, 1976), p.25.

[17] Quoting McEwen: 'Cicero once claimed that he could not make a proper argument indoors, away from the repository of signifiers that was the city with its buildings: "one can use words [Cicero said] to reply to an argument made with words. But how does one reply to the self-evident fact of a building?"' McEwen, *Vitruvius*, p. 81.

[18] According to Carruthers: 'Almost every monastic mnemotechnical scheme – ladders, roses, buildings, maps – was based on geometrical figures: squares, rectangles, circles and complex reformations of these, including three-dimensional structures (like the Ark described by Hugh of St. Victor begins with instructions of how to draw a rectangle mentally and then to trisect it …)'. Mary Carruthers, *The Craft of Thought: Meditation, Rhetoric, and the Making of Images, 400–1200* (Cambridge: Cambridge University Press, 1998), p. 16.

[19] Frances Yates was the first to write a short history of mnemonic techniques from ancient Greece to the Renaissance and identifies among them architectural mnemonics. Frances Amelia Yates, *The Art of Memory* (London: Pimlico, 2003).

[20] Vitruvius, *Ten Books on Architecture*, trans. Ingrid D. Rowland (Cambridge: Cambridge University Press, 1999).

[21] In my *definition of the palindrome* these are the three characteristics of the palindrome. S. Varsamis, *Spatial palindromes/palindromic spaces: spatial devices in Vitruvius, Mallarmé, Polieri, Perec and Libeskind*, (PhD Thesis, University College of London, 2010).

[22] Virginia A. La Charité, *The Dynamics of Space: Mallarmé's Un Coup de Dés jamais n'abolira Le Hasard* (Lexington: French Forum, 1987), p. 32.

[23] According to Charité: 'For example, in the early text, 'Brise marine', he uses the folding-unfolding fan technique to transpose the quayside scene into an exotic dream. The final lines of the text contain the evocation of the voyage and the longing of the poet for adventure: '… sans mâts, sans mâts, ni fertiles ilôts … / Mais, ô mon coeur, entends le chant de matelots!'. By folding the words *mâts* and *ilôts* into *matelots*, Mallarmé creates a mobile image of the sailors and reduces the entire text to an evocation of departure'. Ibid., p.32.

24. According to Charité: 'The texts must be seen to be grasped because they depend primarily on the tactile sense: "dans telle/dentelle", "Cold/Hérolde", "m'accommode/comme ode", "**rêver/ever**", "Commentaire. Comme en terre", "qu'on fit/confit".' Ibid., p. 20.
25. Introduction, Stéphane Mallarmé, *Dice Thrown Never Will Annul Chance*, trans. Brian Coffey (Dolmen Press: Dublin, 1965).
26. 'A reader who reads "transparently", without preconception, as candid as the witness from which that word derives, will perceive these patterns, will understand the connected links which bind together and demonstrate the existence of *l'Idée*.' Roger Pearson, *Unfolding Mallarmé: The Development of a Poetic Art* (Oxford: Clarendon, 1996), p. 3.
27. In the middle of the poem Mallarmé uses the palindromic symmetry of the words: *comme si, comme si*. But there is also the palindromic symmetry between the first and the last phrase of the poem: *Un Coup de Dés*.
28. Heraclitus used the metaphor of a child playing with dice to visualise the concept of time (introducing the order of randomness in the conception of time). One of his most celebrated fragments states:
'Αιών παίς έστι παίζων, πεσσεύων. Παιδός η βασιλίη'
'Time is a child playing the dice. The kingly power is a child's.'
Κώστας Αξελός, *Ο Ηράκλειτος και η Φιλοσοφία* (Αθήνα: ΕΞΑΝΤΑΣ, 1976).
29. The image of the whirlpool appears often in the poem, for example in exactly the middle of the poem where the image is structured around a palindromic symmetry of the words *comme si, comme si*. I am not going to use the quote here as there is not only one way of reading the poem and consequently quoting it. Please refer to the poem itself.
30. 'The ideogram on page 6 represents art expressed as a whirlpool ("tourbillon", in the middle of the page), for art returns upon itself and nature, creating an eddy of its own, a momentary stasis, yet not, which paradox is figured as a spiral, that of artistic production as well as the history of art …' Robert Greer Cohn, 'Mallarmé's *Un Coup de Dés*: An Exegesis [a Thesis. With a Facsimile of the Paris, 1914, Edition of *Un Coup de Dés jamais n'abolira Le Hasard*]' (New Haven, 1949), p. 31.
31. '[O]rientation is the ability to locate oneself in one's environment with reference to time, place, and people. In this respect, Katz speaks of shocking, even shuttering, the standard epistemic security of disciples, and forcing them to *locate* themselves [reorientate] vis-à-vis normal versus transcendental reality.' Reuven Tsur, *On the Shore of Nothingness: Space, Rhythm, and Semantic Structure in Religious Poetry and Its Mystic-Secular Counterpart: A Study in Cognitive Poetics* (Thorverton: Imprint Academic, 2003), p. 208.
32. According to Roland Barthes: 'In the ideal plural text the networks are many and interact, without any of them being able to surpass the rest; this text is a galaxy of signifiers, not a structure of signifiers; we gain access to it by several entrances, none of which can be authoritatively declared to be the main one; the codes it mobilizes extend *as far as the eye can reach*, they are indeterminable (meaning here is never subject to a principle of determination, unless by throwing dice); the systems of meaning can take over this absolutely plural text, but their number is never closed, based as it is on the infinity of language'. Roland Barthes, Richard Miller and Honoré de Balzac, *S–Z* (London: Cape, 1975), p. 5.
33. The constellation is another of the main images of *Un Coup de Dés*.
34. 'Pythagoras and those who followed his sect decided to write down their precepts using the principle of cubes; they thought that two hundred sixteen lines constituted a cube and that there ought to be no more than three cubes in a single written composition [Book V, preface, 1–4]. Now a cube is a body, squared all round, made up of six sides whose plane surfaces are as long as they are wide. When it is thrown, the part on which it lands (so long as it remains untouched) preserves an immovable stability; the dice that players throw onto the gaming board are like this. The Pythagoreans seem to have taken the image of the [literary] cube from dice, because this particular number of lines, landing like dice on any side whatsoever, will there produce immovable stability of memory. The Greek comic poets divided up the space of their plays by inserting a song by the chorus; defining the parts of the play by the principle of the cube they relieve the actor's speeches with these intervals', Vitruvius, *Ten Books on Architecture*, p. 63.
35. Cesare Cesariano, Vitruvius' literary cube. From Marcus Vitruvius Pollio et al., *Di Lucio Vitruuio Pollione De Architectura Libri Dece Traducti De Latino in Vulgare Affigurati: Comentati (Da Caesare Caesariano)*, Como, 1521.
36. Quentin Meillassoux, in his quest to discover the hidden number in *Un Coup de Dés* – although is not taking into consideration the spatial qualities of the poem –.determined that the words of the poem count to the (palindromic) number 707, which also determines other sequences within the poem 7-0-7. Quentin Meillassoux, *The Number and the Siren, a Decipherment of Mallarmé's Un Coup de Dés*, trans. Robin Mackay (UK: Urbanomic, 2012).
37. There are numerous websites providing information about the construction and the use of the Dreamachine. Gysin's original drawings are in the public domain together with step-by-step instructions on how to manufacture one. A description from a website that sells patterns of Dreamachines: 'The Dreamachine is viewed with the eyes closed: the flickering light stimulates the optical nerve and alters the brain's electrical oscillations, producing vivid visions of very bright moving and morphing colours in geometrical patterns to appear "projected" behind the eyelids, covering completely the field of vision. A prolonged session in front of a Dreamachine (time may vary among subjects) can push the experience further, altering the perception of time and space and provoking a dream-like state'. <http://importantrecords.com/visualshop/brion-gysins-dreamachine> [accessed 19/05/2016].
38. Paul Valéry, *Eupalinos or the Architect*.
39. Ibid., pp. 21–22.

List of figures:

Figure 1: A palindromic grid moving in two dimensions is the very well-known Latin palindrome, which was first found depicted in Pompeii's frescoes.

Figure 2: Stills from the video EROS / SORE that is looking at domes as palindromic metaphors. The top of 30 St. Mary Axe (the Gherkin) was filmed while under construction for 24 hours (3 seconds every ten minutes). The footage was edited based on a palindromic mirroring of its movement and time forwards and backwards to infinity. The soundtrack used the original recordings, edited using the same principles, by music producer and composer Robin Morrison. Actors, Stamatis Zografos and Efi Dementi. Voice, Aggelos Abazoglou.

Figure 3: Still from the video *Spatial Palindrome I*. Lubetkin's staircase in Bevin Court was used a spatial palindromic metaphor to explore the temporal and cognitive poetic operations of Georges Perec's *The Grande Palindrome* (1969).

Figure 4: Still from the sound installation *Towards the Flame* in collaboration with Robin Morrison for the *Cities Methodologies, Buildings on fire: Towards a new approach to urban memory*, UCL, 2014. The installation consists of a mental land(sound)scape or a room of thoughts created by the voices of all of my friends that – burning with their breathing – bring form to the Latin palindrome *in girum imus nocte et consumimur igni* and exhaust it by repetition. Photograph by Ståle Eriksen. Event organised by Ben Campkin, installation curated by Incandescent Square: Stamatis Zografos and Elena Papadaki.

Figure 5: Axonometric study of Mallarmé's *Un Coup de Dés*. Produced by author.

Figure 6: Drawings for the first realisation of the *Dream Machine*. Architects Sotiris Varsamis and Petros Ioannou.

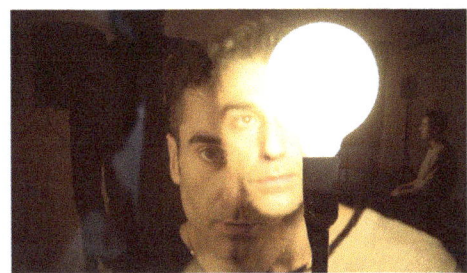

Figure 1

Figure 4

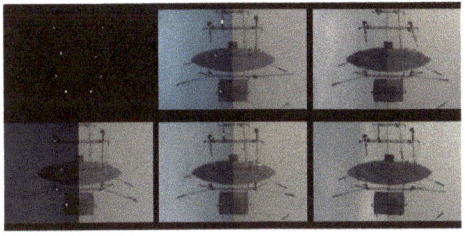

Figure 2

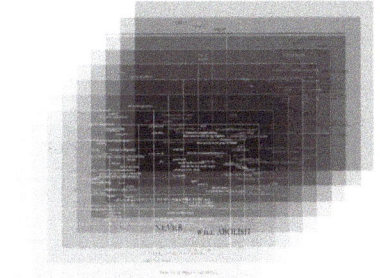

Figure 5

Figure 3

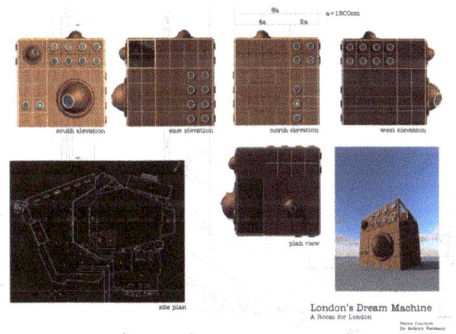

Figure 6

MONTAGE AND MULTIPLE INTERPRETATIONS

CONSTANCE LAU

'Open Work' and Techniques of Montage

The notions of different interpretations have been discussed by Umberto Eco in *The Open Work* (1989) and Walter Benjamin in *The Arcades Project* (1989). In the first, Eco raises the issue of different interpretations concerning modern art, and the concept of 'openness' was considered in relation to authorship and the capacity for user intervention to shape the reading of the work.[1] As a result, the creation of multiple interpretations is inevitable in order for the work to be deemed complete.

In *The Arcades Project* the notion of multiple interpretations is demonstrated through Benjamin's technique of researching, constructing and organising the contents of the work.[2] The resulting montage was essentially Benjamin's representation and critique of nineteenth-century Parisian bourgeois society through his fascination with life beneath the Paris arcades. Benjamin not only considered these arcades to be 'the most important architecture form of the nineteenth-century', but also where the most interesting and relevant depictions of the century's preoccupations occurred.[3] Hence the contents of *The Arcades Project* can be described as one manner of documenting the activities that took place beneath the roofed spaces. More importantly, the narrative can also be argued to be a site-specific reflection on life in Paris during the nineteenth-century.

These indoor arcades that were described as a cross between 'a street and an interior' were complete with living quarters, shops, cafés and theatres, and created different meeting and social places different from the traditional Paris boulevard.[4] This additional street life also extended the boundaries from which the *flâneur*, defined as 'a man about town who strolls around and observes society', could operate.[5] Hence an appropriate way that the basic essence and characteristics of the Paris arcades could be effectively captured was in a working system that respected the differences of the events juxtaposed within the spaces. In addition, this system also had to further Benjamin's argument, as well as respect both the process of material collection and the intended structure of the finished product. For this, Benjamin recognised himself in the role of the ragman and, assuming the character of the materialistic historian, likened his practice of material collection to the task of rag picking. This idea was adopted from Charles Baudelaire's description of the *chiffonier*, or rag picker, as 'he collects and catalogues everything that the great city has cast off'.[6] Hence *The Arcades Project* 'wishes to pick up the refuse of history' through the materialist historian who 'selects from amongst all that is disregarded and from the residues of history'.[7] Benjamin's interpretation of this task was reflected in his choice of research material for the project, stemming from a particular interest in the 'dispersed and frequently arcane sources' in the Bibliothèque Nationale in Paris.[8] His conception of the project as an appropriation of rags further meant complete disregard for material that has been 'accredited as precious and valuable'.[9] This new interpretation of history and choices concerning 'historical refuse' has enabled 'waste materials to enter into significant connections' where fragments of information are 'used to gain a new perspective on history'.[10]

Benjamin arranged for the archival material consisting of quotations and excerpts transcribed into notebooks, note paper and note cards, in addition to draft writings and manuscripts, to be photographically reproduced in the mid-1930s. These images were then sent to the Institute for Social Research, New York, for safekeeping.[11] However, it is not certain whether Benjamin had intended that the material for *The Arcades Project* should become a book. The initial intention was for a few small essays regarding the Parisian arcades, but the eventual project has been described as 'the blueprint for an unimaginably massive and Labyrinthine architecture, a dream city, in effect'.[12] The principles of montage are evident in the arrangement of the six chapters of the book, which are designed to operate independently and enable 'the work to be remade anew' by each reader.[13] More importantly, the published body of work contradicts the commonly accepted layout of the conventional book form that is known for continuity and linearity. In this instance, the structure is discontinuous and the contents juxtaposed, which enables each of the individual sections to be read independently, or against the context of one another. This in effect enables numerous interpretations of the work. Significantly, it in essence also allows the reader to play a part in the process and design of engaging with the project by means of selecting which way to complete the work.[14]

In this analysis, attention can also be drawn to issues of site. As much as *The Arcades Project* is a site-specific documentation of the nineteenth-century Paris arcades, the location of the final product is also the book. This suggestion extends the explorations concerning design methodology to the notion of 'medium'. The comparison between 'the physical nature of architecture' and 'the physical object of a book' starts with the assumption that both are located between the author and the reader and/or user.[15] While the six chapters appear as fragments, the concept of 'openness' is exaggerated by the gaps that are apparent between each of these sections. The qualities of montage are enhanced as the presence of these gaps allows the work to remain unfinished and 'available for endless revisions and appropriations'.[16] The argument concerning montage is especially 'appropriate to user creativity in architecture because the building is not experienced all at once' but in 'moments separated by gaps in climate, space and time'.[17] These experiential moments form part of the exploration concerning architectural fragments.

The reading of architecture over time takes into account the fact that 'buildings long outlive the purposes for which they were built, the technologies by which they were constructed and the aesthetics that determined their form'.[18] These shifts, and the ensuing gaps between form, function and site, create opportunities for differences of opinions concerning meaning and use to emerge. This understanding brings forth the idea of the architectural fragment and - similar to the use of montage in design work - enables a work of site-specific architecture to engage with the user to the extent that new meanings are created. Hence multiple interpretations are inevitable. The architectural fragment can be experiential and/or expressed literally as physical components. Both are of great interest to this discussion, especially in relation to the manner in which narrative is approached in architectural design.

The Architectural Fragment

Buildings have their own inherent narratives, which start from 'the first impulse to build, to their realisation and prime, and to their decline'.[19] Hence chronology, of its own accord, provides different readings and enables multiple interpretations, depending on the physical and/or theoretical contexts in which the works are located at a particular moment. At the most basic levels of interpretation these narratives revolve around programme and function, or are recounted through the marks of the environment and user patterns. In writing, a work of architecture and/or a space is used to support the recounting of the narrative. In architecture, the articulation of this idea can be further communicated through a series of spaces, which can be expressed in various ways. The concept of narrative progression or movement from one point to another implies the existence of 'narrative space'.[20] The relationships between these spaces could be linear or non-linear depending on the approach and manner of use.

As much as narratives serve as useful means to interpret buildings, the notion of narrative in relation to the process of architectural design has wider implications where works of architecture are concerned. The architectural narrative can be additionally used as a means to spatially reinterpret research material. History and/or historical events are not regarded as passive sources of information, but are actively prescribed within current architectural sites and reworked as design proposals. Hence, events that would otherwise be consigned to memory or totally forgotten are retold and given new readings and meanings.

This is also when the notion of the architectural fragment comes into play. The fragment is a spatial interpretation of a precise source and/or reference, which enables particular meanings to be expressed through the articulation of the architecture. These allusions can be spatially considered in their entirety or occur as architectural fragments. The occurrences imbue the spaces with alternative readings and connotations, which are subject to interpretation. This layering of meaning over function allows for the possibility of new dialogue to be created between the design brief, the site and the user to enrich the experience of the work.

In *Narrative Architecture* (2012), Nigel Coates discusses different design methods in relation to binary, sequence and biotopic narratives in architecture.[21] These different approaches to narratives are used as tools to design, interpret and understand works of architecture. Binary narrative refers to the adoption of a parallel identity that is a combination of function and metaphor. The architecture is a symbolic and straightforward representation of key themes.[22] Coates cites the example of the 2005 exhibition piece by Will Alsop for a convention in Toronto, Canada. To advertise the textile industry, Alsop employs the 'narrative of a voluptuous red dress to define enclosure' and creates a work space for the machinists beneath the skirt of this giant dress.[23] This piece of architecture encapsulates the context of the show, the use of machining and the narrative of the dress in one single image.[24] As a single feature, it is complete, but against the context of the entire convention, this construct can be read as an architectural fragment.

Sequence narrative expresses the articulation of spaces along a route, each of which has its own spatial coherence. The unfolding of these prescribed routes may contain sub-narratives, and there could be various ways for the sequences to unfold as one moves through the spaces.[25] This is when the notion of the architectural fragment becomes evident. Lina Bo Bardi's SESC Leisure Centre in Pompéia, São Paulo, Brazil is a non-profit project that was built in stages between 1977 and 1982.[26] Significantly, the narrative references the enormous scale of the city, its disconnected valleys and the unequal social divide between rich and poor. Located in a defunct industrial complex, this multi-purpose building provides leisure facilities like theatres, gymnasiums, galleries, workshops, restaurants and a swimming pool for the community. The inclusion of an artificial beach further hints at the fact that this entity is unreachable for the majority of residents in São Paolo. Spatial navigation is designed around a system of internal 'streets', which connect the visitors to different leisure options. More importantly, every fragment plays dual roles of function and fantasy, where the latter, expressed architecturally by a jungle mural and boardwalk 'beach', creates an unfolding illusion of nature and enables belief to be suspended in one of the most polluted cities in the world.[27]

Lastly, a biotopic narrative refers to a set of interrelated conditions, each with their own logic and dynamics. In architecture, this suggests 'an urban field that includes a variety of functions and storylines that are mutually supporting yet independent'. Examples of places exhibiting these characteristics are university campuses and urban villages. Enric Miralles's 2002 Parc Diagonal Mar in Barcelona, Spain, occupies a large rectangular plot between housing blocks at the end of a major axis, the palm-tree-lined Avenida Diagonal. The wider context of Barcelona is reinterpreted in a landscape consisting of an artificial lake, a rose garden and over-scaled steel vines supporting giant vases covered in broken pieces of ceramic. The approach allows the relative actions of using the city, the park and the elements within the park to overlap, as well as 'inform and invade' each other. While the architectural fragments of 'ludic devices' in the landscape clearly reference nature, they have also been designed to amplify its inherent complexity. The layering of these design concepts and fragments 'exhibits functional clarity' while simultaneously stimulating 'incongruity, form and fiction'.[28] Hence a biotopic narrative occurs when 'a system of narrative components fuses with its system of functional parts'. This subverts the physical reality of a space and, more importantly, allows it to be 'open to multiple interpretations'.[29]

This study demonstrates that the employment of narrative in design practice is able to contribute to the 'basic architectural language'.[30] The new ways in which these existing components can be articulated subsequently enhance the physical and experiential qualities of the resulting works. In relation to notions concerning use, however, carefully considered aspects of the architectural narrative need to be further devised as dialogues with the users to enhance the reading and experiential qualities of the work. One such important aspect concerns issues of site. In addition to current readings, the notion of history in the form of physical elements, or manifested by means of intangible allegorical narratives, can be used to good effect where the architectural site is concerned. This includes an awareness of the inherent non-visible complexity that exists in buildings, and the idea that the physical manifestation of a work of architecture at any given time belies the richness that is hidden. The role of history and the consideration of historical narratives during the identification of site boundaries in the form of physical elements and/or the implied boundaries of associated memories can inform and enrich architectural design. History affects the making and reading of architecture, and the idea of a building being physically located in its current context but also read within the historical context, and vice versa, has different implications. Hence the added complexity in the design process resulting from the conscious allusion to specific site elements or narratives can enhance and give another layer of meaning to the work. This notion of context is an ongoing and important consideration with regards to architectural design.

Site-Specificity and 'Aura'

Site investigative studies are critical to the construction of the architectural narrative, and accurate knowledge of existing conditions acts as a counterfoil for locating the design proposal. In this instance, a work of architecture is defined as the result of the seamless and precise synthesis between the built work and the existing site. This further enables site-specific qualities to become an integral aspect of the design process and the architecture. Hence the architectural narrative serves to confront, place and integrate the chronological shifts between the programme and user, as well as specific site readings at a given moment. The shifts in time, location and event further initiate the notion of multiple interpretations in the meaning, reading and experience of the work. Once again, this demonstrates the idea of the work being made anew in relation to individual responses. In this instance, the extent of site-specific research is broadened to include the ephemeral and experiential qualities, which are as intrinsic to design work as the more common practices associated with documenting the physical attributes of an architectural site.

The term 'antaeic magic' was proposed by the art historian Aby Warburg to describe the 'release of latent memories through direct contact'.[31] The integral relationship between this experience and that of a specific site is furthered by Aleida Assmann, who maintains that 'the antaeic magic is anchored in the authenticity of the historical site', and that this particular argument concerning site is also defined by their 'aura'.[32] This notion of 'aura' is referenced to Walter Benjamin's definition of the term in 'The Work of Art in the Age of Mechanical Reproduction'.[33] His arguments regarding the reproduction of artworks concern the uncompromising suggestion that authenticity results from a reading of the work located within its original physical context. Hence the 'most perfect reproduction' will undoubtedly be lacking in 'its presence in time and space'.[34] This 'unique existence' is defined as the 'aura of the work of art'.[35] The idea of 'historical objects' is further discussed in relation to 'natural objects' and the latter expressed as 'the unique phenomenon of a distance'.[36] The definition of distance in this instance refers to the extent within which the boundaries of the natural objects are located, and is concurrently identified in relation to the notion of nature. This is also when the association to issues of site becomes apparent and the notion of aura, in essence, can be read as the site-specific experiential qualities embedded in a work of architecture. Hence while a building is read and used differently by different people, the permanence and specificity of a particular site enables the unique qualities associated with aura to be induced, recognised and applied.

While uniqueness is inseparable from history and tradition, different interpretations occur as a result of the shifting historical context in which the object is located. Benjamin cites the ancient statue of Venus, which was 'an object of veneration' to the Greeks and an 'ominous idol' to the clerics of the Middle Ages, despite both groups being equally engaged with its aura.[37] This intrinsic pre-secular relationship between the artwork and its ritualistic functions can be compared to that of a building and the notion of repeated use. This idea of use, like a ritual, is habitual and accomplished gradually in fragments. Hence the shifts that occur enable new interpretations each time the building is experienced.[38]

The secular position however, negated all associations with 'cult value', 'dependence on ritual', and emancipated a work of art from its social roles.[39] Hence the notion of art became a creation with entirely new functions, and more importantly, laden with an overstated emphasis on its exhibition value.[40] This alternative emphasis subsequently diluted the importance of site, as the insistence on site-specificity limited the number of places and times a work of art could be exhibited. The ensuing monopoly over the value and perception of a work of art by institutions, as well as the eradication of user participation will now be explored in relation to issues of site and the notion of nonorganic works of art.

This interest is discussed in relation to Peter Bürger's analysis concerning the distinction between organic and nonorganic works of art. In the first, the individual parts of the work of art are considered of lesser importance and hence serve to ensure the harmony of the overall composition. Artists who produce organic work perceive their material as 'something living', 'respect its significance as something that has grown from concrete life situations', and that it is consequently entrenched with meaning.[41] As a result, ideas of totality and unity are very important, and these intentions are reflected in the final works. In a nonorganic work of art, all the parts, their arrangement and the context are distinct and non-hierarchical. The artists isolate their material from the 'context that gives it meaning', and treat it as 'an empty sign, to which only they can impart significance'.[42] The resulting work is composed of fragments and usually put forth as a basis to further discussions. This latter category is also referred to as 'works of the avant-garde' with regards to this analysis.[43]

Bürger's argument against the concept of 'art as an institution' includes the ways in which art is produced, and distributed, and 'also to the ideas about art that prevail at a given time that determine the reception of the works'.[44] The twentieth-century avant-garde movements turned against this idea of 'institution' and contested especially the aspects of control and exploitation. As a result, the avant-garde advocated that the distance between art and social reality should be negated, and that art should be reunited with life. This is mainly with respect to the way in which art functions and communicates with society. The avant-garde also looked back to the arguments of purpose, function, production and reception from which to express their ideas.[45] The result was the development of nonorganic works which focused on negating unity in favour of creating tension between the individual parts and the whole work of art. More significantly, this allowed the work to be autonomous and operate independently with regards to this notion of institution.

The argument was further illustrated by Bürger through two types of avant-garde art, namely collage and montage, in which the latter was explored in conjunction with nonorganic works of art. This is due to the allegorical nature of montage, and the inherent dialectical qualities that enable new meanings to be generated as the work is continuously read and re-read in the new contexts formed. The criticism that art lacked social impact was addressed by means of introducing fragments of material that were considered relevant and symbolic of life. This enabled works of art to be reintegrated into the praxis of life.[46] This notion concerning the practice of life in relation to works of architecture can be read as the integration of site studies with the provision for the user to partake in the creative process. Hence, as previously discussed, the idea of multiple interpretations is especially possible with montage as the recipient becomes an active participant in the creation of the work.[47] This participation can be further enriched with the inclusion of narrative in design practice.

Perspective of Meaning

The properties of montage 'as a language and technique associated with critical intent and used in a number of media' have been raised in this discussion.[48] One example that shows how montage is affected by the medium in which it operates is *The Arcades Project* as previously discussed.[49] Another medium that is highly indicative of the potential of montage is film. In this instance, the presence of the architectural narrative is expressed through sequence, space and time.[50] The construction of deliberate shifts between these factors exaggerates the creation of different interpretations and the consequences of this approach are abundantly reflected in the works of Peter Greenaway. In essence, the nature of his films 'exhibit an architecture which seems to owe less to the unfolding of a coherent narrative than to the demands of visual composition, aleatory sequences, complex language games, taxonomies founded on more arbitrary principles of selection'.[51] These qualities will be further explored through the use of montage in the narrative, the role of the architectural fragment and issues of site-specificity.

In The Draughtsman's Contract (1984) the protagonist, a draughtsman, is hired to execute a series of twelve drawings of the fictional Compton Anstey, a country house and its gardens. This key decision inventively initiates the use, production, description and representation of architecture throughout the narrative which is 'unpacked' from drawing to drawing as the plot unfolds.[52] The ensuing series of events involving adultery, betrayal and murder is told through the cultural and chronologically specific context of aristocratic England during the seventeenth-century, as well as the site-specific qualities of the country house and its landscaped gardens. For instance the film is set in 1694, the year the Bank of England was established and this fact is highlighted by the different ongoing manifestations of attitudes and obsessions with money throughout the narrative.[53] This was also a time when the 'mixing of families and nations' in England was occurring.[54] The Catholic sovereign was banished and this initiated the return of Protestant values but by a Dutch king, whose presence was followed by the arrival of the Dutch, and the Germans.[55] The film expresses the fluidity of this situation by referencing and drawing upon precise traits from these specific historical events. These implications of change and juxtaposition are additionally layered over the English landscape to reinforce the notion of change and simultaneously showcase its changeable beauty.[56] The use of montage in the narrative further results from the gaps in the chronological shifts between the setting of the film in 1694 and the reading of the work in 1984. This is cleverly designed into the language whereby the wordy sentence constructs are juxtaposed against 'the sanction of contemporary diction'.[57] The notion of the visual fragment is additionally heightened by the medium of film and the camera technique of close ups. This procedure is employed to reveal only a small portion of the 'mysterious goings on', and the fragmentation of the narrative is further induced by the constant juxtaposition of numerous shots, which 'prevents the necessary space for a good overview'.[58]

Each of the twelve drawings performs as a 'partial narrative', a fragment of the happenings, which are precisely recorded and contained within the artefact of the two-dimensional drawing.[59] The ideas of 'cutting and montage' are also apparent in this practice as the Draughtsman is 'contracted to fix on a white surface the portions of space that he captures in the frame of his optical device'.[60] The architectural narrative is furthered as a design tool as the process of constructing the twelve drawings creates openings from which the various plots evolve. Together the drawings present Compton Anstey as a whole, but individually they act as architectural fragments, each triggering a slightly different reading and understanding of the narrative.

The recurring conversation regarding perspectives is indicted throughout by the presence of a black edged view-finder, which the draughtsman uses to assist in the production of the drawings. The rules for the construction of these drawings are also precise and require the draughtsman to be at the same location at the same time every day in order to continue working on each particular drawing under similar light conditions. This fragment of the narrative is complete with visual references to the gridded drawing frame in Albrecht Dürer's 1525 engraving 'Unterweisung Der Messung' (Four Books on Measurement) to further allude to the Renaissance ideals of truthful representation. All of these knowing references occur in stark contrast to the underlying questions concerning singular and multiple points of view.

Prior to the Renaissance development of perspective drawing and perceptions of visual accuracy, the term 'perspective of mind' referred to a skill that viewers were trained in and applied to reading the composition and meaning of certain elements in works of art. The use of this knowledge resulted in the ability to comprehend and appreciate the intention and meaning of the works. Also referred to as a 'habit of mind', this approach to vision was manifested through issues of conveyance and included the construction of visual symbols embedded with allegorical references as well as allusions to specific narratives. These works usually appear as a collection of individual objects placed within the picture plane, hence resulting in images that have 'no unity in pictorial design'.[61] This approach disregarded the notion of creating a visually unified picture through the accurate depiction of scale and optical distance and instead, emphasised the placement of these objects within the picture plane. The main idea relied on an aesthetic 'dependent on colour and outline' and the placement of individual objects as opposed to a construction that realistically represents space in its entirety.[62] The treatment of the picture surface as a completely flat and two-dimensional plane enables the work to be 'achieved entirely through pattern'.[63] This technique of arranging individual objects to create a picture has more in common with medieval art than with the techniques of perspective drawing developed during the Renaissance.[64] This 'perspective of mind' approach in medieval art that similarly relied on a flat pictorial organisation was also referred to as a 'perspective of meaning'. The application of this medieval technique of presenting and reading paintings diminished greatly during the Renaissance, during which the belief that vision and truth were inseparable was fostered. Hence the ability to see and understand works of art presented in this manner no longer exists.

This was mainly due to the addition of a mathematical dimension to the development of linear perspective that afforded vision an empirical status during the Renaissance. More importantly, it enabled the ability to calculate and realistically represent three-dimensional spaces on two-dimensional surfaces. Hence the well-placed foreground and background in paintings serve to give a picture depth, and turn the painted surface into a space. This advocated method of constructing and presenting paintings treated the two-dimensional space in the picture plane as an extension of the actual surroundings. In addition, the meaning of the work becomes apparent at a glance, and 'the eye no longer has to wander across the painting and piece the events together'.[65] Hence the demonstration of visual accuracy afforded by the use of linear perspective also ensured that vision was to be regarded as the most important of the five senses. More significantly, this relationship concerning certainty and the sense of sight is still very much assumed currently and influences the way in which works of art are appreciated and understood. This idea of visually constructing a picture plane that realistically corresponds to the surrounding space could not be further from the concept of 'perspective of meaning', where the third dimension of the three-dimensional world constructed in medieval and pre-Renaissance times is one of time as opposed to space.[66] Hence, while the Draughtsman's process of construction and drawing techniques to replicate Compton Anstey may point towards accuracy and truthful representation, the meanings behind each of the drawings are neither straightforward nor truthful.

This questioning of constantly changing views and viewpoints with carefully choreographed gaps between 'perception and comprehension, seeing and knowing' enables the audience to question and decide the roles they assume, from protagonist to actor to bystander, at any given moment in the narrative.[67] This dialogue between the director and audience creates a multitude of possible interpretations. The main argument of drawing what one sees as opposed to what one knows lends itself to another parallel argument in art concerning the structured Renaissance notions of 'truth' versus the Dutch masters' approach of '"seeing" the world empirically for what it is' without the burden of cultural allusions.[68] This difference between the 'reading' of Renaissance art and the newer approach to 'seeing' art further lends itself to the discussion of individual responses and hence, yet again, the notion of multiple interpretations.[69]

The discussion centred on the medium of film and use of the camera has also introduced deviations from assumed understandings with regards to the Renaissance principles of truth. According to Benjamin, 'a man who concentrates before a work of art' is so absorbed to the extent that he 'enters into this work'.[70] Hence the painter adopts a removed stance and 'maintains in his work a natural distance from reality', whereas the cameraman attempts to accurately record nature. Bürger's arguments regarding organic and nonorganic works of art, as well as the notion of montage, are also of relevance in this instance. For while the picture a painter obtains is an interpretation, it is 'total', whereas that of the cameraman 'consists of multiple fragments' that have been assembled.[71] More importantly in the latter, reality is an artefice and ideas of truthful representation are due to mechanical equipment and, significantly, 'the result of cutting'.[72] Hence the kaleidoscope of views in this film can be extended to 'what the camera man sees, what the draughtsman sees and what we as an audience see' and, more importantly, 'the representational difference between the three'.[73] The use of fragments and allusions play substantial roles in informing the narrative of the work and this representational difference is the gap in which multiple interpretations can be derived.

Authorship and Multiple Interpretations

To avoid the argument of multiple interpretations being an accidental and existing by-product of architecture, the role of design authorship ensures that the occurrence of different readings shifts from being an assumption to a working focus. Hence the context of this argument is widened to include works of art that adopt comparable approaches and principles. The notion of 'Open Work' is evident in the manner in which Mark Dion approaches his art projects. His endeavours explore ways in which the narrative, material fragment and issues of site-specificity are designed into a precise working system that exposes the degrees of control given over to the role of authorship and user participation. Hence the consequence of multiple interpretations in this instance is specific and remains a key aim from the onset.

The work of Mark Dion draws on the practice of archaeology, and shares the belief that knowledge and information inferred from material finds enables a study of the human past. His interest in nature as well as issues relating to the history of nature is further explored through a 'fieldwork' model of working, which emphasises the idea of 'raw material' and the 'precise context' from which each find is excavated.[74] Dion is also concerned with 'principles of taxonomy' and the manner 'by which people have sought to bring order to the world' through 'systems of classifications'.[75] Hence the 'meticulous processes of recovery, conservation, classification and installation' are crucial and evident in Dion's work.[76] These interests are illustrated by projects such as *On Tropical Nature* (1991), and *Tate Thames Dig* which is also referred to as *Two Banks* (1999).

In the first, Dion spent three weeks in the Orinoco Basin in Venezuela and sent boxes containing his finds to an appointed museum in Caracas, but with no instructions as to how the contents should be identified, preserved and exhibited.[77] These responsibilities were left to the museum staff and the eventual presentation consisted of three tables where Dion's journals, tools and maps were displayed alongside the dirt, insects, plants and reptiles from the boxes. In addition to the boxes, design research also extended to material associated with arrangements for the project. This included negotiations with a series of South American bureaucracies which were described as 'extremely delicate and expensive'.[78] The procedure raised issues regarding authorship and ownership as each organisation was further depicted as focused on 'protecting their own interests' within the framework of the project.[79] These time consuming processes, while not evident in the presentation of the work remain inseparable from its meaning.[80] Hence notions of ownership and authorship in this project are addressed within issues concerning site-specificity and displacement, conservation and presentation, as well as the idea of the museum as a didactic institution.

Dion's *Tate Thames Dig* in London was designed to coincide with the transformation of the disused Bankside Power Station into the Tate Modern.[81] Two sites along the Thames were identified for the dig. The first was near the existing Tate Gallery on Millbank, and the other in the vicinity of the newly proposed Tate Modern on Bankside. The process of 'beachcombing' the two sites at low tide over two weeks for 'both historical and contemporary flotsam and jetsam' further highlighted the relationship between the two Galleries.[82] The schedule for collecting was precise as tidal patterns only allowed two hour time slots daily. The conditions at both sites varied greatly and this affected the frequency and nature of found material. The presence of thick silt at Millbank coated and obscured surface material which made the process of locating and cleaning objects tedious. Bankside on the other hand, provided better collecting opportunities as the reduced speed of the river at this point consequently deposited many objects.

The salvaged material from both sites was cleaned, catalogued and displayed sequentially in purpose-built cabinets at both the Tates.[83] The discoveries were displayed in a double-sided mahogany cabinet alongside photographs of the beachcombers and tidal flow charts. One side of the cabinet contained items from Millbank and the other, items found at Bankside. This manner of display references the traditional 'Cabinets of Curiosities' or *wunderkammer*, where an 'endless play of meaning' is generated through the visual reading of objects and their placements in relation to each other.[84] Dion frequently engages with this approach of using 'arbitrary visual arrangements' to further the notion of multiple interpretations in his presentations.[85]

In this instance, a profile of the city of London was built up through the found objects in the river. In addition, *Tate Thames Dig* further served as a record of tidal patterns within the particular stretch of the Thames where the digs occurred. The water quality at different points during specific times of the day was revealed through the condition of the material finds. Significantly, the project and resulting documentation presented the Thames as an archive of London and Dion's *Tate Thames Dig*, an archive of the Thames.

Similar to the practice of archaeology, both of Dion's site-specific projects discussed employ 'material remains' to express the 'immediacy of contact with the past'.[86] Multiple readings and interpretations can be derived from the working process, the elements on display, and the manner in which these elements are exhibited. Both projects, while exposing and revealing particular material and historical aspects of their respective physical sites, are also designed to challenge the idea of authority. Design research is approached as a means to juxtapose and create different interpretations of a chosen site and the site-specific material. Decisions to expose the working methods and the structure of the eventual presentations are used to provoke viewers into questioning the exhibition and material on display as opposed to simply accepting an institution's opinion. This is advanced by the lengthy duration of the working process during which the projects go through 'complicated transformations' and generate 'multiple narratives' on many levels.[87] The work in this instance is deliberately constructed to contradict the accepted idea of the museum and/or gallery as a 'neutral viewing environment'.[88] Hence the narratives constructed by the collection and display are designed to encourage personal opinions and readings in order to give meaning to the work.

In Dion's work and working processes, the deliberate relegation of authorship and creation of multiple interpretations through the employment of different places, people and routines, is a key consideration from the outset of the work. This notion of attribution in relation to works of art, and especially Dion's projects, is comparable to the manner by which buildings are conceived, constructed and finally credited to an architect. Similar to the discussions in this study, the working process in architecture is often ambiguous, and the meaning of authorship changes at different stages of the project. This is an important argument as buildings are made by many people, and inherently used and appropriated by different people in numerous ways. Hence the role of authorship contests the straightforward argument that buildings are conceived, constructed and attributed to an architect and/or a singular source and makes the idea of a single claim to authorship questionable. Hence multiple interpretations where works of architecture are concerned are unavoidable.

More importantly, understanding the intrinsic presence of multiple readings and interpretations in works of architecture contributes to the practice of architectural design. In relation to design practice, this discussion simultaneously highlights the idea that there are multiple ways in which to interpret and/or reflect upon research material during the design process. The physical limits of an architectural site and boundaries alluded to in historical narratives are different. Current discussions normally treat historical knowledge as mere background information to support existing readings. The ability to interpret, apply and infer from historical site information, which includes narratives that are current or historical, especially features that are no longer visible, can be used as a means to actively generate design work. The creation of multiple interpretations is further achieved by the apparent juxtapositions between the programme and site studies and allowing the resulting shifts to create new contextual readings of the work. The author edits and decides the mode and manner in which to put forth this information in order to present a particular argument. The outcomes are decisive and the intended experiences are precisely described by means of the design proposals. The precision adopted in this process is reflected in the architecture.

This argument also extends to include the user and the different individual responses a work of architecture induces. The user has a creative role as the different aspects of the architecture are defined by the manner of usage. For instance the role of design authorship is an important consideration in issues regarding restoration during conservation processes in relation to ideas of history and use. This is apparent in the repair as well as redesign of spaces and buildings to suit new purposes and in many instances, decisions concerning the allocation of use in architecture are not necessarily in the best interest of the user. Hence the notions of experiential fragments, continuous change, issues of site and multiple interpretations apparent in design practice can be appropriated to challenge these issues of control with regards to authorship, conservation, presentation and use. This is especially in relation to the shifting role of the recipient concerning ideas of participation and response. The work is designed such that the recipient becomes involved in the working process and, more importantly, their response is required in order for the work to be deemed complete. The meaning of each segment of the architectural narrative as articulated by design authorship and articulated spatially, materially and/or experientially is revealed and individually appropriated by each inhabitant. Hence, in a parallel reading of *The Arcades Project*, the idea of a literary montage is applied to the production of a work of architecture.

[1] Umberto Eco, *The Open Work*, trans. by Anna Cancogni (Cambridge, Mass.: Harvard University Press, 1989).

[2] Walter Benjamin, *The Arcades Project*, ed. by Rolf Tiedeman, trans. by Howard Eiland and Kevin McLaughlin (Cambridge, Mass. and London: Belknap Press of Harvard University Press, 1999).

[3] Eiland, 'Translators' Foreword', in *The Arcades Project*, pp. iv–xiv (p. viiii).

[4] Walter Benjamin, 'The Flâneur' in *Charles Baudelaire: A Lyric Poet in the Era of High Capitalism*, trans. by Harry Zohn (London: New Left Books, 1973), pp. 35–66 (p. 37).

[5] Oxford English Dictionary online, <http://www.oed.com/view/Entry/71073?redirectedFrom=flaneur&> [accessed 18 August 2009]. This role of the *flâneur* was further explored in Benjamin's work *Charles Baudelaire: A Lyric Poet in the Era of High Capitalism*. Baudelaire was a nineteenth-century French poet and art critic.

[6] Michael Schwarz, 'Rag Picking' in *Walter Benjamin's Archive, Images, Texts, Signs*, ed. by Ursula Marx, Gudrun Schwarz, Michael Schwarz and Erdmut Wizisla, trans. by Esther Leslie (London and New York: Verso 2007), pp. 25–265 (p. 262). The original source of this French quote 'tout ce qu'elle a brise, il le catalogue, il collectionne' is noted as '*Du Vin et du haschisch, Oeuvres*, vol. 1, pp. 249–50'. Charles Baudelaire uses the French word 'chiffonier', which carries the dual meaning of 'ragpicker', and also 'chest of drawers for oddments'. The English usage only refers to the latter.

[7] Schwarz, 'Rag Picking', p. 252.

[8] Schwarz, 'Rag Picking', p. 252.

[9] Schwarz, 'Rag Picking', pp. 252–3.

[10] Schwarz, 'Rag Picking', pp. 252–3.

[11] Ursula Marx, 'Tree of Conscientiousness' in *Walter Benjamin's Archive*, pp. 7–27 (p. 9). The last surviving document from Benjamin's briefcase was incidentally an authenticated letter from the Institute for Social Research, New York, dated 8 May 1940, confirming Benjamin's membership and that his researches proved of extreme help for the Institute. Erdmut Wizisla, 'Preface', unpaginated.

[12] Eiland, p. xi.

[13] Jonathan Hill, 'The Montage of Fragments' in *Actions of Architecture, Architects and Creative Users* (London and New York: Routledge, 2003), pp. 93–196 (p. 108).

[14] Hill, 'Conclusion', pp. 199–200 (p. 200).

[15] Nigel Coates, 'The Long Perspective' in *Narrative Architecture* (West Sussex: John Wiley and Sons Ltd., 2012), pp. 13–32 (p. 31).

[16] Hill, p. 200.

[17] Hill, p. 200.

[18] Coates, 'Preface', pp. 8–12 (p. 10). The quote is referenced to Edward Hollis and the original source is noted as 'Joseph Rykwert, *On Adam's House in Paradise, the Idea of the Primitive Hut in Architectural History*, MIT Press (Cambridge, MA), second edition, 1981'.

[19] Coates, p. 10.

20. Paul Cobley, *Narrative* (London and New York: Routledge, 2014), p. 11.
21. Coates, 'Story Buildings', pp. 80–111 (p. 81).
22. Coates, p. 83.
23. Coates, pp. 83–84.
24. Coates, p. 84.
25. Coates, p. 92.
26. This building was previously referred to as the Centro de Lazer Fábrica da Pompéia (Pompéia Factory Leisure Centre).
27. Coates, pp. 93–94. A further reference is indicated as 'Elisabetta Andreoli and Adrian Forty (eds), *Brazil's Modern Architecture*, Phaidon (London), 2004, pp. 91–5'.
28. Coates, p. 100.
29. Coates, p. 100.
30. Coates, p. 15.
31. Mattias Ekman, 'Architecture for the Nation's Memory: History, Art, and the Halls of Norway's National Gallery', in *Museum Making, Narratives, Architectures, Exhibitions*, ed. by Suzanne Macleod, Laura Hourston Hanks and Jonathan Hale (London and New York: Routledge, 2012), pp. 144–156 (p. 100). The original source is noted as 'A. Assmann, *Erinnerungsräume: Formen und Wandlungen des Kulturellen Gedächtnisses*, 3rd edn., Munich: Beck, 2006, p. 174'. The term '*antëische magie*' is also used.
32. Ekman, p. 148. The original source is noted as 'Assmann, *Der Lange Schatten der Vergangenheit*, p. 223'.
33. Walter Benjamin, 'The Work of Art in the Age of Mechanical Reproduction' in *Illuminations, Essays and Reflections*, ed. by Hannah Arendt, trans. by Harry Zohn, 1968 (London: Fontana Press, 1992), pp. 211–244. First English edition published in 1968.
34. Benjamin, 'The Work of Art in the Age of Mechanical Reproduction', p. 214.
35. Benjamin, 'The Work of Art in the Age of Mechanical Reproduction', p. 215.
36. Benjamin, 'The Work of Art in the Age of Mechanical Reproduction', p. 216.
37. Benjamin, 'The Work of Art in the Age of Mechanical Reproduction', p. 217.
38. Benjamin, 'The Work of Art in the Age of Mechanical Reproduction', pp. 217 and 233.
39. Benjamin, 'The Work of Art in the Age of Mechanical Reproduction', p. 218.
40. Benjamin, 'The Work of Art in the Age of Mechanical Reproduction', pp. 218–219.
41. Peter Bürger, *Theory of the Avant-Garde*, trans. by Michael Shaw (Minnesota: University of Minneapolis Press, 1984), p. 70.
42. Bürger, p. 70.
43. Bürger, p. 56.
44. Bürger, p. 22.
45. Bürger, p. 50.
46. Bürger, p. 22.
47. Hill, p. 100.
48. Hill, p. 96.
49. Hill, p. 96.
50. Cobley, p. 15.
51. Bridget Elliott and Anthony Purdy 'On Common Ground: Allegory as Architecture' in *Peter Greenaway, Architecture and Allegory* (West Sussex: Academy Editions, John Wiley and Sons Ltd., 1997), pp. 27–44 (p. 27).
52. Elliott, p. 38.
53. David Pascoe, 'Fields of Vision' in *Peter Greenaway, Museums and Moving Images* (London: Reaktion Books Ltd., 1997), pp. 67–91 (p. 81).
54. Pascoe, p. 82.
55. Pascoe, p. 82.
56. Pascoe, pp. 71 and 82.
57. Pascoe, p. 80.
58. Pascoe, p. 70.
59. Pasoce, p. 70.
60. Pascoe, 'Artificial Light', pp 7–41 (p. 15).
61. Roy Strong, 'The Queen: Eliza Triumphans' in *The Cult of Elizabeth: Elizabethan Portraiture and Pageantry* (London: Thames and Hudson, 1977), pp. 17–55 (p. 43). The original source is noted as 'John White, *The Birth and Rebirth of Pictorial Space*, London, 1957, p. 35'.
62. Roy Strong, 'Icons of Power and Prophecy: Portraits of Queen Elizabeth I' in *The Tudor and Stuart Monarchy, volume II: Pageantry, Painting, Iconography* (Woodbridge: Boydell Press, 1995), pp. 5–7 (p. 5).
63. Roy Strong, 'The Ermine Portrait' in *Gloriana, The Portraits of Queen Elizabeth I* (London: Thames and Hudson, 1987), pp. 113–115 (p. 113).
64. Unless otherwise stated, all mentions and references to the Renaissance in this thesis refer to the Italian Renaissance. This includes both the early and high periods during the fifteenth- and sixteenth-centuries.
65. Anna C. Krausse, *The Story of Painting: From the Renaissance to the Present* (Cologne: Konemann Verlagsgesellschaft mbH, 1995), p. 7.
66. Roy Strong, 'The Elizabethan Image' in *The Cult of Elizabeth*, pp. 111–112 (p. 112).
67. Pascoe, pp. 71–73.
68. Elliott, p. 38.
69. Elliott, p. 38.
70. Benjamin, 'The Work of Art in the Age of Mechanical Reproduction', p. 232.
71. Benjamin, 'The Work of Art in the Age of Mechanical Reproduction', p. 227.
72. Benjamin, 'The Work of Art in the Age of Mechanical Reproduction', p. 226.
73. Elliott, p. 41. The original source is noted as 'Interview with Waldemar Januszczak, *The Studio 999* (April–May 1983), p. 23'.
74. Miwon Kwon, 'Interview, Miwon Kwon in Conversation with Mark Dion' in *Mark Dion*, Lisa Graziose Corrin, Miwon Kwon and Norman Bryson (London: Phaidon Press Ltd., 1997), pp. 8–35 (p. 25).
75. Tate online <http://www.tate.org.uk/whats-on/tate-britain/exhibition/art-now-mark-dion> [accessed 17 December 2011].

[76] Alex Coles, *Mark Dion, Archaeology*, ed. by Alex Coles and Mark Dion (London: Black Dog Publishing, 1999), p. 14.

[77] Kwon, p. 25 and Corrin, 'Survey, Mark Dion's Project: A Natural History of Wonder and A Wonderful History of Nature', pp. 38–87 (pp. 63–65). This project was commissioned by the Sala Mendoza Museum in Caracas, Venezuela for the exhibition *Arte Joven en Nueva York*, which means 'Young New York Art'. The show ran from 9 June to 7 July 1991.

[78] Corrin, p. 65.

[79] Corrin, p. 65.

[80] Corrin, p. 65.

[81] The proposal to use the Bankside Power Station was announced in April 1994, and Tate Modern was officially opened on 11 May 2001. As a result, the existing Tate Gallery on Millbank was renamed Tate Britain.

[82] Coles, ed., p. 27.

[83] The work was first shown at the *Art Now* exhibition, which ran from 20 October 1999 to 26 February 2000 at the Tate Gallery, prior to being renamed Tate Britain. It was subsequently displayed at the Tate Modern from April 2003 to October 2005.

[84] Corrin, p. 53. The German word *'wunderkammer'* literally translates to 'wonder chamber'. Dion's interest and use of this component references the type of cabinets used to display collections of curiosities and rarities during the eighteenth-century.

[85] Corrin, p. 53.

[86] Coles, ed., p. 22.

[87] Kwon, p. 26.

[88] James Putnam, *Art and Artifact: The Museum as Medium* (London: Thames and Hudson, 2009), p. 100.

ACKNOWLEDGEMENTS

First and foremost, I would like to thank Prof Lindsay Bremner for her invaluable advice and support throughout the making of this book.

I am also exceedingly grateful to Prof Jonathan Hill for writing the inspiring foreword and a befitting title, both of which perfectly describes the work we have been doing. Thank you for sharing the title for the book proper. Above all, for always being a mentor and a friend.

Thank you Prof Harry Charrington for your encouragement with my research and teaching.

I am also grateful for the ideas, suggestions and material contributed by many people, especially Dr Claire Harper over the course of producing this book.

I would particularly like to thank the students whose work in this book have served to reinforce the joys of 'Dialogical Designs'. Their passion for design have been proven time and again, and once more during the countless revisions that were requested over the course of assembling the book. They are Loreta Lukoseviciene, Larisa Bulibasa, Panagiota Kotsovinou, Ioana Vierita, Sear Nee Ng, Iga Martynow and especially Kyriakos Eleftheriadis, for the beautiful cover entitled 'Site-Specific Planes'.

A big thank you to the next generation of Studio 3 students, namely Rebecca Billi and Mervin Loh, who have also stepped in to be a part of this wonderful process of research and design.

My gratitude to Associate Prof Tan Aik Ling for her help with the work of Lev Vygotsky.

Last but not least, to a very special person with whom I have had many inspiring exchanges, my friend and fellow researcher, Dr Sotirios Varsamis, for his constant encouragement, advice and for being such an important part of Studio 3.

Dialogical Designs

DS03: 2012-2015

Edited by Constance Lau
Assisted by Larisa Bulibasa

A University of Westminster
Department of Architecture Publication
Designed by Mark Boyce
Printed by Lightning Source

All texts ©2016 the authors
Cover image: Kyriakos Eleftheriadis

This work is subject to copyright. All rights are reserved, whether the whole or part of the material is concerned, specifically the rights of translation, reprinting, re-use of illustrations, recitation, broadcasting, reproduction on micro films or in other ways, and storage in databases. For any kind of use, permission of the copyright owner must be obtained.

ISBN 978-0-9933986-2-9

The Studio as Book series are available to purchase through www.studioasbook.com and other online stores.

The editor has attempted to acknowledge all sources of images used and apologise for any errors or omissions.

Department of Architecture
University of Westminster
35 Marylebone Road
London
NW1 5LS

www.ingramcontent.com/pod-product-compliance
Lightning Source LLC
Chambersburg PA
CBHW040928240426
43667CB00025B/2982